# THE TIMELINE OF AVIATION

# THE TIMELINE OF AVIATION

## THE ULTIMATE GUIDE TO MORE THAN A CENTURY OF POWERED FLIGHT

Jim Winchester

THUNDER BAY
P·R·E·S·S

San Diego, California

**Thunder Bay Press**

An imprint of the Advantage Publishers Group

5880 Oberlin Drive, San Diego, CA 92121-4794

www.thunderbaybooks.com

ISBN-13: 978-1-59223-720-3
ISBN-10: 1-59223-720-7

Project Editor: Sarah Uttridge
Picture Research: Terry Forshaw
Design: Zoë Mellors

Printed in China

1 2 3 4 5 11 10 09 08 07

# Contents

# First Steps

*The dream of flight is as old as civilization itself. Examples from Chinese and Greek literature and from Native and South American legend tell of flying warriors, priests and prisoners – some of them doubtless based on real attempts to fly with self-fashioned wings.*

Documentary evidence of early attempts at manned flight tells of Chinese kite riders (mainly, it would seem, political prisoners), and tower jumpers of various nationalities and faiths – all united by failure. Those few tower jumpers who survived their falls attributed their relative success to their God and their makeshift wings.

Birds offered the most obvious model for mechanical flight. Many would-be aviators built feathered wings, failing to appreciate that, no matter how dressed, human muscle was not enough to support a person for flight. One of the best documented tower jumpers is Brother Eilmer, a monk from Malmesbury, England, who was left lame after his 'flight' in the year 1010. An account by William of Malmesbury, writing about a century later, describes how he jumped from the Abbey tower, about 46m (150ft) high, then glided for a furlong (about 200m/656ft) before stalling and breaking his legs.

*Left: Henri Giffard's steam-powered dirigible flew from Paris to Trappes on 24 September 1852, reaching a maximum speed of 14.5kph (9mph).*
*Right: French engineer Clément Ader's Avion III.*

Eilmer himself put his failure down to the lack of a tail, and in this he had a point. Where he did succeed was in joining his two separate wings with a shoulder brace, to take the strain off his arms. This, historians have speculated, actually prevented him flapping as he had intended, and allowed the fabric of his wings to balloon slightly, giving camber and thus lift.

## Da Vinci

Serious research into the subject of manned flight is usually thought to begin in the fifteenth century, with the work of Italian artist and scientist Leonardo da Vinci. Studying the flight of birds as well as human anatomy, he was he first to realize that a human being could never hope to match the relative muscle power of a bird and fly by direct application of force.

Leonardo drew more than 100 sketches related to flight, including detailed drawings of bird wings. Among his surviving drawings are designs for a parachute, a hang glider and a four-man helicopter that worked by a helical screw arrangement. Modern scientists have proved that the parachute and glider were just about workable, but the helicopter is regarded as impractical. Sometime around 1485, he drew sketches for an ornithopter, a machine designed to achieve flight by means of flapping wings. Leonardo's ornithopter used hand levers, foot pedals and pulleys to reduce the effort required, but, without an engine of some sort, the design would never have worked. As with many of his inventions, Leonardo was ahead of his time, and the world would have to wait until advances in materials and engineering made them possible.

Da Vinci was undoubtedly a genius, but he rarely finished his projects, moving on to the next great idea before he brought the last to fruition. Progress with the ornithopter ended after construction of a small model. His ideas were not disseminated in his lifetime, and had little influence until much later.

## The Montgolfiers

It was to be a further 300 years before significant progress was made, and it was not to come from a scientist or natural philosopher. Brothers Joseph and Étienne Montgolfier were the sons of a papermaker from Annonay in southern France, and achieved the first manned flight – in a hot-air balloon. Unlike many other

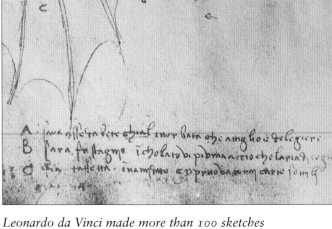

*Leonardo da Vinci made more than 100 sketches related to flight, including detailed drawings of birds' wings, one of which is pictured here.*

**Circa 1010**

EXACT DATE UNKNOWN

Monk Eilmer of Malmesbury survives a jump from the tower of Malmesbury Abbey, using home-made wings.

**1485**

EXACT DATE UNKNOWN

Leonardo da Vinci designs an ornithopter or flapping-wing flying machine.

experimenters, they achieved success quickly. Joseph began tinkering with models for a balloon just seven months before the public demonstration of a full-size balloon.

Their father allowed them use of the family paper works to build their balloons, with the stipulation that neither brother ever fly in one of their creations. (One brother, in fact, did once go aloft; which one is unknown.) Balloon flying was initially reserved for animals, and the Mongolfiers' first passengers were a rooster, a sheep and a duck. When it was clear that these had suffered no physical harm, gentleman adventurers were allowed onboard. On 21 November 1783, Jean-François Pilâtre de Rozier and François Laurent, the Marquis d'Arlandes, lifted off from the Château de la Muette in western Paris and drifted across the city for 25 minutes, landing in open countryside when embers threatened to set the balloon's envelope alight. The Montgolfiers' balloon was elaborately decorated in blue and gold with red

*The first ascent of the Montgolfier brothers' hot-air balloon from the suburbs of Paris. The balloon's first passengers were a rooster, a sheep and a duck.*

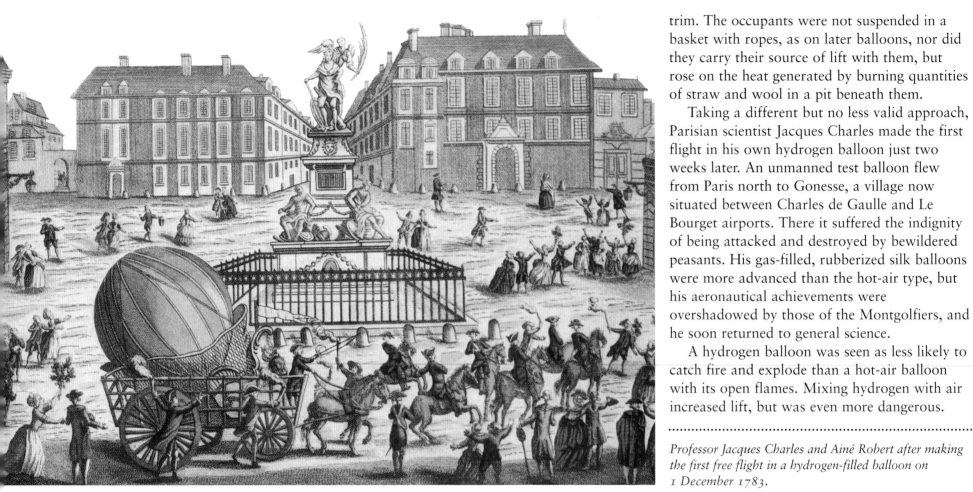

trim. The occupants were not suspended in a basket with ropes, as on later balloons, nor did they carry their source of lift with them, but rose on the heat generated by burning quantities of straw and wool in a pit beneath them.

Taking a different but no less valid approach, Parisian scientist Jacques Charles made the first flight in his own hydrogen balloon just two weeks later. An unmanned test balloon flew from Paris north to Gonesse, a village now situated between Charles de Gaulle and Le Bourget airports. There it suffered the indignity of being attacked and destroyed by bewildered peasants. His gas-filled, rubberized silk balloons were more advanced than the hot-air type, but his aeronautical achievements were overshadowed by those of the Montgolfiers, and he soon returned to general science.

A hydrogen balloon was seen as less likely to catch fire and explode than a hot-air balloon with its open flames. Mixing hydrogen with air increased lift, but was even more dangerous.

*Professor Jacques Charles and Aîné Robert after making the first free flight in a hydrogen-filled balloon on 1 December 1783.*

## 1783

### AUGUST

**27 August** Jacques Charles flies the first manned hydrogen balloon near Paris.

### NOVEMBER

**21 November** The first successful manned flight takes Jean-François Pilâtre de Rozier and the Marquis d'Arlandes above Paris in a hot-air balloon designed and built by the Montgolfier brothers.

It cost the lives of several early aeronauts, including de Rozier, who thus became not only the first man to fly, but also the first to die in an air accident, during an attempt to cross the English Channel in 1785.

Not surprisingly, gas-filled balloons soon took over, and the hot-air balloon was largely forgotten. (Indeed, it did not fly again until the 1960s, when new synthetic materials and propane gas burners brought about their revival for sport, tourism and record-breaking attempts.)

Word of the new balloon spread fast, and ballooning demonstrations became all the rage in Europe and America. Jean-Pierre Blanchard made the first ascents in several countries, including the United States, the Netherlands and Germany. His most notable achievement was to make the first aerial crossing of the English Channel, on 7 January 1785. Flying from Dover Castle to a forest near Calais, he was accompanied by an American passenger, Dr John Jeffries. The flight was marked by desperate attempts to stay aloft, necessitating the discarding of most superfluous items overboard, including much of the occupants' clothing. But it *was* successful, and this was the first hint that flying machines might be good for more than spectacle and amusement. One considerable disadvantage remained, of course – namely that the balloons could not really be steered.

In 1808, Blanchard was to die as the result of a fall from his balloon over The Hague. His widow carried on ballooning, but was killed a decade later when fireworks ignited the hydrogen in her craft. Early ballooning, it must be said, was fraught with hazards, both obvious and unexpected.

A certain amount of scientific experimentation was carried out in the early balloons. Perhaps the most important discoveries concerned the effects of altitude on the human body. A balloon ascent in 1862 reached over 7925m (26,000ft), by which time the occupants, British aeronaut Henry Coxwell and meteorologist James Glaisher, were frostbitten and unconscious at the bottom of their basket. The euphoric and literally mind-numbing effects of thin air disguised the danger until they were incapable of doing anything

........................................................................

*Jean-Pierre Blanchard and Dr John Jeffries successfully crossed the English Channel on 7 January 1785.*

**1785**

JANUARY

**7 January** Jean-Pierre Blanchard and Dr John Jeffries make the first flight over the English Channel in a Montgolfier balloon.

*Sir George Cayley's design for a dirigible balloon, driven by airscrews and powered by a steam engine.*

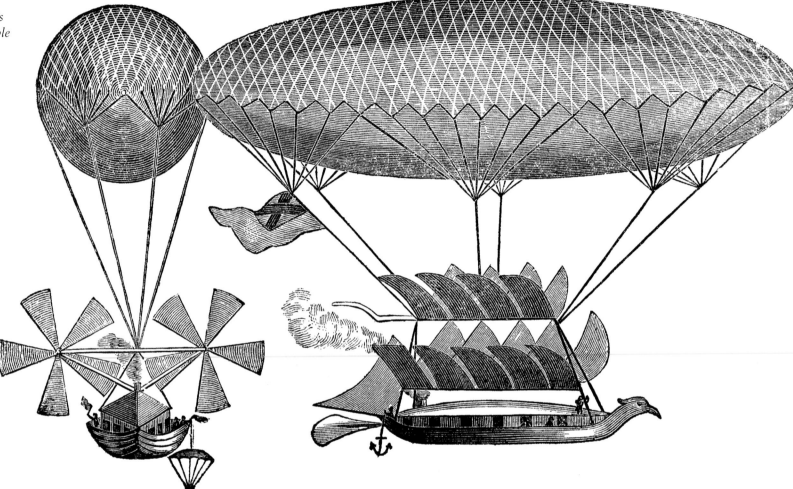

## 1843

### EXACT DATE UNKNOWN

William Henson and John Stringfellow patent an 'aerial carriage' and, with others, incorporate the Aerial Transit Company.

*Henson's Aerial Steam Carriage, designed in 1842, was inspired by the writings of Sir George Cayley, and greatly influenced subsequent developments.*

about it. Both men survived, but such high-altitude flights were discontinued until a method of providing gaseous oxygen to balloonists could be developed.

France again led the way in the field of 'aeromedicine', developing a pressure chamber and bags containing a mixture of nitrogen and oxygen, with a breathing tube. Unfortunately, the need to breathe oxygen continuously at altitude was not immediately understood. In April 1875, two of three French aeronauts aboard the balloon *Le Zénith* succumbed to anoxia despite the use of breathing bags. Rising above 6100m (20,000ft), they became too weak to operate the bags.

Aerial advancement in the nineteenth century was a mixture of theory and experiment. It should be noted that, barring a few notable exceptions, pioneers of the period were reluctant, or unable, to expose their own bodies to hazard or to build full-size machines for carrying people. Generally speaking, though, this was a time of cooperation and the sharing of information between pioneers experimenting in different parts of the globe. Questions of patents and proprietary knowledge were largely left to a later era.

### The Influence of George Cayley

Sometimes known as the true 'Father of Aviation', Yorkshireman Sir George Cayley outlined a practical aeroplane design when he was in his twenties. The inventor of the cambered airfoil, he is credited with discovering the basic principles of flight – lift, thrust, drag and weight.

Dispensing with ornithopters, he established that a fixed wing could provide enough lift to carry a man through trials with some simple gliders, at least one of which briefly carried a small boy. He progressed to a substantial glider with a wheeled bathtub-like hull, and in 1853 he persuaded an employee, possibly his coachman, to fly it across a valley on Cayley's estate at Brompton Dale. Legend has it that the man then resigned, claiming he was hired to drive, not fly, but details are sparse and did not emerge until some time after Cayley's death. Modern replicas have proven that Cayley's design was sound, but it appears he made no more test flights. He did, however, set down his knowledge in the three-part *On Aerial Navigation* (1809), which described helicopters, parachutes and a variety of wing forms.

Inspired by Cayley and others, Englishmen William Henson and John Stringfellow went a few steps further and set out to invent air travel. They drew up a design for a large 'aerial steam carriage', which received a patent in 1843. The same year, they joined with others to form the Aerial Transit Company, to raise money to build their machine. It would have been a truly impressive craft, with a wingspan of 45.7m (150ft), greater than that of a Boeing 707 airliner. The Steam Carriage had many of the elements that featured on

*John Stringfellow was interested in the possibilities of manned flight and went into partnership with William Samuel Henson.*

**1848**

EXACT DATE UNKNOWN

John Stringfellow successfully flies a steam-powered model aircraft in Somerset.

*Coxwell and Glaisher almost succumbed to the effects of anoxia when their balloon reached 7925m (26,000 ft).*

later pioneer aeroplanes – propellers, a wheeled undercarriage and external wire bracing. However, passengers would have been required to climb a tower to board the aircraft, which would have been launched down a steep ramp.

Illustrations were drawn up showing the steam carriage soaring over London and the Pyramids. A prospectus described the purposes of the steam carriage to carry 'Passengers, Troops and Government Despatches to China and India in a few days'. All of this attracted great interest, but not a little scepticism.

Henson built two models in preparation for the aerial carriage: a small one, which had limited success, reportedly flying a short distance under steam power; and a medium one with a 6m (20ft) span, which could not be coaxed to fly. The designers had come up against the perennial problem of power versus weight. As the size of the machine increased, so did the amount of power required and the size of the engine. Increasing pressure requires a stronger, heavier boiler and, before long, the weight of the engine alone is more than the lift that can be generated by the wings.

It seems that the failure of the model to fly proved the impracticality of the scheme, and discouraged investors. The Aerial Transit Company had been wound up by 1848 and none of its principals contributed much more to aviation, but the proposals, and particularly the illustrations left behind, inspired the next generation of inventors to consider the possibilities of flight and aerial commerce.

### Mouillard and Chanute

Another inspirational figure whose practical experiments fell short of powered flight was North African-based Frenchman Louis Pierre Mouillard. He published several books on the subject of flight, the best known being translated into English in 1893 by the Smithsonian Institution as *The Empire of the Air*. A keen observer of bird flight, he built a number of gliders based on natural forms, and one of his most successful designs flew near Cairo for about 28m (92ft) at an altitude of about 9m (30ft), in January 1878.

Mouillard also corresponded with French-born American inventor Octave Chanute, who

**1852**

SEPTEMBER

**24 September** Henri Giffard flies the first powered manned aircraft – a steam-driven, coal gas-filled dirigible (rigid airship) – on a 25km (15-mile) flight from Paris.

**1853**

EXACT DATE UNKNOWN

After years of experiments, Sir George Cayley builds a glider that carries his coachman on a flight of 275m (900ft) at Brompton Dale in England.

began his own gliding experiments in 1896. In letters to Chanute, Mouillard predicted the use of rocket or jet engines as the main future method of propulsion, as well as the use of aluminium for aircraft structure (a material that became available only in the 1890s). He was also very interested in the use of aircraft for military purposes, in part to counter the naval superiority of England.

Chanute chaired a conference in Chicago to discuss the future of aerial navigation, and a year later he incorporated many of Mouillard's findings in his seminal 1894 book *Progress in Aviation*. Chanute's gliders were less birdlike than Mouillard's or others of the period, and were comprised of up to four wings, plus tail surfaces. He worked with Augustus Herring, who also developed his own gliders. Some believe that Herring's compressed air-powered triplane glider made a short hop in 1898. Chanute's most important influence was to act as a kind of clearing house for aerial enthusiasts in Europe and the United States. After they read *Progress in Aviation*, the Wright brothers wrote to Chanute in 1900, and in time he became the main proponent of their work.

## Lilienthal, 'King of the Air'

In Germany, Otto Lilienthal became known as 'King of the Air' for his repeated gliding flights in the mid-1890s. Equally important as the flights themselves was his careful recording of his progress, including which aerofoils and wing shapes gave the best results.

Undaunted by the flat terrain near his home in Berlin, he ordered the construction of a hill at Gross-Lichterfelde in 1894. The conical hill, built from building rubble at no little cost, was about 14m (45ft) high and 61m (200ft) in diameter, and allowed flights into the wind, no matter which direction it was blowing. Working with his brother Gustav, who was responsible for most of the engineering, Otto built a series of gliders between 1891 and 1896. He made more than 2000 flights, hauling the glider back to the top of the hill for the next one. Despite all this effort, he probably logged a total of only about five hours of flying time.

Lilienthal was extremely fit, with a gymnast's physique, which helped him to overcome some

.................................................................

*In April 1875, two French aeronauts died from anoxia during an ascent to 6100m (20,000ft).*

**1861**

JULY

**21 July** Military balloons are used for observation during the First Battle of Bull Run in the American Civil War.

of the limitations of his control method, namely shifting his body weight to effect changes of direction. And by 1895 he was reporting that he was able to soar higher than his starting point on some flights. The Lilienthals found time to build multiple examples of his 1894 standard glider, and eight of these were sold to enthusiasts in America, England, Ireland and Russia.

Lilienthal's progress was covered by the media of the day, and photographs of his flights appeared widely in newspapers and magazines, encouraging builders and experimenters around the world. Lilienthal also assiduously recorded data from his flights and the effects of various aerofoil sections. He was the first to plot lift and drag values for different wing angles of

*Otto Lilienthal was one of the true pioneers of manned heavier-than-air flight. He died in a glider crash in 1896.*

attack, and his data was widely studied by others. Unfortunately, largely due to the limits of his instrumentation, his tables contained many inaccuracies. The Wright brothers later found they had to redo many of his experiments before proceeding.

Sadly, on 9 August 1896, Otto Lilienthal's glider was caught in a gust as he glided from the Stollner Hills. He stalled, and fell from a height of 15m (50ft), suffering injuries that would prove fatal the following day. His dying words were 'Sacrifices must be made.' His legacy was the first controllable flying machine.

*One of a series of gliders designed by Octave Chanute (1832–1910), a US citizen of French origin.*

### Pilcher's Bat and Hawk

In the United Kingdom, Percy Pilcher took Lilienthal's work and advanced it a step closer towards the ultimate goal of powered flight. After building a glider, the *Bat*, in early 1895, Pilcher met Lilienthal in Germany. He then built three more gliders in quick succession, each based on Lilienthal's experience and data. These were not entirely successful, however, and Pilcher modified his *Bat* design into the much more satisfactory *Hawk*.

Pilcher made many flights in the *Hawk*, using a towing system to rise aloft, and eventually considered modifying it for power, even receiving a patent for a version with a pusher propeller. By September 1899, he had an engine,

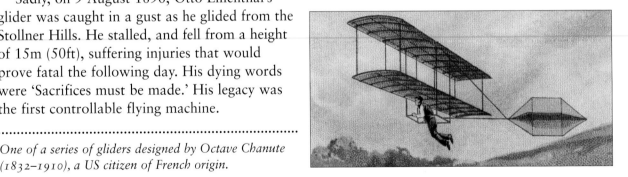

## 1884

### NOVEMBER

**26 November** A British Royal Engineer balloon unit is sent to Bechuanaland in southern Africa (now Botswana).

## 1890

### OCTOBER

**9 October** Clément Ader claims to have flown his steam-powered *Éole* monoplane for a distance of 49m (160ft).

of 3kW (4hp) output, suitable for a triplane aircraft. Unfortunately, the two elements had not been satisfactorily combined by 30 September, when he planned to fly before a group of guests, including potential investors. To avoid disappointing them, he made a gliding flight in the reliable *Hawk*, which on this occasion let him down. The tail of the glider broke off in flight and Pilcher was mortally injured in the subsequent crash. His powered triplane remains unflown.

## *Maxim's* Test Rig

Hiram Maxim may be better known for his machine-gun design, which under the Vickers name proved very important in early military aviation. However, he also made a contribution to aeronautical engineering, even if his most impressive creation did remain essentially earthbound.

Born in Maine, Maxim moved to England in 1881, when the British War Office showed an interest in his machine gun, unlike the US

*Hiram Maxim's steam-powered aircraft, the* Test Rig. *It was mounted on rails and used to test various aerofoils.*

**1891**

Otto Lilienthal begins gliding experiments in Germany. Although he never flies a powered aircraft, he contributes greatly to the study of aerodynamics.

government. Using the considerable proceeds from this and his other inventions, Maxim was free to indulge in his passion for aerial experimentation.

On rented land at Baldwyns Park, Kent, he constructed an enormous steam-powered 'aircraft', which he called the *Test Rig*. Weighing about 3630kg (8000lb) and with a wing area of 372 square metres (4000 square feet), the *Test Rig* was mounted on railway tracks. Another pair of rails was mounted above them to prevent flight above a height of about 60cm (2ft), as the purpose of the *Rig* was to test various aerofoils, propellers and wing planforms at speed rather than to fly. Thrust came from two enormous two-bladed pusher propellers, driven by two lightweight steam engines of Maxim's own design, which had an output of about 134kW (180hp). With all its lifting surfaces fitted, the *Rig* was a quadruplane about 11m (36ft) tall with a span of 33m (107ft). The propellers alone were 5.5m (18ft) in diameter. Although it had elevators for pitch control,

*Hiram Maxim with the invention for which he became most famous, the machine gun.*

directional change was to be made by differential engine control. For all its lift and power, the *Rig* lacked an effective method of control and, as it was, could not be said to be a true aeroplane.

Riding on the *Test Rig*'s short journeys became the fashionable thing to do. The Prince of Wales (the future George V) enjoyed a ride, as did many moneyed gentlemen of the day. This did not translate into great financial

**1894**

JULY

**31 July** Hiram Maxim's *Test Rig* makes an inadvertent 'flight', but is seriously damaged.

*British pioneer Percy Pilcher might have gone on to make the first powered flight had not the crash of one of his gliders cost him his life.*

## 1896

**MAY**

**6 May** Samuel Langley flies his unmanned Aerodrome No. 5 for 800m (875yd) near Washington, DC. This and a subsequent longer flight leads to government funding for manned experiments.

**JUNE**

**June–September** Octave Chanute and Agustus Herring conduct gliding trials at Dune Park, Indiana.

**AUGUST**

**10 August** Otto Lilienthal dies as a result of a gliding accident the previous day.

backing, however, and, even with Maxim's considerable resources, the project was a huge drain on his pocket – probably several million dollars in modern terms. He was forced to move the *Test Rig* to his company's firing range when the local council wanted the original site back to build a mental hospital. And at this point, one of Maxim's assistants, Percy Pilcher, left to pursue his own independent work.

Finally, on 31 July 1894, the *Test Rig* had its greatest moment of glory. On that day, with boilers at maximum pressure, the *Rig* and its three crew steamed off down the track until it reached about 64km/h (40mph) and lifted high enough to strike and break the guardrails. As the *Rig* was on the verge of becoming freely airborne, Maxim shut off the power, just as one propeller was destroyed by flying debris. The *Rig* came to rest in a heap after about 183m (200yd) of 'flight'. It never flew again, but was reportedly rebuilt enough to serve as a fairground attraction at charity events. Maxim's practical experiments more or less stopped at

*Langley's 'Aerodrome No 5' was launched from a spring-actuated catapult mounted on top of a houseboat on the Potomac River near Quantico, Virginia.*

**1897**

OCTOBER

**14 October** Clément Ader makes a hop with his steam-powered *Avion III* (or *Éole III*) aircraft.

this time, although in 1910 he did produce an unsuccessful design for a biplane, long after the Wright brothers' success.

### Ader's Avion

First to claim that he had conquered the problem of powered flight was Frenchman Clément Ader. Although his later claims are debatable, he was indeed the first to complete a full-sized powered aeroplane. A self-taught engineer, he dabbled in ballooning and invented several electrical devices before turning his attentions to heavier-than-air flight. He eschewed the traditional first steps of model-building and gliding, moving straight to powered machines.

Ader made careful observations of birds and bats, travelling as far as North Africa to study the flight of storks. On this journey in 1882, he met Mouillard in Algeria and discussed his progress. This was just one of the many direct connections between the scattered experimenters of the period.

*Frenchman Clément Ader was the person who designed the first aircraft to fly under its own power.*

### 1898

Brazilian Alberto Santos-Dumont builds the first of 14 dirigibles in France.

It was the bat rather than the stork that was to have the more profound influence on Ader. His *Avion No. 3* was not only influenced by the external shape of a bat, but had the internal structure of a bat's wing as well. Also batlike in its wing planform was the *Éole* of 1890, named after the Greek god of the air. The *Éole* can be described as a contraption rather than an aeroplane. It sat on a three-wheeled undercarriage, with another wheel on a short outrigger to prevent it from tipping forward. The powerplant was a vertically mounted steam engine with a large boxlike condenser above the wing. The engine drove a very unusual propeller, with each bamboo blade on a separate shaft. This was an inefficient arrangement, to say the least. The pilot himself sat on a simple stool with just a slight lip to stop him falling backwards, and had no direct forward view past the engine and boiler. The body was covered in blue fabric and two small windows in the sides gave some light and view.

On 9 October 1890 at the estate of a friend at Armainvilliers, Ader claimed to have flown the *Éole* for 49m (160ft) at a low level; however, he was never able to repeat this feat.

*In 1892, Ader began construction of a steam-powered bat-wing monoplane, which he named* Eole *(Aeolus), after the Greek god of the winds.*

**1899**

SEPTEMBER

**30 September** Percy Pilcher suffers a fatal accident while demonstrating his *Hawk* glider. His powered triplane remains unflown.

The French government noticed Ader's work. In recent memory, France had been defeated in the Franco-Prussian War, and the French War Ministry took an interest in any weapon that would offer a decisive advantage in future conflicts. Thus it was that Ader received the first government funding for aeronautical development to be given anywhere. Over time, this led to the *Avion III*, which was tested at the artillery grounds at Satory near Paris in October 1897. For some unknown reason, Ader insisted that a circular runway track be built, which subjected the craft to winds from all directions as it built up speed, rather than having it face directly into the wind as on a straight run.

The *Avion III* was outwardly similar to the *Éole*, but larger and powered by two steam engines, each with an output of about 15kW (20hp). With a weight of about 295kg (650lb), there was theoretically enough power to fly the *Avion III*, but the only achievement was the raising of the tail wheel. With insufficient speed for the rudder to be effective, the lifting of the tail wheel meant that the aircraft was essentially out of control, and by the time it stopped, the *Avion III* was badly damaged. The observing

generals were not impressed, and trials were halted. More pressing matters distracted the War Ministry and Ader's craft did not participate in any further official demonstrations.

Much later, Ader claimed to have made a flight of some 274m (900ft) in 1897 with the *Avion III*. This and other statements, made well after the Wrights had flown in the United States, make it difficult to be sure about who really was the first to achieve powered flight. Samuel Langley, later to become embroiled in similar controversies, visited Ader in 1899 and, while impressed with him as a person, described the *Avion III* as 'simply a giant bat, plus steam engine and propellers'. He dismissed it, noting that it was incapable of flying for 'a single minute without disaster'.

### Hargrave's Trocoided Planes
A small number of individuals worked diligently on the problem of flight far from the main centres of activity, facing ridicule or at least

............................................................

*Alberto Santos-Dumont's exploits were an inspiration to many aeronauts at the end of the nineteenth century.*

**1900**

OCTOBER

**22 October** The Wright brothers make their first gliding flight at Kitty Hawk, North Carolina.

indifference. In Sydney, Australia, Lawrence Hargrave devoted himself to the study of aerodynamics through the testing of models and kites. Working mainly in the early 1890s, he built numerous clockwork and rubber band-powered models that worked well, although they look odd to modern eyes. He was interested in a method of propulsion he called 'trocoided planes'. These were flapping surfaces on stalks, powered by lightweight steam engines or compressed air. Some of these flew nearly 107m (350ft). He also worked on designs for lightweight rotary engines, the main type of air engine used between about 1909 and 1918, but these were frustrated by the quality of materials and machining available to him.

Hargrave believed in sharing his data with others. Independently wealthy like many of the other pioneers, he had no need to increase his fortune from the profits of patents. He corresponded with Chanute, who devoted considerable space to his work in *Progress in Flying Machines*. Hargrave's box kite designs influenced Chanute and Herring, and were his most notable achievement. Although Hargrave himself did not progress beyond person-carrying

*Santos-Dumont achieved fame by becoming the first man to fly around the Eiffel Tower in France.*

kites to full-size powered machines, his invention of the strong but light box kite proved the basis of the biplane and thus the majority of successful aeroplanes up to 1915.

### Pearse's Monoplane
Also working on the far side of the world from the centres of aeronautical progress was New Zealander Richard Pearse. Living in a rural area of the South Island, he turned his natural mechanical aptitude to the problem of flight, but was toiling in almost complete isolation. He did subscribe to various aeronautical and scientific periodicals, but had no access to a technical library and is not known to have corresponded with any of the other pioneers.

Like the Wrights, Pearse began with bicycles and invented his own motor, but he appears not to have bothered with gliding before building a powered monoplane in 1902. This more closely resembled a practical aeroplane than did the Wright Flyer, Santos-Dumont's *14bis*, or many other successful machines of the period. It had a three-wheeled undercarriage using bicycle-type wheels, a wing with a rectangular rather than bird-wing planform, and a two-bladed propeller.

**1901**

AUGUST

**14 August** Gustave Whitehead later claims to have flown four times near Bridgeport, Conneticut, in a powered aeroplane on this date. He will also make claims for flights in 1899 and 1902.

Devices on the wingtips resembling ailerons were indeed control surfaces, although they were unlikely to have been effective in influencing the flight path.

Pearse tested his monoplane as early as March 1902, but he was mostly active in the southern hemisphere winter of 1903. Several straight-line flights seem to have taken place during that period, mainly witnessed by only local schoolchildren. All flights ended in crash landings and it is debatable whether they qualified as controlled, although they were certainly powered. Pearse himself never claimed to be the first to fly. Later he recalled 1904 as the period of his most successful flights, but his champions note that witness reports (taken years later) and other circumstantial evidence point to July 1903.

Thus the 'pre-flight' era ended, with several inventors having achieved a degree of flight, little of which could be called controlled. Many were pursuing the same goal, but it fell to two bicycle makers from Ohio to systematically attack the problem, working up to a controllable craft over several years, then improving and exploiting their invention.

*The son of a very wealthy Brazilian coffee planter, Albert Santos-Dumont was never short of the necessary funds to indulge in his love of aviation. He also had no difficulty in being accepted in Parisian high society.*

OCTOBER

**19 October** Santos-Dumont flies his No. 6 airship on a circuit around the Eiffel Tower, winning a prize of 100,000 francs.

# Pioneers and Perils

*By the late 1890s, numerous inventors had proved that powered flight was possible. The nascent motor industry was producing lightweight powerplants, either petrol-driven or steam-driven, and these were enabling machines to hop and stagger into the air.*

What was lacking was *control*. Some would-be aviators considered this to be a problem that could be dealt with *after* they had achieved straight-line flight – if, that is, they considered it at all. Lilienthal had manoeuvred his gliders by shifting the weight of his athletic body, and various balloonists had tried guide ropes, sails or even oars to steer a course – all methods that were largely impracticable. The first truly controllable aircraft were not fixed-wing aeroplanes, but dirigible balloons, or simply dirigibles – a word derived from the French *dirigeable*, meaning 'steerable'.

Balloons were used to convey both messages and people out of Paris during the Franco-Prussian War, but the problem of getting a balloon *into* the city from outside was never solved. As early as the 1780s, it was understood that a steerable balloon would need to be streamlined and powered.

*Left: Alberto Santos-Dumont and his team working on the engine and attachments of his Dirigible No. 6. Right: The Wright brothers' 1901 glider, which is gradually assuming the configuration of the aircraft in which the first powered flight was made in 1903.*

*Alberto Santos-Dumont's Dirigible No. 6 rounding the Eiffel Tower on 19 October 1901.*

The first success with a powered dirigible came in 1852, when Frenchman Henri Giffard built an airship 44m (144ft) long and flew it from Paris to Trappes, a distance of 27km (17 miles). His intention to return to the start was thwarted by strong winds, but he demonstrated the ability to make turns and orbits. Other flights followed until the airship was irreparably damaged.

The hydrogen-filled Giffard Airship was powered by a 2kW (3hp) steam engine and featured a vertical rudder. The engine itself weighed 180kg (400lb), giving a rather poor power-to-weight ratio. Giffard also experimented with a much larger airship, but this was unsuccessful, and he lacked the funds to continue development beyond captive balloons, which were essentially little more than fairground rides.

In the United States, some unusual but ultimately fruitless machines were built. Most notable were Solomon Andrews's *Aereon* of 1862, which was unpowered but controlled by the distribution of gas and ballast within its hulls, and Frederick Marriott's steam-driven *Aviator* of 1869, which achieved some unmanned flights near San Francisco.

French efforts of the period included Dupuy de Lome's 1872 airship, its huge propellers hand-powered by a team of eight rum-fuelled strongmen, and the Tissandier brothers' electrically powered airship of 1883.

These and other oddities were surpassed by the airship *La France*, built in 1884 by Charles Renard and Arthur Krebs. This, too, had an electric motor, with an output of 6.5kW (8.5hp) supplied by lightweight batteries, making it superior to the Tissandiers' 0.38kW (0.5hp) Siemens motor. At Villacoublay, on 9 August 1884, the airship made a circular 23-minute flight. Some 51m (165ft) long, it flew at an average speed of nearly 24km/h (15mph), achieving the first completely controlled powered flight. It was also the first craft to return to its place of takeoff.

The car of *La France*, which was almost as long as the huge envelope, featured a rudder, an elevator and a ballast shifting system for raising and lowering the nose. Despite the space available, the lift and power were only enough to transport three people. There were plans for a much larger airship, with a 75kW (100hp) engine – but, as with so many follow-ups

## 1903

**MARCH**

**31 March** The New Zealand inventor Richard Pearse reputedly makes a sustained but uncontrolled flight.

**OCTOBER**

**7 October** Samuel Langley's Great Aerodrome fails to take off from its launch platform and crashes into the Potomac River, USA.

**DECEMBER**

**8 December** A second attempt to launch the Great Aerodrome also ends in failure, and Langley ceases its development.

**17 December** Orville Wright makes the first successful manned powered controlled sustained flight in a heavier-than-air machine, when the *Wright Flyer* makes a 12-second flight near Kitty Hawk, North Carolina.

planned to capitalize on an initial success, it was never to come to fruition.

In Germany, progress was being made with petrol engines and smaller airships. Friedrich Wölfert made the first flight by a petrol-engined machine, flying from Tempelhof in Berlin in 1888. He and his mechanic also became the first to die in an airship accident: the open-flame ignition system in a later balloon ignited the hydrogen, in 1897.

The problem remaining now was to prove that flying was safe and reliable, by making repeated journeys. The breakthrough came with diminutive Brazilian Alberto Santos-Dumont, who popularized the airship and later achieved significant feats with the aeroplane. Heir to a coffee plantation, Santos-Dumont moved to Paris in 1891 and was soon dabbling with cars and other conveyances.

Inspired by the writings of Jules Verne, he acquired a balloon and, from 1898, built a series of small non-rigid airships. These were also petrol-powered, but designed for safety, with the envelope protected from engine sparks and flames. His No. 9 airship became a common sight around Paris, with Santos-Dumont

*Samuel Pierpont Langley's* Aerodrome 'A' *comes to grief in the Potomac after an attempted launch from a converted houseboat. After two failed attempts, the project was abandoned.*

## 1904

### MAY

**May** A French copy of the *Flyer,* built as a glider, is the first aircraft to feature ailerons.

### SEPTEMBER

**7 September** The improved *Flyer 2* makes its first flight near Dayton, Ohio.

**20 September** Orville Wright makes the first complete circuit in an aircraft.

**[Date uncertain]** Horatio Phillips' *Multiplane* achieves a short hop in Streatham, south London.

*Orville (left) and Wilbur Wright, the self-taught engineers who made history at Kittyhawk, North Carolina, by becoming the first to make a sustained powered flight in a heavier-than-air craft.*

using it as a runabout and often parking it outside his favourite cafés or his apartment.

After several attempts, Santos-Dumont came to worldwide attention by making a flight from St Cloud to the Eiffel Tower and back on 19 October 1901. This feat won him the Deutsch de la Meurthe prize of 100,000 francs, which he promptly shared between his workmen and the poor.

With this triumph under his belt, Santos-Dumont turned his attention to the aeroplane. However, his success did not come until after the achievements of two American brothers, then experimenting with neither great riches nor government backing at their disposal.

### Samuel Pierpont Langley

One important figure in the last years of the nineteenth century was Samuel Picrpont Langley – a man for whom government money, and the supervision it entailed, was probably more of a curse than a benefit. An astronomer by training, Langley did not begin serious study in aeronautics until his fifties.

Beginning with rubber-powered models in 1887, Langley also constructed a 'whirling

## 1905

| JUNE | JULY | | OCTOBER–NOVEMBER | |
|---|---|---|---|---|
| **23 June** First flight of the *Wright Flyer III*. | | | | **October–November** The Wrights offer their design to the US, British and French governments, but are rejected. |
| | | | **5 October** The modified *Flyer III* flies for nearly 40 minutes, covering 39km (24 miles). | |
| | **14 July** Orville Wright escapes serious injury when the *Flyer III* is badly damaged in a high-speed crash. | | | |

*The Wright brothers testing one of their glider designs. This was just one step in a broad experimental programme that began in 1899 with their first kite and concluded in 1905, when they built the first truly practical aircraft.*

table', a predecessor to the wind tunnel, which allowed him to test various wings and configurations at speed. In the same year, he joined the Smithsonian Institution and by its end was Secretary, a position that offered ample opportunities for experimentation. In 1891, he began his series of 'Aerodromes', a word he coined for the powered flying machine, based on the Greek for 'air runner'. The propulsion for these increasingly large models was, variously, carbonic acid gas, compressed air, and steam and petrol engines.

Langley hired Charles Manly as engineer and test pilot. Manly made many contributions to the design of the Aerodromes. When a commercial firm failed to deliver a gasoline engine to the promised specifications, he modified it to produce a high power-to-weight ratio.

The Aerodromes were large tandem-wing creations with a narrow fuselage structure and twin pusher propellers. To give an advantage at takeoff of height and optimum wind direction, the Aerodromes were launched from a houseboat on the Potomac River. Most trial flights ended immediately, crashing into the water, but eventually better rigging, and bracing in particular,

## 1906

### JANUARY

**17 January** Zeppelin airship LZ2 flies. It is wrecked in a gale the next day.

### NOVEMBER

**November** The first commercial aircraft company is founded in France.

**12 November** Brazilian Alberto Santos-Dumont makes the first officially sustained powered aeroplane flight in Europe.

*Orville Wright becomes the first man in history to make a sustained powered flight in a heavier-than-air machine.*

## 1907

### APRIL

**5 April** The first Blériot monoplane is successfully flown.

### AUGUST

**1 August** An aeronautical division of the US Army's Signal Corps is established.

**24 August** The first (unmanned) rotorcraft is tested in France.

**August–November** Orville Wright takes aircraft to Europe for demonstration flights.

allowed flights of up to a minute. In November 1896, Aerodrome No. 6 flew for 1280m (4200ft).

By 1897, Langley felt that he had gone as far as he could. He concluded his experiments, satisfied that he had proved mechanical flight possible, but weary of the time and effort it had taken to achieve the results.

In 1898, however, President McKinley encouraged Langley to solicit a $50,000 grant from the US Army. This allowed him to experiment towards the goal of a manned aircraft that might eventually have military applications. Working in his free time, Langley proceeded through several more unmanned Aerodromes, culminating with the 'Quarter-sized Aerodrome' of 1900. As its name suggests, this was one-fourth the size of the projected man-carrying machine. This made initial flights of only 45m (150ft) and 90m (300ft) in June 1900, but by August 1903 it had flown over 330m (1000ft).

An inherent problem with Langley's design was the damage suffered by the machines during each flight. It was not simply a matter of adjusting this or that element before making another test; sometimes a complete rebuild was

*Orville Wright lying prone on the brothers' first glider. The Wrights flew this aircraft in October 1900. It was followed by two more, and it was on the third aircraft, the No. 3 glider, that the* Flyer *of 1903 was based.*

needed between launches. Inevitably, this made progress a slow business.

The first of Langley's machines designed for human carriage was the 'Large Aerodrome A', also called the 'Great Aerodrome'. To modern eyes it looks strange, with a configuration that is hard to grasp. The only immediately familiar features are the propellers and the wings, which

although arranged in tandem are also some distance apart. The rest of the airframe consisted of a rail-like 'fuselage', a large hexagonal rudder and many bracing wires. The elevator was an elongated hexagon, but the two wings were equal span and rectangular in planform, the rear wing being slightly higher than the forward wing. The elevator on the tailplane and the rudder

**Exact date unknown** Horatio Phillips' 1907 *Multiplane* design achieves an uncontrolled flight of 152m (500ft) at Streatham.

**SEPTEMBER**

**10 September** British Army Dirigible (steerable airship) No.1 *Nulli Secundus* makes its first flight at Farnborough.

provided yaw and pitch control, but there was no roll control – as effected on later aeroplanes by the means of wing warping or ailerons. Langley valued stability over manoeuvrability, and insisted that his aircraft would 'fly itself' without need for pilot input.

Manly's redesigned motor was a reliable five-cylinder radial, which gave 39kW (52hp) at 950 rpm. Quite an achievement for its day, this one of the best features of the Aerodrome. It drove two large but inefficient propellers.

On 7 October 1903, Charles Manly climbed aboard the Great Aerodrome, mounted high atop the houseboat. Running up his engine, he ordered a workman to cut the rope restraining the catapult. The craft hurtled forward. What happened next is unclear; accounts vary. The craft may have been damaged by the force of the launch before it could develop lift; part of the rigging may have caught on a displaced pin on the catapult; or the aircraft itself may have been poorly balanced, thus being pulled straight down by the weight of its engine as soon as it left the ramp. Manly, who was a strong swimmer, was quickly recovered from the Potomac, but the Great Aerodrome

suffered further damage as it was towed ashore by a tugboat. The event was witnessed by Army officers, who were not impressed, although mollified somewhat by Manly's reassurances and the promise of future success. The press, on the other hand, was largely critical. The *New York Times* called the attempt 'a ridiculous fiasco', suggesting that the failure showed that a practical flying machine would

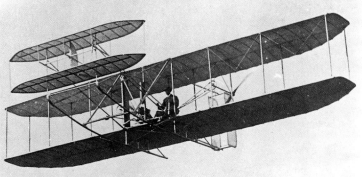

*The* Flyer II *was broken up. and various components used in the construction of the greatly improved* Flyer III. *This was the Wrights' first fully practical aircraft, and it had made some 50 flights by mid-October 1905.*

**1907**

NOVEMBER

**13 November** The first manned helicopter makes a vertical free flight.

**1908**

JANUARY

**14 January** The Wright brothers arrive in Pau, France, where they set up the world's first flying school.

not evolve 'for one million or ten million years'. Even other scientists poured scorn on the idea of flight. Fellow astronomer Simon Newcomb described aerial flight as 'one of that class of problems with which man can never cope'.

By 8 December 1903, the Great Aerodrome had been repaired at the Smithsonian, and preparations for a second manned attempt were complete. In less than optimum weather conditions, with low cloud and gusting winds, the Great Aerodrome was launched again. This time, there was little doubt about what happened. The spring catapult, another invention of Langley's, imparted too much force on the weak structure, and the aft wing spar twisted and fractured with a loud crack. At the end of its run, the Aerodrome pitched up and fell tail-first into the Potomac. Manly had some trouble escaping the wreckage and freezing water, but was pulled aboard the houseboat unharmed.

This time there was no comeback. The press was relentless in its criticism, and so were politicians. 'The only thing that Langley made fly was government money,' fumed a Nebraska congressman. As a result, the War Department, which needed Congressional support, was

*The Wrights' second biplane, or* Flyer II, *was flown for the first time on 23 May 1904, the flying site having now moved from Kill Devil Hills to the Huffmann Prairie.*

reluctant to entertain inventors of flying machines – and remained so for quite some time.

It has been said of Langley that he 'failed at the moment of success'. Perhaps he should not have continued experiments beyond his initial series of successful models. Pressure from no less than the president made him carry on, but his approach of simply scaling up his models was never likely to work. His method of launching the Aerodromes – which lacked effective steering or an undercarriage – over water had outlived its usefulness by the time he put a man aboard.

### MAY

**14 May** The first aeroplane passenger is carried by Wilbur Wright in North Carolina.

**23 May** The first flight is made in Italy by Léon Delagrange, in a Voisin biplane.

### JULY

**4 July** Glenn Curtiss receives a trophy for the first official flight over 1km (0.6 mile), although the Wrights had made longer unrecognized flights.

**July** The US Army buys its first powered aircraft, a Baldwin dirigible.

*Beginning in 1906, Santos-Dumont designed a series of little single-seat aircraft known collectively by the name* Demoiselle *(Dragonfly).*

Langley never quite recovered from this failure, and died a broken man in 1906. His name, however, lives on, in the names of various institutions, including NASA's Langley research facility and Langley Air Force Base.

### The Wright Brothers

In the Midwest town of Dayton, Ohio, two brothers with a lifelong interest in flight read of the events on the Potomac. The younger brother wrote to Octave Chanute, with whom he had been corresponding for some time: 'I see that Langley has had his fling, and failed. It seems to be our turn to throw now, and I wonder what our luck will be.'

These were, of course, the Wright brothers. Sons of a bishop, Wilbur and Orville were printers who opened a bicycle shop during the height of the cycling craze in the 1890s. With only moderate formal educations, they were voracious readers across many fields. They were also mechanically adept, and built a one-cylinder piston engine to power their workshop machines. Their profitable businesses allowed them to hire a gifted mechanic, Charley Taylor, who was to be instrumental in their later success. By 1896, they were considering moving from making bicycles to making automobiles. However, the death of Lilienthal, whose progress they had followed via newspaper accounts, spurred them to pursue their interest in human flight.

The genesis of the Wright Brothers' fascination with flight was a flying helicopter toy, which their father had given to them in 1878. It was designed in 1870 by Parisian Alphonse Pénaud, who is regarded as the father of model flying and is credited with the invention of the rubber band-powered model. None of his full-size designs was ever built, and he took his own life in 1880, unaware that he had lit the spark which would eventually lead to manned flight.

The Wrights had a considerable advantage over their experimental predecessor. Langley worked in the glare of the media and under government oversight, and also held down an important post as the head of the national scientific body. The Wrights, by contrast, could work on the problem of flight unhindered by such concerns. They absorbed as much as possible about other experiments and applied a step-by-step approach until achieving success, which they were then careful to exploit.

## 1908

### AUGUST

**8 August** Wilbur Wright demonstrates an aircraft in France.

### SEPTEMBER

**17 September** The first fatal aeroplane crash kills Thomas Selfridge and injures Orville Wright.

### OCTOBER

**10 October** The *Nulli Secundus* airship is damaged at its moorings by a gale and is rebuilt as the *Nulli Secundus II*.

**16 October** Samuel Cody flies the first aeroplane in England.

An important milestone was a letter written by Wilbur to the Smithsonian in June 1899. Requesting information on the current state of aeronautical research, the earnest young man did not get the brushoff. Instead, the Smithsonian recommended an extensive reading list that described the progress so far: Chanute's *Progress in Flying Machines*, Lilienthal's *Practical Experiments in Soaring*, Mouillard's *Empire of the Air*, and Langley's *Story of Experiments in Mechanical Flight*, as well as further works by these and other practitioners and theorists of flight.

Thus armed with the accumulated wisdom of the age, the Wrights set out to avoid the mistakes of their predecessors. Wilbur likened the process of learning flight to breaking a horse: you can sit on the fence and observe it, or you can climb aboard and master it yourself, learning its tricks by actual trial.

The two brothers were quick to appreciate several points. That control should not be an afterthought, but rather the first priority. That mimicking the forms of birds was unnecessary. That shifting body weight, the method used by Lilienthal and Chanute, was good only for short glides in small aircraft. And, perhaps most importantly, that control worked in three dimensions, making banking as important as climbing, diving and making level turns. Flexing the outer portion of a wing altered its lift and thus rolled the aircraft around its longitudinal axis, allowing climbing and descending turns, with the wind or against it.

In 1901, Wilbur spoke publicly of the need for the would-be aeroplane inventor to climb onboard and risk his skin. The brothers themselves, however, had begun more cautiously two years previously, flying kites. Their kite was

*After a lull of about two and a half years, during which they undertook no flying at all, the Wrights produced the* Flyer A, *which Wilbur took on a demonstration tour of France in 1908.*

**1909**

JANUARY

**23 January** The Blériot XI, the first mass-produced aircraft, flies for the first time.

FEBRUARY

**23 February** John McCurdy makes the first flight in Canada, in the *Silver Dart* at Baddeck, Nova Scotia.

essentially a pair of biplane wings with an elevator mounted on a stalk forward of the wing. This design, now known as a canard foreplane arrangement, was influenced by some of Chanute's 'double-decker' manned gliders. Control lines leading to the wingtips of the kite allowed the brothers to warp the wings, altering the lift and rolling the kite. Tilting the control handles pitched the kite up and down. The 1899 kite design became the core of all the subsequent Wright gliders and aircraft.

The next step was to build a kite near to the size of a man-carrying glider. In September 1900, after studying official weather records, the Wrights moved their experiments to Kitty Hawk on the North Carolina coast. It was a location they chose because of its reliable winds and remote location, which allowed them to work in private. The 1900 kite was smaller than planned due to a lack of local wood to build it, and it had a very short career before being wrecked.

In 1901, the Wrights returned, this time to Kill Devil Hill, some miles from Kitty Hawk. They were now flying a larger glider, initially as a kite, then with one of the brothers aboard. Chanute was there in person for some of the tests, which were not entirely successful, ending in a crash in which Wilbur was injured. The Wrights now realized the limitations of Lilienthal's data and returned to Dayton, Ohio, to rethink.

The need for more reliable data led the Wrights to one of their most significant inventions – a wind tunnel, for evaluating aerodynamic flow. A type of wind tunnel had been built in 1870 by Englishman Frank Wenham, but the Wrights' device was probably the first outside Europe. Essentially a box 1.8m (6ft) long and 41cm (16in) square, it had a fan powered by the workshop's single-cylinder engine. In it, they tested more than 200 models of different types of wings, each 8–23cm (3–9in) long. Experimenting with monoplanes, biplanes, triplanes, and tandem wings like Langley's Aerodromes,

*Count Ferdinand von Zeppelin was the inventor of the rigid airship, or dirigible balloon.*

they gained a thorough appreciation of the advantages and disadvantages of the different layouts, correcting many of Lilienthal's results.

Using this new solid foundation, the Wrights made major breakthroughs when they returned to Kitty Hawk for the 1902 flying season. The outwardly similar 1902 Glider had notable improvements over its predecessors. The tail now had a tall double-vaned rudder and the wing was longer and slimmer, with less camber. Initially the vertical tails were fixed, but the brothers soon realized that these needed to be moveable

## 1909

**APRIL**

**24 April** The first moving pictures are taken from an aeroplane in flight at Centocelle, Italy, by Wilbur Wright's passenger.

**JUNE**

**Exact date unknown** The Handley Page company is formed in Britain.

**12 June** Blériot's Type XII becomes the first aeroplane to carry a pilot and two passengers.

**20 June** Zeppelin LZ3 is delivered to the German Army.

rudder surfaces. The pilot lay prone across the lower wing and adjusted the pitch by moving a horizontal control bar forward and back. Roll and yaw control was achieved by use of a hip cradle, which was connected to the rudders and wing warping. This was a huge step forward because it allowed balanced turns to be made, without sideslip or skidding. Most later aeroplanes divorced the yaw and roll controls into unconnected rudder and ailerons, requiring greater pilot coordination.

The 1902 season achieved controlled flights up to 200m (600ft), lasting up to 26 seconds. Everything was now in place for powered flight, except for the means of propulsion themselves – the engine and propellers.

The power problem was solved with the help of the mechanical genius of Charley Taylor. Built in only six weeks, his four-cylinder inline engine weighed 82kg (180lb) and delivered 9kW (12hp), a remarkable power-to-weight ratio.

Propellers were a trickier problem. Few other pioneers seemed to understand more than that

*Samuel Franklin Cody (on horseback) demonstrating one of his man-carrying kites, used for military observation.*

**JULY**

**19 July** Hubert Latham makes an unsuccessful attempt to cross the English Channel.

**25 July** Louis Blériot makes the first crossing of the English Channel by air.

**25 July** Flying a Voisin biplane, Van den Schkrouff makes the first official aeroplane flight in Russia.

they type of propeller used on a boat would not be suitable. The Wrights looked at all available literature on the theory of propellers, but found nothing of help. They later wrote:

'... so far as we could learn, marine engineers possessed only empirical formulas, and the exact action of the screw-propeller, after a century of use, was still very obscure.

'What at first seemed a simple problem became more complex the longer we studied it. With the machine moving forward, the air moving backward, the propellers turning sideways, and nothing standing still, it seemed impossible to find a starting point from which to trace the simultaneous reactions.'

Eventually they hit upon the principle that a propeller moving in and through the air was nothing more than a wing moving in a spiral course. The brothers rewrote propeller theory and created a propeller design that reached

*Louis Blériot, the first man to fly the Channel in a heavier-than-air machine.*

70 per cent efficiency (a measure of the proportion of the engine power transmitted into thrust). Even the most sophisticated modern propellers can reach only 85 per cent efficiency.

Thus armed, they set out for Kitty Hawk again, in September 1903. Assembling their new powered aircraft took some time, the work hindered by engine problems, cracked propeller shafts and other snags. All the mechanical parts were thoroughly ground-tested before the first trials of the *Flyer*, as the Wrights had prophetically dubbed their craft.

While the Wrights completed their preparations in their workshop at Kill Devil Hill, they received word of Langley's failure on 8 December. It was time for them to have their 'throw'. On the 14th, Wilbur made the first

powered run of the *Flyer*. The craft pitched up almost immediately and fell to the earth, suffering damage that took three days to repair.

### Success at Last!

Thursday, 17 December 1903. A blustery wind sweeps over the sand dunes of North Carolina's Outer Banks. Watched only by the crew of the local life-saving station on the hill above, two young men in tweed suits and flat caps haul their flying machine out of its shed and lay its takeoff rail. By 10 a.m., the wind has died down a little. A flag is raised, a signal to the lifeguards, who haul the aircraft to its takeoff point. Having made the previous attempt to fly, Wilbur now takes his turn to steady the wingtip while his younger brother lies on the cradle and advances the throttle. As the *Flyer* pulls against its restraining ropes, one of the lifeguards, John Daniels, stands by with the hand on the shutter release for the brothers' camera. The restraint is cut and the *Flyer* clatters off down the rail, its two pusher propellers rotating slowly, biting the air. The wood and canvas machine lifts off as Wilbur clicks his stopwatch and John Daniels takes the first photograph of a true aeroplane.

## 1909

### AUGUST

**22–29 August** More than 250,000 spectators attend the first great international air show, held at Rheims, France.

### SEPTEMBER

**7 September** Eugène Lefebvre becomes the first pilot of a powered aeroplane to be killed in a crash.

Just twelve seconds later, and some 39m (120ft) from the launch point, Orville touches down on the sand, the first man in history to make a powered controlled aeroplane flight.

If that had been the sum total of the Wrights' powered flying career, the two brothers would have been forgotten. 'Flights' of equal distance had already been achieved, so this was nothing special. Indeed, it is often pointed out that this first flight could have been conducted entirely within the cabin of an early-model Boeing 747.

However, this was only the beginning of a most successful day's flying. Next it was Wilbur's turn, and he flew 53m (175ft). Orville then flew 61m (200ft). And at about midday, Wilbur made the *Flyer*'s greatest – and last – flight, the aeroplane rising and falling for almost a minute on a more or less straight course, and eventually coming down with a bump after 260m (852ft). The *Flyer* was now caught in a gust as it was being prepared for a fifth flight, and suffered more damage than the brothers wanted to repair before winter really took hold. They cabled their father that they would be home for Christmas and told him to inform the press, then began to pack up for the return to

*A tractor monoplane type, the Blériot XI flew for the first time at Issy-les-Moulineaux on 23 January 1909, powered by an 18.6kW (30hp) REP engine fitted with a crude four-bladed metal propeller.*

**1910**

JANUARY

OCTOBER

**16 October** The first commercial air service is established in Germany, using Zeppelin airships.

Italy and France buy military aircraft and start training pilots.

**22 October** Frenchwoman Elise Deroche makes a solo flight, becoming the first female aviator.

**10–20 January** An air show held is at Dominguez Field near Los Angeles, the first major air event in the United States.

*Louis Blériot after landing at Dover. As British Customs had no provision for a landing other than by ship, Blériot was logged in as a ship's Master and the aircraft as a yacht!*

*Front page of the British newspaper the* Daily Sketch, *showing Blériot's monoplane approaching the cliffs of Dover and the aviator surrounded by well-wishers after his landing.*

## 1910

### MARCH

**10 March** Emil Aubrun makes the first night flight in an aeroplane, near Buenos Aires, Argentina.

**18 March** Escapologist Harry Houdini makes the first controlled powered aeroplane flight in Australia.

**8 March** The Baroness de Laroche becomes the world's first qualified woman pilot, when she receives Fédération Aéronautique Internationale certificate No. 36.

**28 March** The first Hydravion, or seaplane, is flown from a harbour near Marseilles.

Dayton. The total flying life of the *Flyer* had been only a few minutes.

At first, their achievements were not appreciated. The Norfolk, Virginia, paper the *Virginian-Pilot* printed a wildly inaccurate account headlined 'Flying Machine Soars 3 Miles in Teeth of High Wind Over Sand Hills and Waves.' Only one other newspaper showed an interest in the story. By January, the Wrights understood that Langley's failures meant that only scepticism met the claims from provincial amateurs to have solved the problem of flight. So, in May 1904, they invited the press to view flights of the *Flyer II* at Huffman Prairie near Dayton. However, damp weather and a soggy field meant that the newspapermen left without seeing any flying. From here on, the Wrights mostly avoided publicity. The one journalist they trusted to write a reliable account of their activities was the editor of the journal *Gleanings in Bee Culture*. This media-shy approach helped to preserve their secrets, but also fuelled the counterclaims of their detractors who doubted their claims to be the first to fly.

In the following years, the Wrights' made more progress. The *Flyer II* exceeded the original *Flyer's* best flight in September 1904, and became the first aeroplane to make a complete circle. A weight-driven catapult to compensate for the lighter Ohio winds allowed for much longer flights, but was to lead to further criticism that the Wrights' takeoffs were not self-powered.

The 1905 *Flyer III* has been described as the world's first practical aeroplane, but not until it was rebuilt after a serious accident that could have killed Wilbur. The rudder and wing warping were decoupled, the rudder surfaces were much enlarged, and the elevator was moved much further out. In October, several long flights were made, culminating in one of just under 40 minutes.

### Meanwhile in Europe

The period 1903–1905 saw little progress in Europe, where there was no aviator to emulate the Wrights. Indeed, there was widespread criticism that the Wrights had flown at all. Some French papers called them *bluffeurs*. The Paris edition of the *New York Herald* wrote in a February 1906 editorial:

'The Wrights have flown or they have not flown. They possess a machine or they do not possess one. They are in fact either fliers or liars. It is difficult to fly. It's easy to say, "We have flown."'

It was Santos-Dumont who was to restore the pride of the French, who saw themselves as the natural leaders in aviation. In the years 1899–1906, he built a dozen balloons and airships before turning his attention to aeroplanes. He was an experienced aeronaut with lighter-than-air craft, but even so it is remarkable how he progressed to a successful powered aeroplane without the intermediate stages of building gliders or unmanned flying models. In fact, Santos-Dumont's transitional step was to take his No. 14 airship and attach it to the top of his aircraft, to give a guaranteed source of lift. He soon abandoned this idea, but it gave him the odd name for the aircraft – the *14bis*, which can be translated as either '14 Encore' or 'Little 14'.

The *14bis* was very different to the *Flyer*, although it shared the basic canard biplane layout. Santos-Dumont's design used a configuration with the wing at the rear and a long 'neck' – the origin of the word *canard* (French for 'duck') to describe a forward-

**APRIL**

**28 April** Frenchman Louis Paulhan makes the first flight between London and Manchester in the United Kingdom.

**JUNE**

**June** The first airmail is carried, between the governors of New York and Pennsylvania.

**9 June** Two French pilots demonstrate the feasibility of aerial photoreconnaissance.

mounted control surface on an aircraft. The structure was that of the box kite, Santos-Dumont being an admirer of the work of the Australian Lawrence Hargrave, who pioneered this type of construction. Unlike the Wrights' aircraft to date, the *14bis* had a wheeled undercarriage with two main wheels, and sometimes a third, mounted near the centre of gravity. A skid helped to keep the forward elevator surfaces, also built as a box structure, off the ground. The rear-mounted engine drove a pusher propeller. In front of this was the pilot, who stood in a modified balloon basket rather than lying prone. Among its many novel features, the *14bis* was notable for having fabric skinning over all of its main surfaces, including the wing struts.

Santos-Dumont began with short trial 'hops' in September 1906. On 23 October, he flew the *14bis* in front of a large crowd, travelling for 60m (197ft) at a height of 2–3m (6–10ft). This was the first time an aeroplane made a self-propelled takeoff from flat ground using a non-detachable landing gear and without assistance from a headwind. The Aero Club de France verified this as the first true aeroplane flight in

*During the first year of World War I, the Blériot XI was among the most widely used Allied observation aircraft. The type served with eight escadrilles of the French Aviation Militaire, and six squadrons of the Royal Flying Corps.*

**1910**

**AUGUST**

**20 August** The first trials of a gun fired from an aeroplane are conducted by the US Army in New York.

**SEPTEMBER**

**23 September** Peruvian Georges Chavez crosses the Alps in a Blériot.

**NOVEMBER**

**23 November** Flight of the Etrich Taube monoplane, the first aeroplane designed in Austria. It becomes the main pre-1914 German military aircraft and an important trainer.

Europe, and awarded Santos-Dumont the Archdeacon Prize for the first European flight over 25m (82ft). On 12 November, he flew for 220m (772ft) at Bagatelle, wining the Aero Club's prize for the first 100m (328ft) flight. Local papers now claimed that the air had at last been conquered and that, before long, everybody would fly.

Time would make this prediction true, but, in the short term, Santos-Dumont's feats inspired further French efforts. Robert Esnault-Peltrie and Louis Blériot both made short flights in tractor-engined monoplanes. These aircraft, with the engines in the front, were marginally successful, prefiguring the configuration that would eventually come to dominate aviation.

### The Wrights Come to France

By 1907, the Wrights were far ahead of everyone else, and offered their designs in turn to the US, British, French and German governments. In each case, they were rebuffed. The brothers were now in a position to produce multiple examples of the *Flyer III*, and they travelled to Europe with several of them. However, scepticism about aviation in general, and the Wrights' claims in particular, still persisted in higher circles. The two brothers returned to Dayton without having made any sales.

The solution, they decided, was to make public demonstrations, in both Europe and the United States. The first public flight of a Wright aircraft in Europe was made by Wilbur on 8 August 1908 at the racetrack of Le Mans, and caused a sensation. His first flight lasted for only 1 minute 45 seconds, but his ability to make banking turns and to fly in a circle amazed and stunned onlookers, including several pioneer French aviators. No one now could claim that the Wrights were liars rather than flyers.

The French demonstration led to a contract with an ambitious new company, La Compagnie Générale de Navigation Aerienne. It asked the

*The first seaplane designed by Glenn Curtiss, first flown at San Diego on 26 January 1911. Curtiss made a huge contribution to seaplane development and secured early US Navy orders.*

**1911**

JANUARY

**18 January** Eugne Ely makes the first shipboard landing, on USS *Pennsylvania*, moored in San Francisco Bay, California.

**7 January** A US Army Wright biplane drops the first live bomb from the air.

**21 January** A US Army officer sends the first messages by wireless telephony from an aircraft in flight.

brothers to supply four aircraft that could carry a passenger, and to train three pilots to fly solo. The brothers modified the 1905 aircraft into the *Flyer A* and, on 14 May 1908, flew the first ever aeroplane passenger, mechanic Charlie Furnas.

The success of the two-seat *Flyer* led to the establishment of the world's first flying school, at Pau in the foothills of the Pyrenees in southern France. It was set up by Wilbur and Orville in the summer of 1909, helped by sister Katherine, who had the social skills that the brothers often lacked. All three were awarded the Legion of Honour award when they left France.

### The First Air Show

Meanwhile, European aviators had made further progress. In August 1909, La Grande Semaine D'Aviation de la Champagne (The Champagne Region's Great Aviation Week), at Rheims, east of Paris, attracted no fewer than 22 machines. The Wrights did not attend, but sent six aircraft of their design, along with machines by Farman, Blériot, Latham and Glen Curtiss. Despite various crashes and incidents, the Rheims meeting was a great success, attracting more than 500,000 spectators, and it is now regarded

*The paths of the pioneer aviators were strewn with pitfalls. This Blériot XI has met with a tragic end. Crashes in the early years of flight were common, although fatal crashes were not as frequent as might be imagined.*

## 1911

### FEBRUARY

**5 February** Vivian Walsh makes the first officially recognized flight in New Zealand in a Howard-Wright biplane.

**22 February** The first regular airmail service is begun in India.

### MARCH

**24 March** Flights are made in France with up to 12 passengers.

as the world's first air show. Curtiss beat Blériot in the speed competition (for the Gordon Bennett Cup), and one spectator, the British politician (and later prime minister) David Lloyd-George, said afterwards: 'flying machines are no longer toys and dreams … they are an established fact.'

### 1908–9: Glenn Curtiss's Years

Glenn Curtiss made his first flight on 21 May 1908 in the *White Wing*, the second aeroplane built by Alexander Graham Bell's Aerial Experiment Association (AE). This had been founded a year before to bring engineers together to build and test different approaches to flying. The first aircraft controlled by ailerons rather than wing warping, the *White Wing* was also the first American aircraft with a wheeled landing gear.

Curtiss was a skilled engineer, famous for his motorcycle designs. He was tasked with building the group's fourth aircraft, the *June Bug*. A biplane of what would later be called a conventional appearance, it also had the unusual characteristic of its lower wings being set at a dihedral (an upward angle) and its

*Postmaster-General Frank Hitchcock hands an airmail bag to pilot Earl L. Ovington at the start of the first airmail flight in the United States, on 23 September 1911. The aircraft is a Blériot-type monoplane.*

upper wings being set at an anhedral (downward angle). First flown in June 1908, the yellow-winged aircraft was soon making flights of more than 918m (3000ft). On 4 July, Curtiss and the *June Bug* made a flight of 2km (1.25 miles), easily winning the $2500 *Scientific American* prize for the first measured flight of more than 1km (3281ft).

The dissolution of the AEA was announced in late 1908, Graham-Bell having decided that

---

**APRIL**

**12 April** The first flight from London to Paris is made by Pierre Prier in a Blériot.

**12 April** The US Navy's first pilot completes training.

**JUNE**

**18 June–7 July** An 1170km (727-mile) Circuit of Europe air race attracts 42 pilots. Only eight finish.

**21 June** Édouard Nieuport sets a new aerial speed record of 140km/h (87mph).

its aims had been achieved. Curtiss now formed a company with Chanute's old gliding partner, Augustus Herring. With their first aeroplane, the *Gold Bug* (or *Golden Flyer*), Curtiss soon captured another *Scientific American* trophy, this time worth $10,000.

The *Gold Bug* design formed the basis for the *Reims Racer*, with which Curtiss won the Gordon Bennett Cup and then several trophies in Italy, in 1909. The following year, the *Hudson Flyer* won the *New York World* prize for flying 245km (152 miles) from Albany to Governor's Island, New York, along the Hudson River. The rules allowed two landings along the way, and Curtiss made one of these in Manhattan after running low on fuel and oil. Landing on Governor's Island after circling the Statue of Liberty, he then completed one of the first important point-to-point flights in history and won the *Scientific American* trophy outright.

### 1910: Air Shows Take off
Following on from the success of Rheims, similar aerial meetings were organized in the United States. The first was held at Dominguez Field, south of Los Angeles, in January 1910,

and featured many events for aeroplanes and airships (including dirigible races). Many notable figures of the day took part, alongside others yet to achieve fame, including Curtiss, the dirigible pilot Lincoln Beachy (later a famous aerobatic pilot), and the Frenchman Louis Paulham. The latter set several records in his Farman biplane, including

records for altitude, reaching 1269m (4164ft), and one for flight endurance, travelling with a passenger for more than 160km (100 miles).

*A replica of Curtis's June Bug built by Pete Bowyer.*

| **1911** | | |
| --- | --- | --- |
| JULY | AUGUST | SEPTEMBER |
| **22 July–5 August** A 1610km (1000-mile) Circuit of Britain race is held. | **2 August** Harriet Quimby becomes the first American female pilot. | **17 September–5 November** A coast-to-coast flight from New York to Pasadena, California, is made by Calbraith Rodgers. |

Curtiss took the speed prize, reaching nearly 90km/h (55mph). Again, up to half a million people enjoyed the spectacle, and many people were now inspired to involve themselves in the exciting new world of aviation.

An air meet at Boston followed in September, attended by Harriet Quimby, later to become the first American licensed woman pilot. The Wright brothers and Curtiss appeared at Boston, but the main prizewinner was Englishman Claude Grahame-White, who also took the Gordon Bennett Cup.

Belmont Park on Long Island, New York, was the site, in October, for the third and final major air show of 1910. Two dozen aviators from the United States, England and France competed at New York, but American John Moisant was the hero of the event. He was declared the winner of a race from Belmont Park to the Statue of Liberty and back, receiving a prize of $10,000. However, he had actually taken off long after the official start period elapsed, and Grahame-White, who was slower but had competed within the rules, appealed – a process that took until 1912, when he was awarded the cash prize plus interest.

*American pioneer aviator Eugene B. Ely made the aircraft carrier for aeroplanes a reality by flying off the USS* Birmingham *on 14 November 1910. The aircraft touched the water, damaging its propeller.*

**OCTOBER**

**15 October** Walter Wellman attempts but fails to cross the Atlantic Ocean in the airship *America*.

**22 October** The first wartime reconnaissance mission is flown by an Italian pilot during fighting against Turkish forces in Libya.

**NOVEMBER**

**1 November** The first bombs (grenades) are dropped in war, by an Italian pilot in Libya.

### The First Mass-produced Aeroplanes

Various aviators had coaxed an assortment of machines into the air by 1909, and now some of the best aeronautical minds of the age set out to develop a practical aeroplane that could be constructed in series and flown by almost anyone.

After the success of the *14bis*, Santos-Dumont suffered a string of failures, finally getting it right with the *Demoiselle (Dragonfly)* in 1909. Regarded as the first practical light aircraft, the *Demoiselle* was a conventional tractor monoplane and proved extremely popular, particularly when Santos-Dumont made the plans available free of charge. He used the first *Demoiselle* as his personal transport, but it was to be his last design before he contracted multiple sclerosis and retired from aviation.

Also in France, Louis Blériot had joined with Gabriel Voisin to form an aircraft company. By 1905, it had produced a couple of designs, including a floatplane glider, but the two designers split in 1906, with Blériot setting up his own company. The 1907 Blériot V is regarded as the first successful monoplane, but it had a short life before crashing. His

Model VII of the same year flew more than 500m (1640ft) and established the configuration of his later successful designs.

In October 1908, Lord Northcliffe, owner of the *Daily Mail* and one of Britain's first 'press barons', offered a prize of £500 for the first person to cross the English Channel by air. By January 1909, he increased it to £1000. Wilbur Wright, then in France, considered competing for the prize – and also a secret offer from Northcliffe to make the flight himself for a much larger sum. However, he rejected both possibilities: Orville was recovering from an accident and warned against it, partly because he thought Wilbur's current engine was not reliable enough.

This left the field open for two of France's most capable aviators, the 26-year-old Hubert Latham and 37-year-old Blériot. Latham was something of a playboy thrill seeker, who had begun with ballooning before graduating to the Antoinette IV monoplane, with which he was

*Harriet Quimby, seen here swinging the propeller of her Blériot monoplane, was America's first woman pilot.*

**1912**

JANUARY

10 January Glenn Curtiss tests the first successful flying boat, the *Flying Fish*.

FEBRUARY

**February** Jules Vedrine makes the first 160km/h (100mph) flight in his *Monocoque Deperdussin*.

soon inextricably linked in the public eye. Blériot, on the other hand, was a respected businessman, but by 1909 his aviation activities were straining his finances, and he was considering giving up flying when he chose to compete for the *Daily Mail* prize.

With his Model XI, which first flew on 23 January 1909, Blériot at last had a machine that was theoretically capable of a Channel flight. The design of the XI was very clean and pleasing to the eye, with an 18.6kW (30hp) Anzani rotary engine at the front, broad wings with considerable camber, and a single tail fin and rudder. Roll control was by wing warping, but, in most other ways, the Blériot XI had the features that would be found on successful aeroplanes for a generation, including the use of a single control stick for pitch and roll and a foot rudder bar for yaw.

Latham's Antoinette IV, designed by Léon Levavasseur, was larger than the Blériot XI, but broadly similar in configuration. Its delta-shaped tail surfaces were somewhat fussier, as were the controls – two separate wheels were required for pitch and roll control. The wings featured ailerons, although subsequent

*On 16 April 1912, Harriet Quimby became the first woman to fly an aeroplane over the English Channel. She had gained her flying licence in April 1911.*

MARCH

**1 March** American Captain Albert Berry makes the first parachute jump from an aircraft.

APRIL

**13 April** The Royal Flying Corps (RFC) is established.

**16 April** The first licensed US woman pilot, Harriet Quimby, crosses the English Channel by air.

*Glenn Curtiss in the cockpit of his first successful flying boat, the* Flying Fish, *which featured a stepped hull. This design reduced drag as the aircraft moved through the water.*

Antoinettes reverted to wing warping. The engine, also called an Antoinette, had an innovative steam cooling system.

In the months before the Channel attempt, Blériot used the Model IX to make several record cross-country flights, including one of more than 35km (22 miles) – enough to cross between Calais and Dover if all went well. Both aviators set up camp near Sangatte in the Pas de Calais. A wireless telegraph station was established on the clifftops to receive weather information from England, and a French Navy destroyer was stationed to point the way to Dover and provide search-and-rescue assistance if necessary.

## 1912

### MAY

**May-June** The US Army conducts trials with an aerial machine gun.

**30 May** Wilbur Wright dies from typhoid fever.

### AUGUST

**10 August** The US Army Signal Corps uses aeroplanes in military manoeuvres.

### SEPTEMBER

**19 September** The Zeppelin LZ13 begins the world's first international commercial passenger air service, between Hamburg, Copenhagen and Malmo, Sweden.

Latham was the first to make an attempt, on 19 July, circling for height, then heading for England. All went well until nearly one-third of the distance across, when the Antoinette's engine began to give trouble. It soon gave out, and Latham glided down to a smooth landing on the water. The aircraft floated well and Latham barely got wet before he was brought aboard the rescuing destroyer. The Antoinette, though, was less fortunate and was too badly damaged by the water and the recovery to be readied for another attempt, so a new aircraft was ordered – an Antoinette VII with a more powerful engine and wing warping.

The new aircraft arrived on July 22, but by now Latham had stiff competition, for Blériot was almost ready to make his own attempt. Meanwhile, along the

coast near Boulonge at Wissant, the Comte de Lambert was preparing his Wright Type A to join the fray. Unfortunately, an accident on a test flight forced him to withdraw injured.

Strong winds on the evening of 24 July saw both aviators retire to bed early, but one of Blériot's assistants roused him at 2.30 a.m., the winds having dropped. Blériot dispatched his wife and several journalists on a warship bound

for England and set off for the takeoff field, where the XI was quickly readied. At 4.15 a.m., he made a short test flight and at sunrise, just 20 minutes later, he set off.

The little monoplane took off over the cliffs, leaving nothing but the rasping noise of its radial engine behind. The noise awoke Latham, who rushed out as Blériot disappeared. Latham's crew hurried to ready his aircraft, but the

*The* Deperdussin Monocoque *Racer of 1913. With its fuselage shell of moulded plywood, the racer was a very advanced design for its day, as well as being a very attractive one.*

## 1913

### JANUARY

**13 January** The first regular aerial cargo service is established between Boston and New York.

**24 January** Swiss pilot Oscar Bider reaches 3500m (11,483ft) when he flies over the Pyrenees in his Blériot monoplane.

### MAY

**13 May** First flight of Sikorsky's *Russky Vitiaz*, or Le Grand, the world's first four-engine aircraft.

weather changed again, and quickly became unsuitable for the fragile Antoinette.

Blériot carried on, making about 64km/h (40mph) at a height of 75m (250ft), and within a few minutes he had passed the destroyer carrying his wife and the reporters. For a while, he could see neither French nor English coasts, but was hanging between sea and sky – and feeling, he said later, as if he were in a balloon. Eventually, the famous white cliffs came into view. Establishing that he had drifted north, he turned to follow the coast until Dover Castle came into view. There stood two journalist friends from the newspaper *Le Matin*, waving a tricolour flag to guide him in.

Blériot was not known for his smooth landings, and the one he made in a meadow near Dover was no exception, breaking his undercarriage and propeller. Nevertheless, just 37 minutes and 34km (21 miles) after takeoff, Blériot had become the first man to cross the Channel, and the first to make an over-the-water international flight. Thirty minutes after his landing, the escorting destroyer docked at Dover, emphasizing (as if it were needed) just how much of a revolution had been heralded by Blériot's

*The Avro 504, which first flew at Brooklands in July 1913, was a straightforward development of the Type E, which was already on order for the Royal Flying Corps.*

## 1913

### SEPTEMBER

**9 September** The first loop is performed by a Russian Army pilot.

**9 September** The first German Navy airship, Zeppelin LZ14 (L1), crashes into the North Sea, killing 14 crew.

**17 September** The Avro 504 flies. More than 8000 are built and used for many purposes, most notably for training.

**23 September** Roland Garros makes the first nonstop crossing of the Mediterranean.

*Igor Sikorsky's* Russki Vitiaz (Russian Knight) *was the world's first four-engined aircraft. On 2 August 1913, it was airborne for 1 hour 54 minutes with eight people on board, and went on to make 53 flights before being dismantled.*

## The Price of Progress

The pioneering years of aviation up to 1914 saw many people attempt to build flying machines – and most of them fail. Those who achieved success – whether by their designs, their daring or both – became the heroes of the age. Some went on to old age and financial success, but many others paid for progress with their lives. Harriet Quimby became the first woman to fly the Channel, just three years after Blériot, then enjoyed a glittering flying career that ended when she fell to her death at the 1912 Boston Aviation Meet. John Moisant was killed when his Blériot crashed in December 1910, only a few weeks after his disputed triumph in New York. Lincoln Beachey was killed at the height of his fame as an exhibition pilot. Hubert Latham made a second attempt to cross the Channel, but came down in the water again and abandoned aviation. Turning to other forms of adventure, he was gored to death by a water buffalo in Africa in 1912.

Others were inspired by the pioneers to take flight, and became the heroes of the second age of aviation, when flying stopped being a rich gentleman's pastime – to become initially a tool of war and, only secondly, a means of commerce.

modest flight. The next day, the *Daily Mail* trumpeted: 'Britain is no longer an island' – the message Lord Northcliffe had been trying to get across from the start. Others said that the flight marked the moment when Britain would need to look further than to its navy for its defence.

Within two days, Blériot had received orders for 100 Model XIs, and his financial worries were over. His monoplanes became the first mass-produced aeroplanes and were built under licence in many countries. Blériot's later company, Société Pour Aviation et ses Derives (SPAD), built thousands more aircraft for the Allied air forces in World War I.

### NOVEMBER

**5 November** In the United States, an aeroplane is used for the first time to correct the fall of artillery fire.

**30 November** American pilots flying in Mexico fire pistols at each other in the first aerial combat.

### DECEMBER

**28 December** The first flight at an altitude of more than 6096m (20,000ft) is achieved in France.

# Bloodied in Battle
# 1914–1918

*The first practical uses for the aeroplane were for military purposes rather than for trade or communication. Apart from a few token airmail flights and exhibition flying, aeroplanes had done little to pay their way before much of the world was thrown into turmoil by the events of 1914.*

**M**ilitary aviation began in the 1860s, when both sides in the American Civil War used tethered balloons for observing each other and correcting the fall of artillery. A Union barge even conducted observation flights while sailing down the Potomac River, thereby becoming the world's first aircraft carrier. One disadvantage of the balloon was that it tended to attract artillery itself, which mainly fell among the soldiers gathered near its tethering point. As a result,

balloons lost favour with the generals of both sides, so it is not surprising that they had no effect on the outcome of the war. The concept was revisited by the British during several colonial campaigns in the late Victorian era, which led to the formation of the first military aviation units, such as the Balloon Section of the Royal Engineers. Observation balloons and, of course, airships would go on to play important roles in World War I.

### The First Military Aeroplane
In 1908, while Wilbur Wright was promoting the aeroplane in Europe, his brother, Orville, was undertaking the

*Left: Although observation balloons had been used experimentally during the Napoleonic Wars, their first use on a regular basis was in the American Civil War. Right: Samuel Franklin Cody assembling an aircraft.*

equally important task of convincing the US government to use it. Although initially indifferent, the US Army agreed to a series of trials, which began at Fort Myer, Virginia on 3 September 1908.

There now followed a series of successful flights, including some that carried passengers and some that lasted for over an hour, but on 17 September tragedy struck. Lieutenant

Thomas Selfridge was riding with Orville Wright over Fort Myers when a propeller fractured. Little could be done before the *Military Flyer*, as it was known, plunged to the ground from a height of about 23m (75ft). Both men were thrown from the aircraft, but Selfridge struck his head on a strut and suffered fatal injuries, becoming the first person to die in a powered aircraft crash.

Selfridge was an experienced aviator at a time when the number of people ever to have flown was probably fewer than 100. The official US government observer to Graham-Bell's Aerial Experiment Association, he had flown several of the AEA's unorthodox craft. Indeed, he had designed and flown the *Red Wing* for the AEA and also served as the group's secretary. He was also one of the first two pilots trained to fly the US Army's first dirigible in 1908.

The crash could have ended the Wrights' hopes of selling the US military an aeroplane. The trials showed enough promise, however, for the government to extend the trials until Orville had recovered from his injuries, which included broken ribs and leg bones, and could fly again.

Eventually, in 1909, the US government bought an aircraft from the Wrights. The *Military Flyer* cost $30,000 and became the first military aeroplane in the world. Even so, the US Army was unsure about how exactly to use it. Wilbur instructed the first two US Army pilots in October 1909. By early 1911, the first aircraft had been damaged and rebuilt several times, and it was retired.

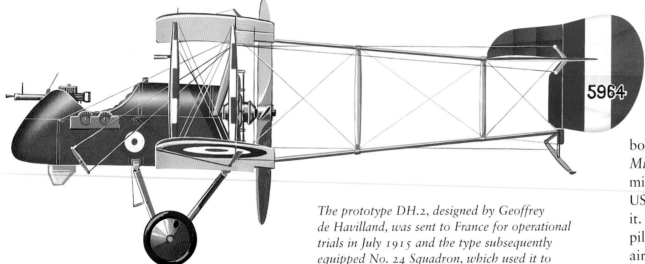

*The prototype DH.2, designed by Geoffrey de Havilland, was sent to France for operational trials in July 1915 and the type subsequently equipped No. 24 Squadron, which used it to counter the Fokker Monoplane.*

**1914**

MARCH

**22 March** The first commercial aeroplane passenger service is begun between St Petersburg and Tampa, Florida.

APRIL

**25 April** US Navy seaplanes make the first operational military flights by American aircraft during the Vera Cruz Incident with Mexico.

## Fledgling Air Forces

Progress was also occurring beyond the United States. The first aeroplane to be flown in Britain was piloted in October 1908 by American-born showman Samuel Cody (born Franklin Cowdery, and no relation to 'Buffalo Bill'). Known as British Army Aeroplane No. 1, the aircraft was of the box-kite type, and drew on earlier experiments. Cody had been working with large, and even man-carrying, kites since 1901, and by 1906 he was serving in the British Army as an instructor in the art of kiting. He was also tasked with the formation of two kite sections for the Royal Engineers – which would later become the Air Battalion of the Royal Engineers and, eventually, No. 1 Squadron of the Royal Flying Corps and Royal Air Force.

After kites came airships, and Cody was involved in the construction of the British Army's first such machine, *Nulli Secundus* (*Second to None*). The airship made a spectacular flight from Aldershot to London in October 1907, circling St Paul's Cathedral, but being forced by strong headwinds to land at Crystal Palace, south of the city. Damaged in a subsequent gale, the airship was rebuilt as the *Nulli Secundus II*. However, it had a short flying life: the government declared that there was no foreseeable use for aircraft in the military and stopped funding Cody's experiments.

Undaunted, Cody carried on privately, his experiments culminating with the *Flying Cathedral* of 1911. This won the British Army's

*The Voisin 3 of 1914 was the standard French day and night bomber during the early part of World War I.*

*The Fokker E.I was the military designation of the Fokker M5K monoplane, fitted with a simple engine-driven system that enabled a Parabellum machine gun to be fired through the aircraft's propeller arc.*

Military Trials on Salisbury Plain in 1912, earning him a prize of ££5000. Sadly, he was to lose his life in August 1913, when his new floatplane design crashed. More than 100,000 people lined the route of his funeral procession.

By 1911, military aviation was well established. In that year, the first trials with guns and small bombs were conducted in the United States, and grenades were dropped in action during Italy's campaign against the forces of the Austro-Hungarian empire in Libya. The same conflict also saw the first operational reconnaissance missions – a role that seemed to offer the most promise to the army air services then being formed in various parts of the world. The year 1911 also saw the first landings aboard a ship, and hence the birth of naval aviation, as well as the first uses of wireless radio to communicate between aircraft and the ground.

Because the first air services were usually formed as adjuncts of national armies, their initial roles were to observe enemy movements and positions, and to spot the fall of artillery. Generals did not consider using them as a means of attack or to destroy enemy observation machines.

## 1914

### AUGUST

**15 August** The first (inconclusive) air combat is recorded between French and German aircraft.

**30 August** A German Taube drops five bombs on Paris.

By August 1914, when the 'War to End all Wars' began, France had the largest air force, followed by Imperial Russia. Great Britain, Belgium, Denmark, the Netherlands, Germany, Italy, Austro-Hungary, Serbia, Spain, Sweden and Turkey were also among the nations to have army (and, in some cases, naval) air arms. Further afield from Europe, air services had been formed Argentina, Australia, Japan and Thailand.

within one unit. As well as French models and the products of nascent British manufacturers such as Blackburn, Airco and Avro, the RFC received aircraft from the government-owned Royal Aircraft Factory. These were designated by their basic type: the craft of the BE series, for example, were regarded as 'Blériot Experimentals', while the SEs, of which the SE.5a is the most famous, were known as 'Santos Experimentals'.

*The Sopwith One-and-a-Half-Strutter, so called because of its unusual wing bracing, was originally designed as a high-performance two-seat fighter.*

The first air combat ever recorded took place in a forgotten theatre of war – Mexico. In November 1913, two American pilots, each fighting for opposing factions in the civil war, took pot shots at each other with revolvers. Earlier that year, the first aerial attack on a ship was recorded, when a Mexican pilot used a Glenn Martin pusher biplane at Guaymas. The results of these actions were not decisive in any way, but they pointed to the way aviation would develop over the trenches of the Western Front.

### The First Fighter Planes
Assorted French aircraft types, many of them already obsolete, made up the bulk of military aircraft in Europe. In the United Kingdom, the Royal Flying Corps (formed in 1912) was equipped with aircraft of many types. Indeed, there were sometimes several types serving

*The Avro 504 served as bomber, reconnaissance, fighter and training aircraft during World War I.*

---

**SEPTEMBER**

**24 September** RFC pilots use aerial photography and wireless telegraphy for artillery spotting at the Battle of the Aisne.

**NOVEMBER**

**22 November** An RFC Avro biplane shoots down the first German aircraft in aerial combat.

The outbreak of war saw the production and purchase of aircraft expand exponentially. It needed to for, within a month of the outbreak of war, the RFC had 63 aircraft deployed to France, representing about two-thirds of its strength. The mainstay of the RFC in 1914–15 was the BE.2, a stately biplane that offered the stability and clear view required by an observation platform. The two-man crew included an observer, who studied the terrain, made notes or took photographs with a bulky camera, making his report to headquarters upon landing. Radio was in its infancy; when it was fitted experimentally to BE.2s, it occupied so much space and weight that the observer had to stay behind.

The BE.2's slow speed and lack of manoeuvrability made it a handy observation and photographic platform, but these same characteristics counted against it when the enemy defences adapted to deal with threats from the air. At first, the threat came from anti-aircraft guns, modified from field artillery pieces (and known to the RFC crews as 'ack-ack' or 'Archie'). Before long, it came from enemy aircraft, whose own observers arrived over the front armed with pistols, rifles or whatever

*The Bristol Bullet was rejected for large-scale production on the grounds that its landing speed was too high for the small French airfields from which it would be operating. The real reason was that it was a monoplane, a configuration against which there was much prejudice in the RFC.*

## 1914

### DECEMBER

**21–25 December** The first bombing attacks are made on Britain, by German Navy seaplanes.

## 1915

### JANUARY

**19–20 January** The first airship raid on Britain causes damage and casualties in Norfolk.

weapons came to hand. Tales of aircraft destroying each other with well-aimed bricks or other hand-thrown projectiles are probably indeed just tales, but improvised bombs, sometimes made from tin cans, were dropped on the enemy from time to time.

The first successful air combats took place within weeks of the outbreak of war. RFC BE.2s met German Air Service Taube monoplanes and forced them down by manoeuvring or, in some cases, lucky rifle shots. This quaint state of affairs lasted into the spring of 1915, when aircraft fitted with machine guns began to appear in significant numbers. Most had a gun in a rear position fired by the observer, requiring the pilot to manoeuvre to give a rear gunner a shot. However, some types, such as the Airco DH.2,

designed by Geoffrey de Havilland, had a pusher propeller and a gun position in the nose. This offered a clear field of fire and allowed the aircraft to be flown aggressively after an opponent, an obvious advantage.

Then, in April 1915, French pilot Roland Garros came on the scene in a Morane Parasol Type L, designed in collaboration with Raymond Saulnier. This was a monoplane with its single wing mounted above the fuselage – a characteristic of Morane aircraft that continued into the 1930s. More importantly, the aircraft was fitted with a fixed, forward-firing machine-gun. This made it the first aircraft specifically designed to destroy others – in short, the first fighter plane. The gun was mounted to fire forward, but could easily be reached by the pilot to clear jams (a common problem with early machine guns).

Garros's Parasol was fitted with brass deflector plates on the propeller blades, which prevented the bullets shattering the wood. Although Garros quickly brought down five

*Two early Zeppelins of the type that took part in the first successful attack on the British Isles in January 1915.*

**MARCH**

**4 March** Zeppelin *LZ37* becomes the first to be destroyed by aircraft when brought down by a Royal Navy aircraft near Calais.

aircraft designer Antony Fokker. Analysing its strengths and limitations, he developed a better aircraft and system, including the synchronization gear, sometimes called the interrupter gear. This worked on the principal of preventing the gun from firing at the moment the propeller blades passed the muzzle. The story goes that he came up with a prototype in just a few days. In fact, he used many of the features of a patent filed in 1913 by Swiss inventor Franz Schneider.

This synchronization gear, when allied to a Fokker Eindecker unarmed single-seat monoplane, created the first truly successful fighter. A Morane Type L was the first

*First flown on 19 September 1916, the Bristol F.2A two-seat fighter made its operational debut in World War I, during the Allied spring offensive of 1917. The F.2A was succeeded by the F.2B, an upgraded version.*

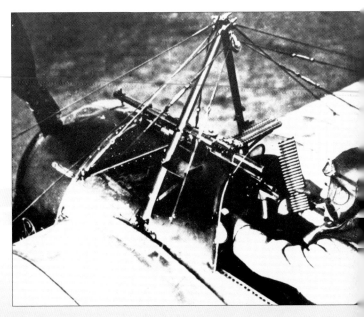

*Roland Garros in his Morane monoplane. His deflector arrangement was crude and only partially effective.*

German aircraft with the Morane, he was not the first 'ace'. That honour fell to Alphonse Pegoud, an aviator famous for being the first in the West to perform a loop. Garros himself was captured by the Germans after his aircraft was forced down behind enemy lines due to engine failure. The secrets of his mount fell into German hands, and were studied by the Dutch

## 1915

### APRIL

**26 April** William Rhodes-Moorhouse is the first airman awarded the Victoria Cross.

**1 April** French pilot Roland Garros shoots down a German aircraft with a forward-firing gun, using deflector plates to protect the propeller.

unconfirmed victim of a Fokker on 1 July 1915. A month later, Max Immelmann forced down a B.E.2c, opening a period that became known as the 'Fokker Scourge'.

The main production version of the Fokker Eindecker (single-decker or monoplane) was the E.III, armed with a single Parabellum machine gun. (A few E.IVs, with two guns, were built, and some with three guns were also tested.) In the hands of experts such as Immelmann, the agile Fokkers ruled the skies for nearly a year. As with many Fokker aircraft, though, the structure of the E.III was not strong, and Immelmann was killed in June 1916 when his E.III broke up in flight. He had scored 15 victories and was credited with inventing the basic combat manoeuvre that bore his name, in which the aircraft reverses direction by beginning a loop, but rolling upright at the top.

The Allies countered the Eindeckers by inventing their own version of the synchronization gear and by fitting guns outside

*Zeppelins in their shed. The later generation of Zeppelin could carry 3624kg (8000lb) of bombs, the average load carried by a Lancaster bomber in World War II.*

MAY

**31 May** The first Zeppelin raid is made on London.

the propeller arc, such as on top of the wing, using a mount that allowed for reloading and clearing jams in flight. The first British aircraft to use synchronization gear was the Sopwith One-and-a-Half Strutter, which arrived in April 1916. Its odd name came from its wing strut configuration, and it was built in both single-seat and twin-seat versions and as fighters and bombers. As a fighter (or in the parlance of the time, a 'fighting scout'), the Strutter was no great shakes, but its basic configuration was adapted for the Pup and later the Camel, the most famous Allied fighter of World War I.

The British also developed a second approach to fighter armament, as typified by the Royal Aircraft Factory SE.5a. This had a Lewis gun mounted atop the wing, as well as a Vickers gun firing through the propeller.

*Early bombing was primitive, the missile being hand-dropped by the pilot or observer.*

It is notable that the success of the Eindecker did not lead to a proliferation of low-wing monoplanes. One exception was the Bristol M.1C, which was more streamlined and strongly built, and a better performer all round. The Bristol failed to find official favour, however. Its landing speed of 80km/h (49mph) was regarded as too fast for the average pilot, and the M.1s were largely assigned to out-of-the-way theatres of war, such as the Middle East.

Two-seat aircraft were the machines of choice for observation and light bombing. As noted earlier, stability was usually chosen over manoeuvrability and speed, leading to heavy losses. Soon reconnaissance aircraft could fly only with a strong escort, and destroying them required a large force of fighters to neutralize the escorts, leading to huge, swirling battles over the Western Front.

To provide a two-seater that had a chance of defending itself, the Bristol Aeroplane Company came up with the R.2B reconnaissance aircraft, powered by a 142kW (190hp) Rolls-Royce

*The Fokker E.I monoplane secured air superiority for the Germans over the Western Front in summer 1915.*

**1915**

**JULY**

**1 July** The Fokker EI monoplane appears on the Western Front. Its synchronized forward-firing machine gun gives it a huge advantage over Allied types.

**AUGUST**

**12 August** A Royal Naval Air Service seaplane sinks a Turkish ship with a torpedo.

Falcon inline engine. Showing potential as a fighter, the R.2B was renamed the F.2A and flew as such in September 1916, becoming known as the Bristol Fighter. The Fighter's combat debut in April 1917 was a disaster, however, four being lost in short order to German fighters. The fault was not with the aircraft, but in its tactical use, relying on straight and level flight to give the rear gunners clear shots.

Nonetheless, the Bristol Fighter had potential for use in an aggressive role, with a fixed forward-firing Vickers gun and twin Lewis guns in the observer's position. The design was therefore improved with revised flying surfaces and a variety of more powerful engines as the F.2B. The extra power allowed the 'Brisfit', as it came to be called, to be flown more as a scout, and it soon became highly successful as a fighter as well as a light bomber.

The Bristol Fighter was flown by many aces. The Canadian Andrew McKeever downed the highest number of enemy planes – 31. New Zealander Keith Park downed 20 – and would go on to have a vital leadership role in World War II, commanding RAF forces in the Battle of Britain and the defence of Malta. More than 3000 Bristol Fighters were built and served the Royal Air Force throughout the interwar period, particularly in the colonial policing role in the Middle East.

### The New Bomber

The bomber can be used for three distinctive roles: close air support, where attacks are directed against forces in the field to help friendly ground troops; tactical bombing against enemy infrastructure or communications behind the front line; and strategic bombing against major bases, industry or population centres on the enemy's home territory.

Close air support and tactical bombing in World War I tended to be conducted by two-seaters, using weapons that could be lifted by a single ground crewman – up to a weight of about 20kg (44lb). Other weapons used

*The Junkers J1 was the first all-metal aircraft to become operational anywhere in the world.*

---

**DECEMBER**

**2 December** The Junkers J1 all-metal monoplane is flown in Germany.

included anti-personnel darts, or *flechettes*, and three-pointed spiked stars designed to hobble horses. A few aircraft, such as the Airco DH.5, were well suited to trench strafing, a hazardous occupation given the many thousands of rifles and machine guns that were available to be pointed skywards.

Although lighter aircraft were mainly used for close air support (CAS), the newly formed Royal Air Force used large bombers for bombing and strafing trenches in the Battle of Amiens in August 1918.

In the beginning of its use as a bomber, the aeroplane had no specialized equipment. Bombs themselves were often artillery shells or mortar rounds adapted with stabilizing fins. The observer simply carried the bombs with him in the rear cockpit and threw them overboard at what he judged to be a suitable moment. The first refinements made were simple tubes that were angled in the direction of flight; the observer looked down these, waiting for the target appear to before he let go. The next development was

*Barrage balloon 'curtains' were used to protect London against air attack. They were quite useless.*

the bomb rack, which carried rows of small bombs under the wings and released them mechanically. Eventually, more sophisticated bomb-aiming devices were developed.

With light bombers such as the British DH.4, Bristol Fighter, French Breguet 14 and German LVG, the strategy of interdiction developed – the destruction by firepower of the enemy's lines of communication. Attacks could be made beyond the front lines at enemy encampments, rail junctions, airfields and supply lines.

### Strategic Bombing and Defence

The proponents of air power considered aircraft to be more than an adjunct to the army, offering the ability to strike well beyond the range of the navy's big guns. Within months of the outbreak of war, the combatants found themselves in entrenched positions, making it impossible to capture or strike targets within the enemy's heartland by conventional means. The first long-range bombers were, in fact, airships, a development in which Germany had the lead.

Count Ferdinand von Zeppelin had flown his first rigid airship in 1900, and, through a series of trials and tribulations, had developed a series

## 1916

### JANUARY

**3 January** RFC aircraft make the first supply drops in wartime, to British forces besieged in Iraq.

### APRIL

**April (exact date not known)** French pilots use Le Prieur air-to-air rockets for the first time in combat. They prove effective in destroying observation balloons.

*The Handley Page O/100 originated in a British requirement, issued in December 1914, for a 'bloody paralyser of an aeroplane' for the bombing of Germany.*

of reliable military airships, in service with both the German Army and Navy. The Schutte-Lanz Luftschiffbau company also supplied airships to the military. These had better streamlining, which was soon adopted by Zeppelin, and also a wooden rather than aluminium internal structure. To the Allies, however, all enemy airships were Zeppelins, or 'Zepps'.

The Zeppelins in service in 1914 were about 150–160m (492–524ft) long, with volumes up to 25,000 cubic metres (883,000 cubic feet) and a lifting capability of about 9000kg (19,840lb). Most had three Maybach diesel engines of up to 410kW (550hp) each, giving top speeds of approximately 80km/h (50mph).

The German Army's war experience with Zeppelins was brief and unsuccessful. Using them against tactical targets in the first weeks of World War I, they lost four airships – wrecked, shot down by anti-aircraft fire or captured. Airship operations were therefore left to the Navy, which saw great promise in using them to attack England.

While Zeppelins had comparable speeds to fighters of the day, they did enjoy an advantage. Taking off from bases on the North Sea, they were flying at a considerable height by the time they had reached their targets and were able to climb higher once they dropped their bombs, leaving the defences far below. That said, the high altitudes were harsh on the crews, who operated in freezing cold and thin air. Navigation was extremely difficult and bombing accuracy poor. Nonetheless, the effect of the bombing raids on civilian morale, however inaccurate, prompted governments to redirect a disproportionate amount of resources to counter them.

The Zeppelins attacked at night, and night-flying by aeroplanes was a new art, mastered by only a few. Initial attempts to intercept Zeppelins over the United Kingdom cost the lives of more defending pilots than airship crews or civilians, the pilots crashing on takeoff and landing. The coordination of defences took time, but eventually areas of priority were established for anti-aircraft guns, searchlights, barrage balloons and fighters. Standing patrols were set up so that aircraft were already at altitude by the time the airships arrived. Observer stations and even sound locators provided a limited degree of early warning of approaching attack.

The first Zeppelin raid on England took place in January 1915, and the first on London

**15–29 April** First sustained resupply of troops by air in Mesopotamia, Iraq.

**20 April** A squadron of American volunteers (later named Lafayette Escadrille) is formed as part of the French Air Service.

at the end of May. The latter raid caused considerable damage and seven fatalities. The public clamour to do something about the 'Zepp menace' grew, and fighters and guns were held back in England to defend the capital and other strategic locations. It was not over England, however, that the first Zeppelin was brought down. Royal Navy pilot Sub-Lieutenant Reginald Warneford, flying a Morane-Saulnier Type L, pursued LZ37 from Ostend to Ghent, Belgium, then destroyed it by dropping six 9kg (20lb) light bombs on it from above. The resultant explosion flipped Warneford's aircraft upside-down and stopped his engine, forcing a landing in enemy territory. Fortunately, he was able to restart his engine before the enemy arrived and return to his home airfield. Warneford was awarded the Victoria Cross, in recognition of the fact that he was the first airman to destroy an airship in air combat.

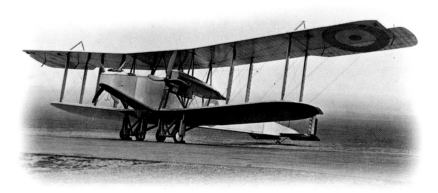

*The Handley Page o/400 was developed from the o/100, and in the summer of 1918 it was the backbone of the RAF's strategic bombing force.*

..............................................

*A Lohner Type L flying boat in the markings of the Austro-Hungarian Navy. The Type L seated a crew of two side by side.*

Airships made a difficult target. They were well defended by several machine-gun posts and, although filled with extremely flammable hydrogen, were hard to ignite with conventional ammunition. Pilots therefore had to climb above them and attack with incendiary bombs, a difficult task for the pilot of a single-seater. Later, two types of incendiary ammunition were introduced, Buckingham and Pomeroy, which were much more effective against airships and also observation balloons.

Zeppelin raids in 1916 killed almost 300 people in Britain, and it was not until September that

---

**1916**

| JUNE | SEPTEMBER | |
|---|---|---|
| **29 June** The first Boeing aeroplane, the B&W, is flown near Seattle, Washington. | | **15 September** A French submarine is sunk in the Adriatic by Austrian Lohner flying boats. |
| | **2 September** Radio communication between aircraft in flight is successfully tested near San Diego, California. | |

the first night-fighter victory was scored against an airship – in this case, the Schütte-Lanz SL 11. Again, the successful pilot, William Leefe-Robinson, was awarded the Victoria Cross, his feat made all the more remarkable for being carried out in an obsolescent BE.2c.

Eventually, the tide turned. Improved fighters such as the Sopwith Camel, SE.5a and DH.4 could counter even the improved 'Super Zeppelins' – also known as 'Height Climbers' for their ability to operate at altitudes of 5500m (18,000ft). Forcing the Zeppelins higher protected them from interception, but the altitude also meant colder temperatures and less oxygen for the crew, and made navigation more difficult and less accurate. Only 11 raids took place in 1917 and 1918 – the last, on 5 August 1918, was marked by the loss of LZ70 off the Norfolk coast and the death of Peter Strasser, head of the Naval Airship Department.

The airship campaign caused nearly 2000 casualties and considerable, if scattered, damage. The cost was heavy, though, at more

*Rittmeister Freiherr Manfred von Richthofen, the top-scoring pilot of World War I with 80 victories.*

than 60 airships, and most of their crews. A Zeppelin cost about the same as a battleship to build, was vulnerable to attack both in the air and on the ground, and could carry only a small warload if it was able to fly above the defences. Their principal advantage was their long range – a fact that would give them new life in the 1920s and 1930s, serving in the commercial sphere.

### Bombers

After the early disappointing airship raids, the German Army Air Service concentrated on bombers in its campaign against England. The first small-scale raids were mounted before the end of 1914, but had little more than nuisance value. In 1915, specifications were issued for a series of large aircraft, or *Grosskampfflugzeug*, for bombing. Most of the tendered designs were ordered in small numbers, the result being that the fleet ended up with half-a-dozen designs. These early aircraft were mainly used tactically, but in early 1917 a special unit was set up to carry out attacks on England, equipped with new bombers built by Gotha.

The principal model was the GIV, a twin-engined machine with a three-man crew and a

**17 September** Rittmeister Manfred von Richthofen, the 'Red Baron', scores the first of his 80 victories.

**22 September** The U-boat *U-32* is sunk by bombs dropped by a Royal Naval Air Service aircraft.

warload of up to 500kg (1100lb). To reach London, however, it was restricted to six 50kg (110lb) bombs. The bomber attacks on England began in June 1917, comprising up to 20 aircraft and leading to significant civilian casualties. The worst raid killed 162 people, including 16 schoolchildren. The Gothas were faster than the Zeppelins, although lower-flying, and operated in daylight. Experienced fighter squadrons were temporarily withdrawn from the Western Front to bolster the home defences, but had no better luck in bringing them down than did existing units. The failure to stop the Gotha attacks led to a major shake-up of the United Kingdom's air defence system – such as it was. A new system of gun and searchlight belts and aircraft patrol areas was established, and RFC aircraft were dedicated to defence, becoming separated from the needs of the British Army in the field. Thus the seeds of a fully independent air force were sown.

The Gothas returned in August, this time at night, and in September they were joined by a handful of *Reisenflugzeugen*, or giant aircraft.

*The Handley Page V/1500 was designed to attack targets in Germany from bases in Britain.*

## 1917

### FEBRUARY

**11–12 February** A German crew scores the first aerial victories at night.

### APRIL

**April** More than 350 Allied aircraft are lost in air battles during what is known as 'Bloody April'.

The most notable of these was the Zeppelin-Staaken RIV, which had no fewer than six engines and a wingspan barely smaller than that of the World War II B-29 Superfortress. Incendiary bombs were added to the arsenal in October 1917.

Despite these new tactics and aircraft, losses became increasingly heavy due to bad weather, mechanical problems and landing accidents. The odd anti-aircraft shell also found its mark, although falling shrapnel sometimes did more damage

than enemy bombs. And the Allied night-fighters were finally beginning to score, led by pioneers such as Gilbert Murlis-Green, who proved that even a twitchy single-seater such as a Camel could be flown at night.

The final German raid came in late May 1918. A force of 38 Gothas and three Giants was met by 30,000 anti-aircraft shells and numerous fighters. The anti-aircraft guns and fighters accounted for three bombers each, and the bombs caused little damage. By this time, the situation on the Western Front had deteriorated for Germany, so the remaining bombers were directed to attack British forces in the field during the last campaigns of the war. The first air campaign against Britain was over, but the experience was to stand the nascent Royal Air Force in good stead when Germany again attacked in 1940.

### British Bombers

The British Admiralty ordered large bombers within months of the outbreak of war in 1914. In contrast to many other aircraft that moved from suggestion to front line in the space of a few months or even weeks, however, these were to take almost two years to enter service.

Answering the Admiralty's demand for 'a bloody paralyser of an aeroplane' (the memorable requirement made in December 1914), the Handley Page company flew its twin-engined, two-seat O/100 bomber prototype a year later. This aircraft featured an enclosed cockpit and considerable armour plating, but these features were dropped for the subsequent 40 production aircraft. One novelty that remained was the ability to fold the wings back, for storage in the standard hangars of the day. The production aircraft also had a four-man crew and up to five defensive machine guns.

Handley Page's O/100s were initially used by the Royal Naval Air Service for sea patrols off Flanders. Then, starting in March 1917, they

*William E. Boeing, who founded the famous aircraft company at Seattle, Washington. Boeing originally worked in the timber industry.*

**18 April** The Boeing Airplane Company is formed in Seattle.

were used for night attacks on industrial and military targets in Germany itself. Three were used in the Middle East and Mediterranean theatres against Turkish forces. The improved O/400 soon followed, some 550 being built before the war's end.

The availability of many large bombers allowed the formation of the so-called 'Independent Force', which carried out strategic attacks separate to the British Army's campaigns. Alongside smaller aircraft such as the de Havilland DH.10 Amiens, which flew day missions, the Handley Page bombers struck at night deep into Germany. They also struck coastal targets such as U-boat bases and ports. The lifting capacity of the O/400, in particular, allowed much heavier bombs to be carried. From July 1918, the 748kg (1,650lb) SN bomb was used. The heaviest bomb of the war, it was said to have destroyed entire munitions factories and streets of houses with a single hit.

Night-flying was certainly hazardous, and the four night-bomber squadrons suffered almost

*Lieutenant Edwin Dunning touches down on HMS* Furious *to make the first landing on a ship at sea.*

## 1917

**MAY**

**3 May** RFC aircraft are used for the first time on close air support missions, during the Arras Offensive.

**AUGUST**

**2 August** RNAS pilot Edwin Dunning makes the first landing on a ship at sea, landing a Sopwith Pup on HMS *Furious*.

four times as many aircraft wrecked as missing over enemy territory (114 to 34) in 13 months of strategic bombing. At the same time, however, the five day-bomber squadrons lost 103 aircraft to enemy action and 201 to crashes. The vulnerability of aircraft daylight raids should now have been obvious, but the point was somehow missed, and the lesson would only be learned, at great cost, during World War II, by the RAF crews sent against German targets in 1940–41.

An even bigger bomber, the Handley Page V/1500 was readied for attacks on Berlin in November 1918, but the Armistice came before it was utilized. Its only use came in May 1919, when an example named *Old Carthusian* dropped a single bomb on the Emir's palace in Kabul, immediately ending a local insurrection.

### Russian Bombers

Beginning a tradition of large Russian aircraft, which continues to this day, was the Sikorsky Ilya Muromets. Although smaller than the V/1500 and the Zeppelin Giant, it had four engines and entered service before its counterparts in the West. Derived from Sikorsky's *Le Grand* of 1913, the world's first four-motored aircraft, the Ilya Muromets was produced by the Russo-Baltic Wagon Factory (RBVZ in Russian). It was built with a variety of powerplants (sometimes more than one type on each aircraft), and was successfully used against German and Baltic targets from 1915 until the Russian Revolution of October 1917. In this time, only one was lost to enemy action and two to crashes, while several others were destroyed to prevent capture by the Germans. The RBVZ Ilya Muromets proved a sturdy and reliable bomber, and could also act as a long-range reconnaissance aircraft. Its resistance to battle damage and its bombing accuracy were superior to most of its counterparts.

*The Fokker Dr.I (the 'Dr' denoting Dreidecker, or triplane) was introduced into service in August 1917.*

**21 August** The Fokker Dr.1 triplane enters service on the Western Front.

## Air Combat

Aviation in World War I is usually associated with aerial combat and duels between fighter aces in brightly coloured fighter planes. To a degree, this picture is true, but one-on-one engagements between opposing fighters were the exception rather than the rule, and dogfighting was a sideshow compared to the serious business of reconnaissance, bombing and close air support.

Fighter aircraft began as fighting scouts – essentially, armed observation aircraft – and most combats began when opposing scouts met. The need to escort two-seat scouts and slower bombers led to the first meetings of large formations fighters and the first mass combats. Basic combat tactics and formations were developed at this time, largely by the first great German flying aces Max Immelmann and Oswald Boelcke.

At the start of the war, the Germans enjoyed air superiority. Following Immelmann's death and the introduction of Allied fighters with

synchronized forward-firing armament such as the Sopwith 11/2 Strutter and the French Nieuport 17, however, this superiority was lost. Boelcke was given a free hand to organize the first dedicated fighter squadrons, known as *Jagdstaffeln*, or hunting squadrons, but usually abbreviated as *Jastas*. Unlike bomber and observation units, which usually occupied the same bases for relatively long periods and moved only as the Army required, the Jastas were sent where needed. This meant a nomadic existence for the pilots, who lived out of tents, and it is for this reason, rather than the colourful markings later adopted, that the units were dubbed 'flying circuses'.

The first of these new fighting units, Jasta 2, entered combat in September 1916. It was

eventually to claim more than 330 victories and a ten-to-one ratio of kills to combat losses. The initial pilots were hand-picked by Boelcke, and were soon racking up an impressive string of victories. Boelcke himself was the leading German ace at the time of his death in October 1916, the result of a collision with his wingman.

Boelcke's legacy was a set of fighting rules known as the *Dicta Boelcke*. These laid down the basic tenets of aerial combat:

1. Always try to secure an advantageous position before attacking.
2. Try to place yourself between the sun and the enemy.
3. Do not fire the machine guns until the enemy is within range and you have him squarely within your sights.

*The Airco DH.4 was a very versatile and reliable machine.*

**1918**

FEBRUARY

**February** The Airco DH4, the first American mass-produced combat aircraft, begins production.

4. Attack when the enemy least expects it or when he is preoccupied with other duties such as observation, photography or bombing.
5. Never turn your back and try to run away from an enemy fighter.
6. Keep your eye on the enemy and do not let him deceive you with tricks.
7. Foolish acts of bravery bring only death. The Jasta must fight as a unit, close teamwork being required between all pilots. The signal of its leaders must be obeyed.

Even today, in the age of jet fighters and guided missiles, these principles largely hold true for visual air combat.

One of Boelcke's protégés was a young observer and former cavalry officer of noble birth named Manfred von Richthofen. He joined Jasta 2 in the autumn of 1916 and scored his first victory on 17 September.

*The giant Ilya Muromets gave Russia a strategic bomber force and became operational in 1915.*

.............................

*The Airco DH.9 was intended to supplant the DH.4, but it was underpowered.*

By the end of the year, he had 15 kills, all of which were scored in the Albatros D.II and against RFC two-seat scouts. Von Richthofen followed Boelcke's rules rigidly, although he simplified them even further: 'The duty of the fighting pilot is to patrol his area of the sky, and shoot down any enemy fighters in that area. Anything else is rubbish.'

**MARCH**

**Exact date unknown** First flight of the Airco DH.9A, a revised and improved version of the DH.9, which sees much service with the RAF in the Middle East and India.

**11 March** An international airmail service is established between cities in the Austro-Hungarian Empire.

The Jastas' greatest success came in as April 1917, known as 'Bloody April' by the Allies for the losses inflicted by the German fighters. Von Richthofen himself scored 21 victories that month before being wounded by a lucky shot from a British gunner. The balance of combat switched only when the RFC and RNAS introduced the Sopwith Camel to the front. A more powerful and better armed development of the same manufacturer's Pup, the Sopwith Camel wrested air superiority from the German Albatros fighters once its pilots had become used to its handling idiosyncrasies. The powerful rotary engine and short wingspan led to a powerful gyroscopic effect, making turns to the right much quicker than those to the left. However, there was a notable downward pull, and although this could be used to the pilot's advantage in combat, it could also be deadly close to the ground. More Camel pilots were killed in spin-related accidents in training than were lost in combat, and the difficulties in training new pilots to fly it delayed its introduction until June 1917.

······································································

*In March 1917, a shipboard version of the Sopwith Camel, the 2F.1, underwent trials.*

## 1918

### APRIL

**1 April** The Royal Air Force (RAF) is created from the RFC and RNAS and becomes the world's first fully independent air arm.

**1 April** A German pilot becomes the first to save himself by use of a parachute in combat.

**13 April** An Argentine Army pilots crosses the Andes from Argentina to Chile.

## Triplanes

A predecessor of the Camel was the Sopwith Triplane. Flown by some highly skilled naval pilots, it had a disproportionate impact on the air war during World War I. Only about 150 'Tripes' were built, all serving with the British and French naval air arms on the Western Front. An advantage of a triplane design is that it has a greater wing area (and therefore lift) for a given wingspan, and the Sopwith Triplanes proved both manoeuvrable and easy to fly. Canadian Raymond Collishaw was the main exponent of the Triplane and scored 33 victories, but the type's career was short.

The design excited the Germans, however, and a 'triplane frenzy' broke out in the German Army's air technical department and industry. At least eight manufacturers produced designs for triplanes, of which only two entered production, one from Pfalz and the other from Antony Fokker. His V.3, better known as the Dr.I (an abbreviation of Dreidecker, or triplane), was directionally unstable and subject to torque

......................................................

*Officers examine the remains of von Richthofen's Fokker Triplane after it had been stripped by souvenir hunters.*

**21 April** Baron Manfred von Richthofen, the 'Red Baron' and the top ace of World War I, is shot down and killed.

effects, like the Camel – but in the hands of experienced pilots, the Dr.I was a match for any Allied fighter.

Von Richthofen first scored with one of the pre-production prototypes in September 1917, marking his sixtieth victory. Returning briefly to Albatros biplanes, Richthofen had another break from combat before adopting the first of his own Triplanes. Between 12 March and 21 April

1918, he increased the number of his kills to 80, shooting down single-seaters, including several Camels. Now the leader of Jasta 2, the 'Red Baron' was increasingly fatigued and the most sought-after target on the Western Front. Finally, on 21 April 1918, he violated his own rules and dove to low level in pursuit of a Camel flown by Wilfred 'Wop' May. In turn, he was pursued by May's fellow Canadian Roy Brown,

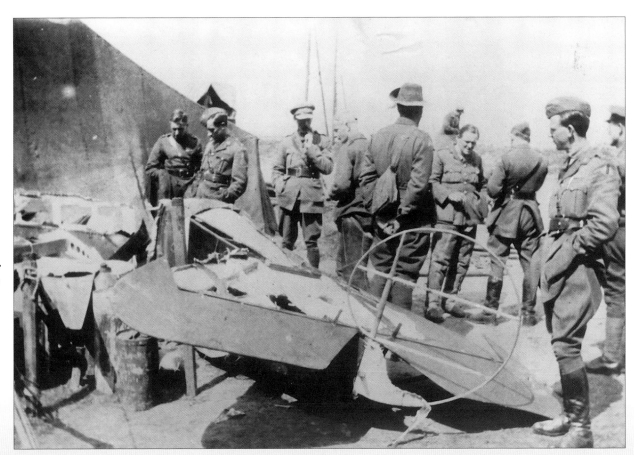

*Although it had a relatively short operational career, the Sopwith Triplane performed well and could outclimb contemporary German fighters.*

who fired several bursts at the red Triplane as it skimmed the rooftops of villages in Picardy. The combat drew the Red Baron over several Australian machine-gun positions, which also let off bursts of fire, and it was probably one of these that struck the fatal blow. The most famous pilot of World War I was dead, aged 25.

The combat record of the Red Baron – 80 confirmed kills – is often held up as a superhuman achievement in an era when a fighter pilot could expect to last only a few weeks in combat. However, a number of Allied aces approached this tally, including Frenchman René Fonck with 75 victories and Canadian

Billy Bishop with a reputed 72. Of the top ten aces, in fact only two were German, with the majority being from Britain and its colonies. It was the flamboyance of von Richthofen and his perceived chivalry, however, that will for ever make him the archetypal figure of the first age of aerial combat.

## 1918

### MAY

**15 May** An airmail service is established between New York and Washington, using Army Signal Corps aircraft and pilots.

*Built in its thousands, the famous Curtiss JN-4 'Jenny' was the result of a US Army specification of 1914, calling for a biplane trainer with a tractor engine.*

### The United States Enters the War

When the United States entered the war in April 1917, its armed forces and industry were unable to field their own fighting machines. This deficiency can partly be attributed to ongoing patent disputes between the Wrights and other manufacturers, and partly to a fragmented procurement system marred by too many vested interests. The result was that the most modern American-built aircraft by 1917 was the Curtiss 'Jenny' trainer, which was hardly suitable for a combat role. As a result, the air component of the American Expeditionary Force mainly adopted French fighter designs and some Italian Caproni bombers when its first aircrews and mechanics graduated from French training schools in late 1917.

One group of American aviators had already tasted combat by this time, however. Like the

JULY

**19 July** The first carrier-launched air strike is made by RAF Sopwith Camels attacking Zeppelin sheds.

famed 'Flying Tigers' in China in World War II, a group of volunteers travelled at their own expense to fight while their nation remained neutral. In late April 1915, this group was formally established as the Escadrille Americaine within the French Air Service, and was later renamed the Lafayette Escadrille in honour of the French general who fought with the American Revolutionary Army. This unit bred a number of aces of its own, who became leaders in the US Air Service when it formed its own squadrons in early 1918.

The unit relied on the Nieuport and SPAD S.VII and S.XIII, fine fighters of French manufacture. A few units were also equipped with Sopwith Camels at one time or another. Some American-built aircraft appeared before the war's end: about 200 examples of the Liberty-engined licence-built version of the British DH.4 light bomber were flown, and the type was to form the backbone of the Air Service for several years, as well as becoming an important mailplane. The first American design

of fighter, the Thomas-Morse MB-3 (usually called the 'Tommy Morse'), did not fly until February 1919.

The top US ace was 'Eddie' Rickenbacker. Between April and November 1918, he scored 26 victories, including a number of Fokker D.VIIs (the type regarded as Germany's best wartime fighter). He also struck several observation balloons, which were considered harder to destroy than aircraft because of their proximity to the ground and the strong anti-aircraft defences arranged around them for protection. Frank Luke, another of the top US aces, scored 14 of his 18 victories against

balloons, and was brought down while attacking another, dying in a shootout with approaching German troops.

Another notable American pilot was Raoul Lufbery, one of the volunteers of the Lafayette Escadrille. Before his death in combat in May 1918, Lufbery had invented several fighting tactics, including the 'Lufbery Circle', a formation where several aircraft provide mutual defence. Such men were to become the inspiration for the nascent US military air services and the founders of many of the traditions that were carried through World War II into the present-day US Air Force.

*HMS* Argus *was one of the Royal Navy's first aircraft carriers to feature an unbroken flight deck.*

**1918**

AUGUST

**August** German Fokker DVII fighters kill 565 people over the Western Front.

### The War's Legacy

It can be argued that World War I advanced aviation by spurring designers to build the strongest and highest-performing machines. In the process, a rich man's novelty was turned into something that involved tens of thousands of people, whether to fly, maintain or build the aircraft. Many people were won over by the perceived glamour of air combat and grew up dreaming of flight.

There is a counterargument, however, that the war held back progress. Stifling commercial aviation, it diverted the best talents into designing and building highly specialized machines of war rather than practical transports for people and goods. Indeed, many considered the war in the air to be as horrifying as the slaughter in the trenches, particularly when bombing was directed at civilian populations.

Certainly, aviation took some time to recover from the stain of war and become part of daily civilian life. And then a Golden Age dawned.

*Captain Eddie Rickenbacker was the US Air Service's leading air ace of World War I, gaining 26 victories in the summer of 1918.*

**SEPTEMBER**

**6 September** HMS *Argus*, the first aircraft carrier with a full-length flush deck, is commissioned.

# The Birth of Passenger Aviation 1919-1938

*World War I over, commercial considerations took over from military matters. The first passenger services began to be operated, often using majestic seaplanes, and the first modern monoplanes appeared. Meanwhile, British and American military aircraft design stalled, although Germany forged ahead with innovations that would prove their worth in the war to come.*

The first paying passenger services, and thus the origins of today's enormous commercial aviation industry, were flown by Zeppelin airships, predecessors of those used to scatter death over Britain in World War I. The designer of these magnificent machines, however, was a man of peace who hated to see airships used as weapons. Unfortunately, Ferdinand von Zeppelin often had to rely on military and politically tainted money to keep his enterprise afloat.

*Left: Pan American World Airways pioneered its trans-Pacific routes with the Sikorsky S-42, pictured here. Right: Count Ferdinand von Zeppelin's first airship, the LZ1, over Lake Constance, Germany.*

Having observed Union observation balloons in the American Civil War, von Zeppelin returned to his homeland determined to develop a steerable balloon. He built his first small airship, the LZ1, in 1899, flying it from his home at Friedrichshafen on Lake Constance. Success was not immediate, although the early experiments did capture public interest.

When the LZ1 was wrecked on an early flight, von Zeppelin received support and contributions from the public. Almost by accident, a local journalist, Hugo Eckener, became

*Zeppelin LZ4, seen here emerging from its shed at Friedrichshafen, Germany, flew for the first time on 20 June 1908. On 1 July it made a 12-hour endurance flight, covering 298km (185 miles).*

destroyed in a fire or a gale within a year; however, the LZ11 had nearly a year of passenger service, transporting more than 4350 passengers between German cities in 224 flights during 1911–12.

The LZ13, or *Hansa*, was the first to make regular international flights, to Denmark and Sweden. Altogether, the DELAG airships travelled approximately 200,000km (124,274 miles), and transported about 40,000 passengers up to 1914, when all surviving civil airships were forced into military service. As a military man, Count Zeppelin was keen to see his craft at the forefront of the armed forces, but Hugo Eckener considered the war to be a disaster that stood in the way of his dream of a worldwide fleet of civil airships.

### The First Aeroplane Airliners

The first paid point-to-point service using aeroplanes is generally agreed to be that of the St Petersburg–Tampa Airboat Line, set up by Tony Jannus in 1914. The aircraft used to take passengers across Tampa Bay, Florida – nowadays spanned by long bridges – was a Benoist 'Safety First' flying boat. This small

involved with Zeppelin's dreams to build an aerial ship. Working first as a publicist for the company, he later became probably the greatest-ever airship pilot, and he headed the business through its glory years.

The Zeppelin Company as a commercial concern did not form until 1908 – ironically in response to the wrecking of the LZ4. A witness started a collection, and this soon grew into a nationwide campaign that raised more than

6 million marks. A Zeppelin Foundation was set up for the promotion of airship travel, and the Luftschiffbau-Zeppelin GmbH company was established to build the airships themselves. In the same year, the LZ2 was sold to the German government.

In November 1909, a group of investors set up Deutsche Luftschiffahrts-AG (DELAG), a company that was to become the world's first airline. Each of its first three airships was

| 1919 | FEBRUARY | MARCH | MAY | JUNE | JULY |
|---|---|---|---|---|---|
| **Exact date unknown** The International Air Traffic Association (IATA) is formed to set standards for airlines, ticketing and passenger rights. | **Exact date unknown** The first sustained daily scheduled airline passenger service is opened by Deutsche Luft-Reederei between Berlin and Weimar. | **22 March** A weekly service between Paris and Brussels is started by Lignes Aériennes Farman. | **8-31 May** The US Navy's NC-4 flying boat crosses the Atlantic in stages. Three sister ships fail to complete the journey. | **14 June** John Alcock and Arthur Whitten Brown make the first nonstop aerial crossing of the Atlantic. They leave from St John's, Newfoundland, and land in a bog at Clifden, Ireland. | **1 July** The British airship R34 makes the first transatlantic round-trip flight. |

aircraft had capacity for only one passenger alongside the pilot. The first passenger was the ex-mayor of St Petersburg, Abraham Pheil, who bid $400 for the honour. The regular passenger fare was $5 and the flying boat made two flights a day, six days a week across the 34km (21-mile) route, carrying both people and freight. In the four months of its operation, 1205 passengers were safely carried, but the line was not profitable. After it ceased operations, no one raced to establish another airline in the United States, while the ongoing war in Europe prevented development there.

After the war, Florida again became the base for the first international air service. In 1920, entrepreneur Inglis

*Commercial aviation was boosted by airmail after World War I.*

*Charles Lindbergh was the first man to fly solo across the Atlantic.*

Uppercu began flying passengers between Key West and Havana, a distance of 145km (90 miles). Before long, he offered connecting services to New York, Cleveland and Detroit in his Aeromarine flying boats. He eventually operated 15 different models of this flying boat, from which the company took its name. Aeromarine Airways carried nearly 10,000 passengers in its 'flying limousines' up to 1924, but a fatal accident that January forced it out of business.

Apart from passengers, these early flying-boat services carried freight and mail.

**1920**

AUGUST

**25 August** The British Aircraft Transport and Travel company begins daily scheduled flights from London to Paris.

OCTOBER

**7 October** Dutch airline KLM is formed.

DECEMBER

**10 December** Australian brothers Ross and Keith Smith reach Darwin to win the England-to-Australia air race in a Vickers Vimy.

JANUARY

**24 January** A French Army pilot flies across the Sahara Desert.

FEBRUARY

**7 February** A Nieuport-Delage 29 fighter achieves a record speed of 275km/h (171mph).

SEPTEMBER

**28 September** The Dayton-Wright *RB-1 Racer*, entered in the Gordon Bennett Air Race, had the first practicable retractable landing gear.

The first sanctioned airmail service was in 1918, a joint operation between the US Post Office and Army. As part of the operation, lines of navigation beacons were established between several cities, the forerunners of the electronic 'nav-aids' in use today. In 1920, the first transcontinental link was established between New York and San Francisco. Mail now took as little as 29 hours to cross the United States, compared to three to four days by rail.

In 1925, the mail service was handed over to the private sector, but the US government continued to subsidize the airlines, leading to a proliferation of small carriers. These were just about profitable, but the early days of airmail flying were dangerous – 31 of the first 40 pilots hired to carry the mail died in crashes. Bad weather contributed to the risk, as did unreliable old aircraft, some of which had reputations as 'flaming coffins' for their propensity to catch fire after a crash. Night-flying was then a very new skill, but one that was essential to carry the mail between railheads, where most trains stopped for the night. Navigation was by beacon – when they could be seen – and by dead-reckoning

*Famous French aviator Jean Mermoz pioneered France's mail routes across the South Atlantic. In December 1936 he vanished without trace on a transatlantic flight in a Latécoère 300.*

## 1920

### NOVEMBER

**1 November** The first overseas flights are operated from the USA – by Aeromarine West Indies Airways from Key West, Florida, to Havana, Cuba.

## 1921

### JUNE

**8 June** A modified Airco DH.4 is tested with a pressurized cabin.

### JULY

**21 July** Brigadier General 'Billy' Mitchell demonstrates that capital ships can be sunk by aerial bombing.

### AUGUST

**24 August** The British rigid airship, the R38, is wrecked. Forty-nine crewmembers die.

**31 August** The first aerial pest-control experiments are carried out in Ohio using a converted Curtiss Jenny.

### NOVEMBER

**12 November** A Jenny is refuelled in flight by a wing-walker climbing from another aircraft with a can of fuel.

measures, such as following railways and spotting distinctive features such as towns, barns and river bends.

One of the more intrepid early airmail flyers was Charles Lindbergh, later to become famous as the first man to fly solo across the Atlantic. He received a mail messenger's certificate in April 1926 and in September made the first of two emergency parachute jumps while flying the airmails. Having become lost in snow and rain during a night flight, he ran out of fuel and was forced to abandon his DH.4B over rural Indiana. A similar incident happened that November. In both cases, mail was recovered from the wreckage and delivered.

At one point, more than 40 small carriers were involved in delivering airmail. The mail was so highly subsidized that it was profitable for airlines to mail heavy objects to themselves: they received government payments well in excess of the postal charge.

In 1928, the US Postmaster General was charged with rationalizing the system. Under the Airmail Act of 1930, he forced the merger of the small carriers into larger entities. The successful companies later merged to become

United Airlines, Transcontinental Air Transport (later TWA), Eastern Air Lines and American Airways (predecessor of American Airlines), and formed the backbone of the US domestic airline fleet for the next 60 years.

The basis of mail carriage was changed, moving from weight carried to space available. This encouraged the purchase of larger aircraft

*The DH.34's baggage hold had a door that was almost triangular in shape.*

......................................

*Two DH.34s were ordered by Daimler Hire Ltd, the first of them making its first flight from Stag Lane on 26 March 1922.*

## 1922

**1922** The first purpose-built civil airport and terminal is opened at Konigsburg, Germany.

### FEBRUARY

**21 February** The explosion of the US airship *Roma* leads the USA to switch to helium instead of hydrogen for buoyancy.

### MARCH

**20 March** The first US aircraft carrier, the converted collier USS *Langley*, is commissioned.

**13 March–16 June** After many trials and three aircraft, two Portuguese pilots make an Atlantic crossing from Portugal to Brazil.

### APRIL

**7 April** A French Farman and British de Havilland collide over northern France, killing seven passengers and crew.

### JUNE

**9 June** The first airliner night flight is made from Paris Le Bourget to Croydon, near London.

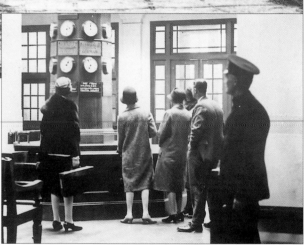

*Croydon aerodrome underwent a great deal of expansion to accommodate civil aviation activities in the 1920s, and new facilities such as a passenger lounge (right) were opened.*

that had provision for passengers as well as mail. There were also bonuses for night-flying and bad-weather flying. Mail planes moved on from war surplus DH.4s and Curtiss Jennies to larger multi-engined aircraft such as the Boeing 80A biplane, Stinson and Ford Trimotors, and the Fokker Universal. Eventually, passengers became more important than mail, but every jetliner of today carries mail in its holds, and international courier companies such as Federal Express and UPS have large fleets of aircraft – continuing the spirit of the original airmail pioneers.

| **1922** | **1923** | | | |
|---|---|---|---|---|
| NOVEMBER | JANUARY | APRIL | AUGUST | SEPTEMBER |
| **30 November** Japan's carrier *Hosho* begins sea trials. It is the first carrier built as such from the outset. | **January** Juan de la Cierva's first successful autogyro, the C.4, is flown. | **20 April** Air refuelling trials with a hose system begin in San Diego, California. | **27–28 August** In-flight refuelling allows a US Army DH4B to stay aloft for over 37 hours. | **4 September** The US Navy's large rigid airship *Shenandoah* makes its maiden flight. **28 September** The first Schneider Trophy for seaplanes is won by US pilots in Curtiss CR3s. |

## Europe–Africa–South America

In southern France, industrialist Pierre Latécoère was quick off the mark at the end of hostilities, establishing a passenger service between Toulouse and Barcelona before the end of 1918. By March 1919, this was extended to Alicante, Spain, and to Casablanca, Morocco. The company was Lignes Aeriennes Latécoère, usually called 'the Line'. Initially using Breguet designs, the company soon adopted Latécoère's own flying boats and expanded its services into Algeria and France's colonies in West Africa.

The next logical step was to jump the shortest span of the Atlantic and set up services in South America. Among those who pioneered the mail routes was a young Frenchman named Jean Mermoz. He became legendary for his daring and his narrow escapes, such as rebuilding a crashed aeroplane on top of an Andean peak and keeping its battered engine running long enough to glide onto the Chilean plains. He pioneered air routes in Brazil, Argentina and Chile, also helping to establish a

*The Armstrong Whitworth Argosy was the company's first venture into the commercial aviation field.*

## 1924

**NOVEMBER**

**4 November** The world air speed record is set at 429km/h (267mph) by a US Navy Curtiss RC21 seaplane.

**1924** Four smaller airlines are merged to create Imperial Airways, Britain's first national airline.

**MARCH**

**17 March** Four Douglas World Cruisers set off from Seattle, Washington, in an attempt to circumnavigate the world.

**MAY**

**19 May** A Royal Australian Air Force crew completes the first flight around Australia.

**SEPTEMBER**

**28 September** Two of the Douglas World Cruisers complete the first aerial circumnavigation of the world, taking 175 days.

**NOVEMBER**

**20 November–18 March 1925** Alan Cobham and crew make a return flight from England to Rangoon, Burma.

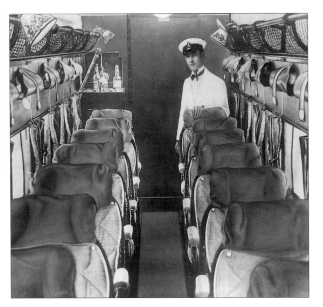

*The interior of the Armstrong Whitworth Argosy airliner. Passenger comfort was very important.*

point, it went bankrupt and was absorbed into Air France.

Another of the pioneering pilots was Antoine de Saint-Exupéry, later famous as one of the first to write seriously about the experience of flying.

### Imperial Airways

British airline services began in August 1919, when a DH.4A of Aircraft Transport & Travel (AT&T) set off from London for Paris with various sorts of perishable cargo, newspapers and a single passenger – a journalist. This marked the first daily scheduled international service. AT&T was an offshoot of Geoffrey de Havilland's de Havilland Aircraft Company, manufacturer of the DH.4A and DH.9. Surplus bombers with capacity for freight and one or two passengers were the mainstay of early British airlines such as AT&T and Instone Air Line, which used the Vickers Vimy Commercial, another converted bomber design.

By 1921, these few small airlines were in financial crisis, and ceased operating. Only a few people could afford to fly to France or Belgium, and it was an uncomfortable, not to say risky, business in poor weather. The

occasional accident and frequent delays did little to inspire confidence. The government reluctantly stepped in to offer subsidies to keep services running, allowing four small companies to offer some internal flights and a limited international service to Paris and Amsterdam.

Financial stability allowed investment in new purpose-built aircraft, such as the Handley Page W.8B and the de Havilland DH.34, which was able to carry about eight passengers. In 1920, Croydon Airport was opened south of London

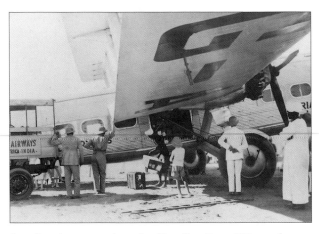

*Loading baggage aboard a Handley Page HP.42 of Imperial Airways. The HP.42 was an admired aircraft.*

regular service from Dakar to Natal. During a transatlantic flight, his plane disappeared, probably due to a propeller flying off and severing the fuselage.

Latécoère's stake was bought out and his company renamed Aéropostale, which continued under that name until 1933. At that

---

**1924**

**DECEMBER**

**15 December** The first successful hook-up in-flight is made between an aeroplane (a Sperry Messenger) and an airship (the US Navy's TC3).

**1925**

**FEBRUARY**

**3–4 February** A French Breguet 19 makes a nonstop straight-line flight of 3166km (1967 miles).

**APRIL**

**April** The first in-flight movie is shown, on an Imperial Airways flight.

**SEPTEMBER**

**3 September** The US Navy airship *Shenandoah* crashes in Ohio, killing 14 crew.

**OCTOBER**

**26 October** American Jimmy Doolittle wins the Schneider Trophy flying a Curtiss seaplane, and sets a world speed record of 394km/h (245mph).

**NOVEMBER**

**16 November– 13 March 1926** Alan Cobham and two crew fly from London to Cape Town and back in a de Havilland DH50.

as the city's commercial air hub. With the growth of traffic, it was rebuilt in 1928, and featured the first purpose-built air terminal building in the world, a hotel for travellers, and other amenities later adopted as standard around the world.

In 1923, the British government decided to stop subsidizing airlines and to nationalize them instead, creating a single entity named Imperial Airways. The four constituent parts were Handley Page Transport, Instone Air Line, Daimler Airways (successor to AT&T), and the British Marine Air Navigation Company, the sole flying-boat operator of the group. Imperial was tasked with expanding air services across the British Empire, linking Britain with Egypt, India and South Africa. It adopted a mixed fleet of landplanes and flying boats, and its first new aircraft was an Armstrong Whitworth Argosy, a roomy three-engined machine which had 20 passenger seats.

The landplane service to India was extended in stages. To connect Cairo and Basrah in southern Iraq, way stations were set up at remote forts in the desert. To help crews navigate across the trackless wastes, a furrow

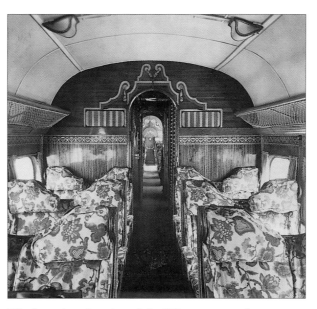

*The luxurious interior of the HP.42 was much appreciated by its passengers.*

500km (310 miles) long was dug in the desert, leading most of the way from Amman in Transjordan to Baghdad. This route was initially established by the RAF for its desert airmail service, but it was handed to Imperial Airways in 1926. Pilots called it 'flying the Furrow' and passengers experienced various privations,

staying in basic accommodation and sometimes helping with refuelling and other necessary tasks.

From 1931, the route was flown by the magnificent Handley Page HP.42 airliners. These were some of the largest biplanes ever built, with four engines and capacity for up to 38 passengers and four crew, including two stewards. Imperial operated two versions, one for European destinations and one for the long-range routes with 24 passenger seats. A novel feature was that they were largely of metal construction, with fabric being used only on the lifting surfaces and the rear fuselage. Only eight were built, and they operated for a decade without suffering a fatal accident. Passengers appreciated their luxurious interiors and relative quietness. The airliners also cut out a lengthy sea journey for many civil servants and businessmen working in India, reducing a Karachi–London trip to five days rather than several weeks. Their performance was stately, with a top speed of about 204km/h (125mph), but usually cruising closer to 153km/h (95mph). In hot weather, they struggled to reach cruising altitude, but the fact that they were unpressurized and the necessity to keep the Furrow in view on trans-Arabian

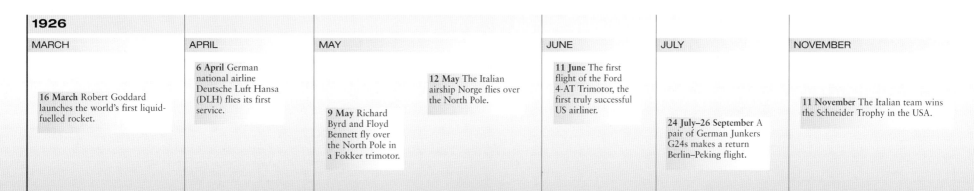

## 1926

| MARCH | APRIL | MAY | JUNE | JULY | NOVEMBER |
|---|---|---|---|---|---|
| **16 March** Robert Goddard launches the world's first liquid-fuelled rocket. | **6 April** German national airline Deutsche Luft Hansa (DLH) flies its first service. | **12 May** The Italian airship Norge flies over the North Pole.<br><br>**9 May** Richard Byrd and Floyd Bennett fly over the North Pole in a Fokker trimotor. | **11 June** The first flight of the Ford 4-AT Trimotor, the first truly successful US airliner. | **24 July–26 September** A pair of German Junkers G24s makes a return Berlin–Peking flight. | **11 November** The Italian team wins the Schneider Trophy in the USA. |

flights meant that high altitudes were rarely necessary, except to avoid sandstorms. Faster monoplanes such as the Armstrong Whitworth Atlanta and de Havilland Albatross eventually replaced them. However, they came into service only shortly before World War II, when all civil airliners were grounded or impressed into military service.

Imperial also operated flying boats, particularly to southern Africa. The first type used in Africa was a three-engined 12-passenger biplane called the Shorts Calcutta. Flying boats did not require runways or the infrastructure of landplanes, and they could land in Alexandria's harbour, say, or on the Nile near Cairo, or on Lake Victoria. The flying boats also extended the eastern route to Australia.

In 1936, the first of the great Empire- or C-class flying boats began operating. These monoplanes with four powerful radial engines on the wing were the height of luxury. With their capacious hulls, they were the 'wide-bodies' of the day, but carried only 24 people as well as a lot of mail. With a full load, they could carry 1361kg (3000lb) of mail or freight, but, by reducing passenger numbers to 17, the cargo capacity went up to 1814kg (4000 lb).

Mail was still at least as important as passengers, and various methods were tried for extending the range of the Empire boats to achieve a transatlantic airmail service. One of these was in-flight refuelling, but the most notable was the building of a composite aircraft. This was known as the Short-Mayo, and consisted of a large flying boat named *Maia*, with a much smaller and sleeker mailplane called *Mercury* attached to the top. When loaded with fuel and mail, *Mercury* could not take off by itself, but once launched by *Maia*, it was able to span the Atlantic nonstop, from Imperial's base at Foynes in Ireland to Montreal, Canada.

The first test of the composite in July 1938 was the first commercial aeroplane flight across the Atlantic. The same combination allowed *Mercury* to fly from Scotland to Walvis Bay in what is today Namibia. The pilot on both these

*The majestic Short C-class flying boats really opened up the Empire air routes. G-ADHL was the first of the so-called 'Empire' boats and was named* Canopus.

## 1927

| MARCH | MAY | | | SEPTEMBER | | OCTOBER |
|---|---|---|---|---|---|---|
| **14 March** Pan American World Airways (Pan Am) is formed by entrepreneur Juan Trippe. | **8 May** French ace Charles Nungesser and co-pilot vanish while attempting an east–west Atlantic crossing. | **20 May** An RAF Hawker Horsley makes a flight of 5472km (3400 miles) from Cranwell, Lincolnshire, to the Persian Gulf. | **20–21 May** Charles Lindbergh makes the first solo Atlantic crossing from New York to Paris in the Ryan NYP *Spirit of St Louis*. | **1–28 September** South African pilot R.R. Bentley makes a solo flight from London to Cape Town. | **26 September** Schneider Trophy is won by the British with a Supermarine S.5. | **19 October** Pan Am operates its first service, a mail flight from Key West, Florida, to Havana, Cuba. |

record flights was Don Bennett, who was to earn fame during the war as the head of the RAF's 'Pathfinder' bombing force. The outbreak of war in September 1939 brought an end to both the air refuelling trials and the Mayo composite operations. The same year, Imperial was merged with its domestic counterpart, British Airways (formed in 1935 from four small airlines), to become British Overseas Airways Corporation (BOAC).

## US Flying Boats

Pan American World Airways was founded in 1927 in Key West, Florida, beginning with services to Cuba and the Caribbean. Soon the company expanded into South America, led by entrepreneur Juan Trippe. He commissioned Russian emigré Igor Sikorsky to build new flying boats, the first of which was the S-40. He named this the *American Clipper*, setting a tradition for names that continued for more than 60 years.

The four-engined S-40 was the first four-engined flying-boat airliner and featured a luxury interior for 28 passengers. A maze of struts connecting the engines to the wings, the

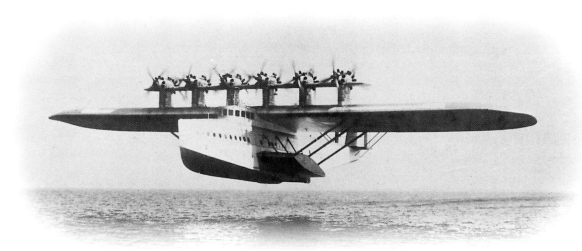

*The Dornier Do X was by far the largest aircraft in the world when it made its first flight on 25 July, 1929. In October 1929 it made a one-hour flight with 169 people on board – including nine stowaways.*

floats and the fuselage gave rise to the nickname of 'flying forest'. The S-42 was an improved version with 50 seats and the engines mounted in the wings, reducing the struttage somewhat. Both had twin fins and porthole-type cabin windows. The S-42s were used to establish a service from continental United States to Hawaii, and were joined by the Martin M-130 in 1935. The first of these was named *China*

*Clipper*, which gave its name to the whole class. Soon, service was extended to China on the route Honolulu–Midway–Wake Island–Guam–Hong Kong–Manila.

The next stage was the South Pacific, and an island-hopping route was established in 1938 by Edwin Musick. At one time, the famous Pan Am captain held more aviation records than any other pilot. Sadly, on the return flight from

| NOVEMBER | **1928**<br>FEBRUARY | MAY | SEPTEMBER | DECEMBER |
|---|---|---|---|---|
| **6 November** The Italian Army makes the first experiments with dropping parachute troops. | **7-22 February** Australian Bert Hinkler flies an Avro Avian solo from England to Australia. | **31 May-10 June** Charles Kingsford Smith and crew make the first trans-Pacific flight from Oakland, California, to Brisbane, Australia. | **10 September** The Fokker FVII *Southern Cross*, flown by Charles Kingsford Smith, makes the first Australia–New Zealand flight, from Brisbane to Christchurch. | **23 December** The first large-scale airlift begins when nearly 600 civilians are evacuated from Kabul, Afghanistan, by the RAF during tribal fighting.<br><br>**28 December** Sir Hubert Wilkins and Carl Ben Eielson pilot a Lockheed Vega in the first flight over Antarctica. |

Auckland to Pago Pago, the *Samoan Clipper* disappeared, probably destroyed by an explosion caused by leaking fuel.

The world was finally circled by air routes in 1940, when TEAL (Tasman Empire Airways Limited) was established as a joint venture between BOAC, Qantas of Australia and the New Zealand government. Using Empire-class flying boats across the Tasman Sea, it completed the link between the Pan Am Clippers and the Qantas flying boats on the 'Kangaroo Route' to England via Singapore. Many of these services were suspended when World War II extended into the Pacific, but the TEAL flights between Australia and New Zealand continued and expanded throughout the war years.

### Germany – Aircraft and Airships

German attempts to compete for influence in South America with the French and Americans saw the construction of one of the most extraordinary flying machines of all time, the huge Dornier Do X flying boat. With no fewer than

12 engines (paired above the wing in push-pull units) and a crew of 10, the Do X could accommodate more than 150 passengers. On an early flight, it carried a record 169 people, including nine stowaways. For long-range flights the Do X was laid

*The Junkers G.38 was the biggest landplane of its time when it entered Lufthansa service. Two were built.*

out for 66 passengers in a style befitting a luxury cruise liner.

In November 1930, it set out for its first transatlantic trip. A fire at Lisbon, Portugal, delayed its progress for six weeks and further incidents slowed its progress down the West African coast. While leaving Las Palmas in the Canary Islands, it was badly damaged by the sea swell and spent another three months there undergoing repairs. Finally reaching South America in June 1931, the giant flying boat was enthusiastically greeted during an extensive tour of the Atlantic coast and the Caribbean. Finally arriving in New York in August, the crew found that the Dornier Company was in bankruptcy. Dornier was bailed out by the German government, and, after eight months in dry dock, the Do X arrived back in Berlin in May 1932. In all, the round-trip journey had taken 19 months.

After only a few further local flights and having incurred more damage, the Do X was retired to a museum. Two further examples were built for Italy, but made few flights before disappearing into obscurity.

| 1929 | | | | | 1930 |
|------|------|------|------|------|------|
| JANUARY | AUGUST | SEPTEMBER | | NOVEMBER | MAY |
| | **8-29 August** The airship *Graf Zeppelin* circumnavigates the globe in 21 days with only three stops. | | **24 September** Jimmy Doolittle flies a course 'blind', proving the viability of instrument flight. | | **5–24 May** Amy Johnson completes the first solo flight by a woman from Britain to Australia, using a de Havilland DH.60 Moth. |
| **9 January** Pan Am makes its first passenger flight, from Key West, Florida, to Havana, Cuba. | | **7 September** The Schneider Trophy is retained by the British with a Supermarine S.5. | | **28 November** Richard Byrd with pilot Bernt Balchen and crew make the first flight over the South Pole. | |

Another German experiment of the interwar years was the Junkers G 38 of 1929, a massive landplane with four engines and 38 seats. Its wings were so broad and thick at the leading edge that some of the seating was located here, the windows offering an excellent forward view. Mechanics could service the engines in-flight from inside the wing. Two were built in Germany and a version was produced in Japan as a bomber/transport. The two German aircraft set a number of weight-carrying records and served Lufthansa on the Berlin–London route for nearly a decade. The G 38 used Junkers's trademark corrugated stressed-skin construction. This was lighter and stronger than conventional metal construction, but created a lot of drag, giving a top speed of 225km/h (140mph).

The most famous of Junkers's pre-war designs was the Ju 52 trimotor. This began in 1930 as a single-engined design, but with one engine in the nose and two in the wings it had the performance to carry 17 passengers from Berlin to Rome in eight hours. Ju 52s were widely exported and

*The Junkers G 38 was a great technical achievement, but passengers preferred smaller aircraft.*

**Exact date unknown** Jean Mermoz, in a Latécoère 28 mailplane, makes the first aeroplane flight across the South Atlantic.

**15 May** The first air hostess begins work with United Airlines.

**18 May** The German airship *Graf Zeppelin* begins services from Europe to South America.

**SEPTEMBER**

**11 September** The first Junkers Ju 52 flies. Initially a single-engined aircraft, the design is modified to a trimotor in 1932.

**OCTOBER**

**5 October** The British airship R101 crashes in France on a pioneering flight to India, killing 54 people.

**25 October** Transcontinental and Western Air (TWA) starts the first US coast-to-coast air service.

fitted with a variety of engines. Airlines throughout Europe operated them, including British Airways. By 1935, the Nazi government wanted military aircraft, not airliners, and forced

*The Junkers Ju 52/3m served in large numbers as a military transporter.*

the nationalization of the company. The Ju 52 design was adapted to be a troop transport and, occasionally, a light bomber; it was used during the Spanish Civil War and throughout World War II. Versions were built in Spain and France even after the war, and a few continued to serve with the Swiss Air Force into the 1980s.

### USA – Domestic

A similar machine to the Ju 52 was the Ford Trimotor, introduced in 1928 in the first of many versions. Known as the 'tin goose' for its corrugated metal construction, the Trimotor was hot in the summer, cold in the winter and noisy all year round.

From the start of its service, male air stewards, or sometimes the co-pilot, offered some assistance to the passengers, but only in 1930 did Boeing Air Transport introduce a dedicated female flight attendant, air hostess or stewardess to the crew. Registered nurse Ellen Church was the first stewardess with Boeing's airline; other carriers followed suit from 1933. Pan Am resisted this new-fangled idea, hiring only male attendants until 1944. In the same period, meals were first offered on domestic flights, and other innovations such as in-flight movies were also tried.

High-wing aircraft such as the Ford Trimotors and various Fokker designs slowly gave way to more modern designs. One spur for better, faster, higher-climbing airliners was the crash of a TWA Fokker Super Universal in 1931. Among the passengers and crew killed

## 1930

### DECEMBER

**17 December–15 January 1931** Italian General Italo Balbo leads a formation of 12 SM.55 flying boats from Rome to Rio de Janeiro, Brazil.

**Exact date unknown** Two-way radio between control tower and aircraft is introduced in the USA.

## 1931

### JUNE

**23 June–1 July** Americans Wiley Post and Harold Gatty fly around the world in a Lockheed Vega.

### SEPTEMBER

**7 September** Jimmy Doolittle wins the Bendix Trophy transcontinental point-to-point race.

**13 September** The Schneider Trophy is won outright by a Royal Air Force team with the Supermarine S6B.

**29 September** Flight Lieutenant G.H. Stainforth sets a new world speed record of 654km/h (406 mph) in the Supermarine S6B.

*The Ford Trimotor became one of the immortals of air transport history, serving for more than 40 years with more than 100 operators.*

**OCTOBER**

**27–28 October** A Fairey Long Range Monoplane flies a nonstop flight from Cranwell in Lincolnshire to Abu Sueir in Egypt.

## 1932

**Exact date unknown** Russian rocket pioneer Sergei Korolev tests a rocket-propelled glider.

**MAY**

**20–21 May** Amelia Earhart makes the second solo flight across the Atlantic and the first by a woman pilot.

**AUGUST**

**24–25 August** Amelia Earhart makes the first US coast-to-coast solo flight by a woman.

## 1933

**JANUARY**

**January** The US military's first monoplane fighter, the P-26 'Peashooter', enters production.

was the famous football coach Knute Rockne. The aircraft's wooden wing had failed in flight and the aircraft broke up. Structural faults had been a feature of Antony Fokker's designs back to the Eindecker. After the accident, metal was the preferred construction material.

Boeing now built the Model 247, a twin-engined streamlined machine with a then-novel retractable undercarriage, and other modern features such as an autopilot. This was the first airliner with the basic configuration and features that are still found today. The 247 entered service in 1933. The better aerodynamics gave it a cruising speed of 305km/h (189mph) and helped take eight hours off an east–west transcontinental journey. The cabin held only 10 passengers, while the wing spar intruded across its middle, and had to be stepped over to progress from front to back. Only 75 Model 247s were built, mostly for Boeing Air Transport and United Air Lines.

Lockheed followed suit with the Lockheed 10 and 12 Electras, which again were small capacity, carrying ten and six passengers, respectively. By 1939, the company was working on a four-engine pressurized airliner that would

*The Boeing 247 was based at least in part on the B-9 bomber. United Airlines placed an off-the-drawing-board order for 60 examples, paying $3.5 million – in those days, a fantastic sum for an aircraft that had not even flown.*

become the Lockheed Constellation, but the war intervened and the Constellation did not enter commercial passenger service until 1946.

At Santa Monica, California, the Douglas Company entered the all-metal airliner field with the 12-passenger DC-1. First flying in 1933, it had bigger engines than the 247 and three-bladed propellers. The DC-2 was somewhat more pleasing to the eye than the Model 247 and had room for a toilet

## 1933

### FEBRUARY

**6–9 February** Jim Mollison makes the first solo UK–South America flight.

**8 February** The prototype Boeing Model 247 flies; it is the first airliner with a stressed metal skin and retractable undercarriage.

### APRIL

**3 April** Two Westland biplanes become the first aircraft to fly over Mount Everest.

**4 April** The US Navy's airship *Akron* is lost in a storm over the Atlantic Ocean.

### JULY

**1–15 July** General Italo Balbo leads a fleet of 24 flying boats from Italy to Chicago. Large aircraft formations are nicknamed 'Balbos'.

**1 July** First flight of the Douglas DC-1, predecessor of the DC-3.

**7–8 July** Amelia Earhart sets a new transcontinental speed record, flying from Newark to Los Angeles in 17 hours 7 minutes.

compartment and galley of reasonable size. It had a wider, taller cabin with no intrusions by the wing spar.

Even today, greater cabin volume and more width, even if only of a few inches, determines the commercial success of airliners. TWA liked the DC-1, but wanted a larger version, resulting in the 14-seat DC-2, which flew in May 1934. A total of 156 was sold, including a number to European airlines. The Dutch national carrier KLM entered its first example in the 1934 London–Melbourne air race and came first in the handicap section and second overall, giving both the design and the company great publicity.

American Airlines was looking for a new airliner that had the volume of its current Curtiss Condor biplanes – and greater speed. In the summer of 1934, it approached Douglas for a version of the DC-2 with sleeping berths, to enable nonstop overnight travel between New York and Chicago.

Douglas was initially reluctant to build such a specialized aircraft, which required a wider and longer fuselage and a larger fin, but an order for 20 from TWA was enough to give it the incentive to proceed. The new airliner was

*The Lockheed Aircraft Company pinned its hopes on the Lockheed Electra airliner following the Great Depression, and they were justified. The Electra was designed for fast, economical airline operation.*

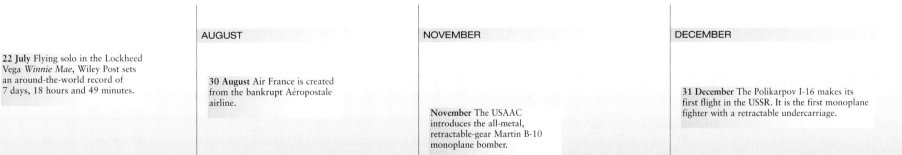

**22 July** Flying solo in the Lockheed Vega *Winnie Mae*, Wiley Post sets an around-the-world record of 7 days, 18 hours and 49 minutes.

**AUGUST**

**30 August** Air France is created from the bankrupt Aéropostale airline.

**NOVEMBER**

**November** The USAAC introduces the all-metal, retractable-gear Martin B-10 monoplane bomber.

**DECEMBER**

**31 December** The Polikarpov I-16 makes its first flight in the USSR. It is the first monoplane fighter with a retractable undercarriage.

called the DST, or Douglas Sleeper Transport, and had 14 seats that converted into sleeping berths at night. A day version was offered with 28 seats as the DC-3. The DST first flew on 17 December 1935, the anniversary of the Wright Brothers triumph at Kitty Hawk – a date often chosen for first flights. While the DST did not sell in great numbers, the DC-3 proved an instant hit.

.................................................

*The Douglas DC-1 set up several speed and distance records.*

Comfortable and fast with a cruising speed of 274km/h (170mph), the DC-3 reduced the time for a New York–Los Angeles flight from about 26 hours to less than 18. The DC-3 was popular with

passengers and was the first airliner to make a profit on passenger tickets alone rather than from mail contracts and subsidies.

Most of the main US airlines soon adopted DC-3s for domestic services, and it was widely sold abroad. Pre-war foreign airlines operating the DC-3 included KLM,

## 1934

### FEBRUARY

**3 February** The first transatlantic airmail service is established, from Stuttgart to Buenos Aires.

**19 February** After a series of crashes, the US government cancels private airmail contracts and brings in the Army Air Corps to carry the mail.

**23 February** The first flight of the Lockheed Electra airliner.

### MAY

**11 May** The Douglas DC-2 makes its first flight at Santa Monica, California.

### AUGUST

**August** The RAF's first rotorcraft, the Avro Rota autogyro, enters service with the School of Army Co-operation.

### SEPTEMBER

**5 September** Using a special pressure suit, Wiley Post sets an altitude record of 12,192m (40,000ft) over Chicago.

*Much of the DC-2's success on the export market was due to its winning the 'MacRobertson' air race from England to Australia in 1934, flown by a KLM crew and carrying three passengers and 30,000 airmail letters.*

Swissair, Air France, Sabena and LOT in Europe, and Panagra and Panair do Brasil in South America. By the time the United States entered World War II in December 1941, 507 civil DSTs and DC-3s had been produced, an unprecedented number for the time. Many of these were drafted into military service, and dedicated military versions were also ordered, including the C-47 Skytrain and C-53 Skytrooper, more often known by its British name, the Dakota.

More than 10,000 Dakotas were built during the war and many re-entered civil service after 1945. A small number are still in service today, flying freight and passengers in remote areas and being used as parachute jump ships and for other specialized tasks.

Boeing's answer to the DC-3 came with the Model 307 in 1938. Resembling a four-engined DC-3, the 307 had the wings of the B-17C bomber and a larger fuselage. Its main claim to fame is that it was the first pressurized airliner able to fly above bad weather in comfort, as high as 6090m (20,000ft). Despite this, the 307 was a poor seller, with only 10 being built and used by TWA and Pan Am.

## 1935

### OCTOBER

**20 October** The Mac Robertson England to Australia Air Race attracts 20 entries. A de Havilland DH.88 Comet wins the speed section in 71 hours 18 minutes, while a KLM DC-2 wins the passenger section.

**21 October–4 November** Charles Kingsford Smith and P.G. Taylor make the first east–west crossing of the Pacific Ocean.

### JANUARY

**11–12 January** Amelia Earhart makes the first California–Hawaii flight, solo in a Lockheed Vega.

### FEBRUARY

**12 February** The US Navy's airship *Macon* crashes off California, ending experiments with 'parasite' fighters.

**26 February** Trials are conducted in the UK to detect aircraft using radio waves (radar).

*First flown in December 1935, the Douglas DC-3 went on to become the best-known twin-engine transport aircraft of all time, and many examples are still flying today in various parts of the world.*

### Zeppelins Return

Following World War I, Germany was forbidden to build dirigibles or produce hydrogen for military purposes. The Zeppelins that were not destroyed by their crews were handed over to the victorious European powers. Two small airships were built for DELAG in 1919, but the company was forced to hand them to the Allies as war reparations.

The US Navy became interested in airships and built one based on Zeppelin technology, the

*Shenandoah*. A British ship, the R38 (also largely copied from German wartime Zeppelins) was completed for the US Navy, but was lost during a proving flight before delivery. To replace it, the US Navy ordered a new ship from Zeppelin, which became *Los Angeles* in 1924. The USN changed its lifting gas to helium, which was safer than hydrogen, but had lower lifting capacity. *Los Angeles* operated safely for eight years before being retired as an economy measure – a better record than most of its contemporaries.

The USN's order put the Zeppelin Company on a better financial footing, but it was not until 1928 that it completed a new ship, the Graf Zeppelin. Dr Hugo Eckener was now the head of the company and decided to promote airship travel by a series of spectacular publicity flights. He took the *Graf Zeppelin* to the United States and around Europe, and in 1929 he embarked on the first aerial circumnavigation of the world. Sponsored by Hearst newspapers, the epic flight first ferried reporters, explorers, diplomats and the very rich on a journey from Friedrichshafen to Lakehurst, New Jersey, where for publicity reasons the 'round-the-world' trip officially began. The *Graf Zeppelin* then returned to Berlin, before continuing nonstop over the largely uncharted Soviet Union to Tokyo. After a rapturous reception, the giant airship, nearly 229m (750ft) long, crossed the Pacific (in the first nonstop transpacific flight) to Los Angeles, then back to Lakehurst. After 12 days of flying, the *Graf Zeppelin* had completed the first circumnavigation of the world by air, and travelled 31,400km (19,500 miles) from Lakehurst to Lakehurst, and a total of 49,618km (30,831 miles) by the time it

## 1935

### MARCH

**9 March** Existence of the Luftwaffe, in violation of the Versailles Treaty, is announced.

**28 March** Robert Goddard launches a successful experimental rocket.

### MAY

**18 May** The enormous *Maxim Gorky* propaganda aircraft collides with a small fighter near Moscow, killing 56.

**28 May** The Bf 109V1, prototype of the Messerschmitt 109 series, makes its maiden flight.

### JULY

**28 July** The Boeing Model 299, prototype of the B-17 Flying Fortress, makes its first flight in Seattle, Washington.

### NOVEMBER

**6 November** The prototype Hawker Hurricane is flown at Brooklands.

returned to Friedrichshafen 21 days after setting out. The journey attracted worldwide attention and made heroes out of pilot Eckener, his crew and the Zeppelin.

Eckener's dream was a regular passenger service from Germany to the United States, but commercial flights began with a service to Brazil, where there were many German colonists. Following test flights in 1930 and 1931, a scheduled service between Friedrichshafen and Recife, Brazil, was opened in April 1932 by Luftschiffbau Zeppelin. The operator later became Deutsche Zeppelin-Reederei, a company formed by the airship manufacturer and Lufthansa. The *Graf Zeppelin* made regular flights to South America until 1937 without serious incident. In all, it flew more than 1,600,000km (1,000,000 miles) and made 144 ocean crossings, carrying more than 13,000 passengers.

The success of *Graf Zeppelin* led in March 1936 to an even bigger airship of an all-new design – the LZ129, or *Hindenburg*. Its internal construction was the alloy duralumin and it was 245m (804ft) long. Its 16 internal gas cells contained 200,000m³ (7,000,000cu ft) of

hydrogen. With its later sister ship, the *Graf Zeppelin II*, it was the largest flying machine ever constructed. Four 890kW (1200hp) diesel engines gave a maximum speed of 135km/h (84mph). The *Hindenburg* was originally designed to be filled with helium, but the world's helium supplies were controlled by the United States, and the rise of the Nazi party in Germany had caused an embargo on goods with a possible military use, including helium. The design was therefore revised to take hydrogen, which also offered an extra 8 per cent of lift.

The *Hindenburg* was the last word in luxury air travel. Passengers were accommodated within the hull. There was a promenade, and lounges on both sides. A lightweight

*The Graf Zeppelin made the first circumnavigation of the globe by air.*

baby grand piano made of aluminium was carried on most flights. There was also a pressurized smoking room, which was isolated from the rest of the ship, where smoking was forbidden and where extreme measures were taken to prevent sparks.

An entirely civilian craft, the *Hindenburg* was nonetheless adopted as a tool of the Nazi regime almost as soon as it first flew in May 1936. Much to Dr Eckener's disgust, Nazi propaganda chief Josef Goebbels insisted that the airship carry the swastika national marking on the fin. Goebbels actually wanted huge swastikas on both sides of the envelope, but could not get his way. Nevertheless, *Hindenburg* was required to fly the Nazi flag on all takeoffs and landings, and it was often used to drop propaganda leaflets over German towns.

In May 1936, the *Hindenburg* made her first flight from Germany to the United States, landing at Lakehurst after 61 hours in the air. This began a successful season of scheduled flights, in which 10 round trips were made. The *Graf Zeppelin* continued to ply the South Atlantic route to Brazil. During the winter of 1936–7, the *Hindenburg* was refitted and its

passenger capacity was increased to 72 by the installation of more berths.

By the time the 1937 summer season was due to begin in May, the giant airships still attracted a great deal of interest whenever they appeared in American skies. Growing disquiet over the Nazi regime, however, meant that they were not always welcomed, and occasionally threats were made against the Zeppelins. The *Hindenburg* was still enough of a spectacle and a novelty that the media, including press photographers, newsreel cameramen and radio reporters, were at Lakehurst on 6 May, when the giant airship arrived for the beginning of the new season.

After circling to avoid nearby thunderstorms, the *Hindenburg* approached the airfield, and hundreds of US Navy sailors made ready to grab lines and guide the enormous craft to its mooring mast. Suddenly, a flicker of flame was seen at the stern of the ship, which quickly ran along its length, engulfing the fabric structure as the millions of cubic feet of hydrogen erupted. Terrified ground handlers ran for their lives as

.................................................................

*The commercial airship* Hindenburg *explodes and burns at her mooring mast at Lakehurst, New Jersey, in 1937.*

---

**1936**

| JULY | AUGUST | SEPTEMBER | OCTOBER |
|---|---|---|---|
| **20 July** More than 7000 Spanish Nationalist troops are transported from Morocco to Seville by Ju 52s in the first large-scale military airlift. | **14 August** An altitude record of 14,843m (48,698ft) is established by a Potez 50 flown by Frenchman Georges Detre. | **28 September** An experimental aircraft, the Bristol Type 138, achieves an altitude of 15,223m (49,944ft). | **5–16 October** New Zealander Jean Batten flies solo from Lympne in Kent to Auckland, New Zealand, in a Percival Gull Six. |

**1937**

| APRIL | |
|---|---|
| **6–9 April** A Japanese Mitsubishi Type 97 named *Kamikaze* flies from Japan to England in 51 hours 17 minutes. | **12 April** Frank Whittle makes the first ground runs of the first gas-turbine (jet) engine. |

the newsreel cameras rolled. Passengers and crew jumped to the ground as the flaming giant sank to the earth. Thirty-four seconds after the first sighting of flame, the *Hindenburg* was a crumpled skeleton on the Lakehurst airfield. Of the 97 passengers and crew, 35 perished in the disaster; one sailor also died on the ground.

Speculation continues to this day about the cause of the disaster – to that point, the worst to have involved a commercial flight. A build-up of static electricity igniting a leaking hydrogen cell is the most common theory; some scientists suggest that the coating of aluminium-impregnated dope and other highly flammable compounds was the initial source of the fire. There are many, however, who believe that the airship was sabotaged.

Although this was the only incident of loss of life or serious injury to befall a passenger Zeppelin, it spelled the end of the commercial airship in its original form. From the 1980s onwards, various helium-filled craft have been constructed of modern materials and used for a

*Britain's R.34 rigid airship made the first east–west crossing of the Atlantic by air.*

variety of tasks, but not yet for scheduled passenger service.

The last of the pre-war airships was the *Graf Zeppelin II*, which first flew in September 1938. It saw no passenger service and little flying, although it was used in a electronic 'ferret' role on the eve of World War II, cruising up and down off the English coast in an attempt to record signals from the new British radar stations. Hermann Goering ordered its scrapping in May 1940 and its materials were reused for aircraft production.

## R34

Britain's postwar passenger airship development was a mix of triumph and tragedy, mostly the latter. The R34 was a military airship built for the Royal Air Force during the last year of World War I, but it was never fitted with armament. Soon after its completion in early 1919, it was used to make the first east-to-west crossing of the Atlantic, from Scotland to New York. This was only two weeks after fellow Britons Alcock and Brown flew a Vickers Vimy from Newfoundland, Canada, to Ireland,

| MAY | JUNE | JULY | | SEPTEMBER |
|---|---|---|---|---|
| **6 May** The airship *Hindenburg* explodes at Lakehurst, New Jersey, killing 33 of the 97 passengers and crew. | **30 June** The Bristol 138 is flown to an altitude of 16,440m (53,937ft). | **2 July** Amelia Earhart and Fred Noonan disappear near Howland Island in the Pacific while attempting a round-the-world flight in a Lockheed Electra. | **12–14 July** A Soviet Tupolev ANT-25 flies from Moscow to San Jacinto, California, over the North Pole, a nonstop distance of 10,148km (6306 miles).<br><br>**3 September** Airborne ASV (air-to-surface vessel) radar is tested by the RAF, and successfully detects large warships. | **24 September** The first air-defence radar system becomes operational at Bawdsey Manor, England. |

crossing the Atlantic in the other direction.

Although not designed as a passenger craft, the R34 carried 30 crew and one stowaway across the Atlantic and back, becoming the first aircraft to make a round-trip journey. Its success led to plans for a luxury transoceanic airship, which was not built. Postwar economic conditions also saw the scrapping of the next large British airship, the R80, even though plans had been drawn up to use a commercial version on inter-European routes. The R34 itself served on for another two years after its transatlantic flight as a training ship, but was then lost in an accident without loss of life.

In 1924, an Imperial Airship Scheme was set up. Its ambitious plans involved building flying troop ships and aircraft carriers to allow colonial outposts to be quickly reinforced from the United Kingdom, and producing commercial versions to cut out the long sea journeys for

*The spacious interior of the R.100. A good airship, she was designed by Barnes Wallis, later of 'bouncing bomb' fame.*

administrators, bureaucrats and businessmen. It was estimated that airships would need to be bigger than the *Hindenburg*, with a capacity of more than 27,000m³ (8,000,000cu ft), but smaller prototypes were built first. Two similar designs were ordered, designated the R100 and the R101.

To promote innovation, the former was built by private enterprise and the latter by the government's airship works at Cardington. The R101 was the first to be completed, in late 1929, and was the largest airship of its time, falling between the *Graf Zeppelin* and *Hindenburg* in terms of length and volume. Despite its great size, it proved to have less lifting capacity than expected during early flight trials. The solution was to cut the hull in half and insert an extra gas cell, and this was done over the winter of 1929–30, extending her length by 11m (35ft). The modifications took longer than expected, and there was strong political pressure for the ship to be completed.

Lord Thomson, Secretary of State for Air, was about to take up a new appointment as Vice Consul of India, and he wanted to arrive in style, in the airship he had commissioned. Further flight trials were rushed and preparations for the flight went ahead, despite poor weather

| **1937** | **1938** | | |
|---|---|---|---|
| OCTOBER | JANUARY | JULY | AUGUST |
| 18 October A new Australia–England record of 5 days 18 minutes is set by Jean Batten. | 20 January Aerial refuelling trials are conducted using Imperial Airways flying boats.<br><br>26 January A Boeing 247 lands at Pittsburgh, Pennsylvania, making the first landing by a scheduled airliner using the Instrument Landing System. | 10–14 July Howard Hughes and a crew of four make a round-the-world flight in 3 days 19 hours, in a Lockheed 14 Super Electra.<br><br>17 July Claiming to have intended to fly to California, Douglas 'Wrong Way' Corrigan flies solo from New York to Ireland. | |

10–11 August A Lufthansa Focke Wulf Fw 200 airliner makes a nonstop flight from Berlin to New York.

forecasts. Weight was still an issue and every passenger was restricted to about 14kg (30lb) of baggage each. Not Lord Thomson and his new bride, though: some of the extra freight included a 32kg (70lb) cask of ale, two cases of champagne weighing 24kg (52lb), and a roll of carpet to be used at state dinners in Egypt and India, weighing 59kg (129lb).

The R101 was to inaugurate an Imperial airship service that would take five days outbound and six more to return to Karachi (then in India) – rather than the eight days each way for an aeroplane or the four weeks for a ship. Airship masts and hangars were built at Ismailia, Egypt, Karachi and elsewhere in preparation for what was hoped eventually to be a commercial service to most of the British Empire. With many events planned for the inaugural journey and Lord Thomson's reputation riding on its success, the R101 set off from England on 4 October 1930 – and promptly crashed. Near Beauvais in

northern France, it encountered strong gales and rain, and could not manoeuvre to escape. Six of the 54 on board survived, but not Lord Thomson. His successor at the Air Ministry cancelled the Imperial Airship Scheme, effectively ending the British airship programme.

*In contrast to the R100, the R101, a government project, was badly designed and paid the price. Her tangled, burnt-out wreckage lies on a hillside near Beauvais.*

The competing design, the R100, was also stretched for extra lift. It was completed first and made a successful flight to Canada in August 1930. Designed by Barnes Wallis (later to find wartime fame as the inventor of the 'bouncing bomb') and Nevil Shute-Norway (later to shorten his surname and become a successful novelist), the R100 had a short career. It was put into storage after the Beauvais disaster, and its fabric deteriorated. In November 1931, the decision was taken to scrap it.

By 1939, the airship's career as a passenger transport was over. Even if structural issues had been overcome, as well as the use of volatile hydrogen (a problem that was always more political than practical), there were already faster airliners on the drawing board, designed to climb above the weather and span the oceans. Once again, though, war was to intervene. And, again, it is debatable whether the technology it spawned benefited civil aviation.

---

**SEPTEMBER**

**14 September** Igor Sikorsky's VS-300 helicopter makes a tethered test flight.

**OCTOBER**

**14 October** The Curtiss XP-40 first flies. Nearly 14,000 of the P-40 Kittyhawk/Warhawk/Tomahawk series are built up to 1944.

**22 October** An Italian Caproni 161-bis reaches 17,083m (56,046ft) – an altitude record for piston-engine aircraft, and one that still stands.

**NOVEMBER**

**5-7 November** Two Vickers Wellesleys of the RAF's Long Range Development Flight fly nonstop from Ismailia in Egypt to Darwin in Australia, a world record distance of 11,520km (7158 miles).

**DECEMBER**

**31 December** The Boeing 307 Stratoliner flies. It is the first airliner to have a pressurized cabin.

# From Biplanes to Jets: World War II 1939–1945

*September 1939 saw the world plunged again into war. By now, the major powers were well equipped with fighting aircraft and theories about how to use them. Germany had tested its machines and methods in the Spanish Civil War; Italy in the Horn of Africa; and Japan in China. Only the Western powers had little or no experience of modern aerial warfare.*

The late 1930s saw the larger air forces make the leap from the biplane era to that of the all-metal monoplane, but all except Germany, France and Britain still had a significant proportion of biplane fighters at the outbreak of war in 1939. Polikarpov in the Soviet Union and Fiat in Italy continued to produce biplane fighters until well into the war. Nearly 20 different types of biplane fighter were used during the war, as well as numerous seaplanes, transports, ground-attack aircraft and, of course, the Fairey Swordfish torpedo bomber, which remained in service throughout the conflict and in production for most of it.

The war was so vast in scope, and the air war barely less so, that it is impossible to describe all the significant aircraft types. What can be described is the general progress of aviation during the war years, by reference to the most significant combat types, beginning with those from the biplane era and ending with the first steps into the jet age.

*Left: The Polikarpov I-153 featured a retractable undercarriage. It fought in the Spanish Civil War and in the battles against the Japanese in the Far East. Right: The Curtiss P-40 was one of the leading Allied fighter-bombers in the Mediterranean theatre.*

## Soviet Aircraft

The Polikarpov design bureau in the Soviet Union was a leader in biplane design, and created one of the few biplanes to have a retractable landing gear. The I-153 (where the 'I' stood for *Istrebitel*, or fighter) actually came after their first monoplane, the I-16, and remained in production for longer. Nonetheless, the I-16 was a significant aircraft in its own right, being the first cantilever (non-externally braced) monoplane fighter with a retractable undercarriage to enter service.

The prototype for I-16 first flew in December 1933 and a pre-series batch entered service in early 1935. The basic structure of the I-16 was a laminated wooden monocoque fuselage, attached to metal wings with fabric-covered control surfaces. The radial engine was enclosed in a metal cowling, which extended to cover the forward surface, and moveable louvres allowed cooling air to reach the cylinders.

Nearly 500 early I-16s were supplied to the Spanish Republicans from October 1936. The Nationalists soon gave the I-16 the nickname 'Rata' ('rat'), the Republicans called it 'Mosca' ('fly'), and the Soviets themselves called it 'Ishak' ('little donkey'). In the Spanish Civil War and in Chinese hands, the I-16 proved superior in climb and dive to all enemy biplanes, and was also better at turning than some of them. Only the arrival of the Messerschmitt 109 in Spain and the Mitsubishi Zero in China prevented the I-16s winning air superiority for the Spanish Republicans and the Chinese Nationalists, respectively.

By the launch of Operation Barbarossa in June 1941, more than 60 per cent of the Soviet fighter force was comprised of I-16s. Several thousand aircraft were lost in the opening days and weeks of the German invasion; however, significant numbers of I-16s were to remain in service until 1943.

*The Polikarpov I-116 was the first monoplane fighter to have a retractable undercarriage. By the summer of 1941, it was outclassed by the Messerschmitt 109 and suffered heavy losses in the early fighting on the Eastern Front.*

## 1939

### JANUARY

**January** The Nakajima Ki-43 Hayabusa Oscar for the Imperial Japanese Army is flown.

**26 January** The twin-boomed Lockheed XP-38 Lightning first flies.

### FEBRUARY

**12 February** Grumman's XF4F-3, the first of the Wildcat family, begins test-flying.

## RAF fighters

During the interwar years, the Royal Air Force had moved slowly in the fighter field. Its fighters of the 1920s and early 1930s were little different than those of World War I. Aircraft such as the Sopwith Snipe and Bristol Bulldog were better built and wonderful to fly, but only slightly faster and no better armed than their predecessors that had duelled over the Western Front.

This was particularly highlighted by the introduction of the Hawker Hart two-seat light bomber. The streamlined inline-engine Hart could outpace the RAF's fighters and led to a series of derivatives, including the Fury fighter. This was faster again, but more expensive than its contemporaries, and it equipped only three 'elite' squadrons of RAF Fighter Command.

The RAF did not embrace monoplanes until 1936, when it introduced the Avro Anson, a twin-engine trainer. Despite its modern outline, it was still constructed of fabric-covered metal tubing and powered by engines with fixed-pitch propellers, which were most efficient only in a small band of the flight envelope. The novel retractable undercarriage had to be cranked up laboriously by hand.

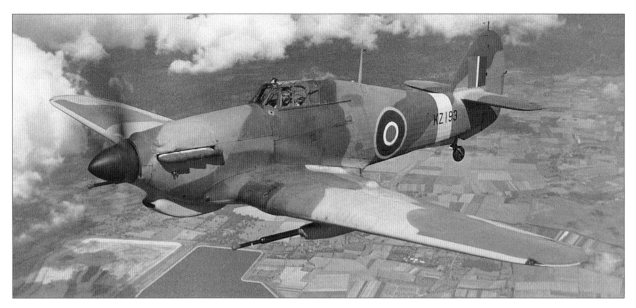

*The Hawker Hurricane Mk IV was armed with two 40mm cannon and was effective in the anti-tank role in the Western Desert. In 1944, it was also used against enemy shipping in the Balkans.*

The first British fighter with a monoplane wing and a retractable gear was the Hawker Hurricane. Developed in 1933 as the Fury Monoplane, it came from Sir Sidney Camm's drawing board. Based on the biplane Fury fighter, it was powered by a steam-cooled 495kW (660hp) Rolls Royce Goshawk engine.

The availability of the new 671kW (900hp) Rolls-Royce PV 12 (later to evolve into the famous Merlin) gave extra impetus to the project. Redesigned around this engine, it emerged in late 1935 as a larger and more modern aircraft. In June 1936, the Air Ministry ordered an unprecedented 600 examples of the

**MARCH**

**3 March** The first Boeing 314 flying boat for Pan Am is named *Yankee Clipper* in Washington.

**30 March** The XB-24 Liberator makes its maiden flight. More than 18,000 Liberators will be built.

**APRIL**

**1 April** Mitsubishi's A6M1 Rei-Sen Zero, or 'Zeke', is flown in Japan.

**26 April** The one-off Messerschmitt Me 209V1, flown by Fritz Wendel, sets a speed record of 755km/h (469mph), the last official piston-engined speed record for 30 years.

Hurricane, as it was officially named. The initial Hurricane Mk I model, now with the 768kW (1030hp) Merlin II and armed with eight 7.7mm (0.303in) machine guns in the wings, entered service in December 1937.

The Hurricane was of fabric-covered metal and wood construction, sharing many features of the earlier Hawker biplanes. It has been said

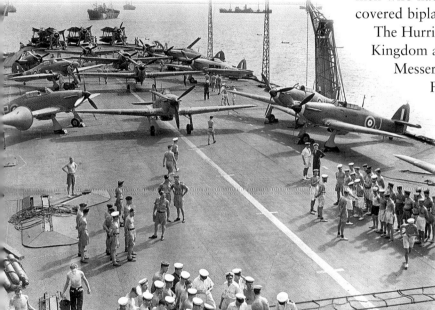

that British aircraft were designed to be assembled by craftsmen, and American ones by high-school graduates. The Hurricane is a case in point: it had almost no interchangeable parts, and many complex ones, all of which needed special equipment to produce. On the other hand, maintenance and battle damage repair was easy for a generation of NCOs and enlisted men who had learnt their trade on fabric-covered biplanes.

The Hurricanes were withdrawn to the United Kingdom after suffering heavy losses against Messerschmitt fighters in the Battle of France. In the Battle of Britain, it was less manoeuvrable than the Spitfire, but it proved to be a more stable gun platform and was more effective in destroying the Luftwaffe's bombers. Its thick gave its best performance at medium altitudes and complemented

.....................................................

*In 1941 the Hawker Hurricane went to sea as the Sea Hurricane.*

the Spitfire with its better high-altitude performance. In the final reckoning, Hurricanes destroyed more enemy aircraft during the battle than all other defences combined – fighters, anti-aircraft guns and barrage balloons.

### The Spitfire

Developed later than the Hurricane, and with the benefit of the next generation of airframe technology, the Supermarine Spitfire was to become the symbol of Britain's resistance to Nazi Germany and is perhaps the most famous fighter of all time.

Certainly, with 22,000 examples built, the Spitfire became the most numerous fighter ever produced in Britain or the United States. It underwent constant development throughout the war, and later versions had almost nothing in common with early Spitfires apart from the name. At two and a half times the weight and almost twice the power, it was also 160km/h (100mph) faster.

The Spitfire's designer, R.J. Mitchell, used his experience in creating high-speed seaplanes for the Schneider Cup races in the 1920s and 1930s. In 1934, he created the fixed-gear gull-

**1939**

| MAY | JUNE |
|---|---|
| | **1 June** The Focke-Wulf Fw 190V1 first flies. |
| **1 May** The Yakovlev I-26 flies, the predecessor of the Yak-1 Soviet fighter and more than 37,000 derivatives. | **20 June** The Heinkel He 176 becomes the first aircraft to fly powered by a liquid rocket motor alone. |

winged Type 224, an ungainly design that was by no means successful. The mistakes made were corrected by an entirely new

design featuring retractable gear, an enclosed cockpit and an elliptical wing of very thin section. Like the Hurricane, this fighter was designed around the Rolls-Royce PV 12, a water-cooled 12-cylinder engine that was soon to be renamed the Merlin and which would power tens of thousands of Allied fighters and bombers during World War II.

The thin wing, lower drag and lighter weight of the new fighter, which first flew in March 1936, gave it better climb performance, higher speed and better manoeuvrability than the Hurricane. Named 'Spitfire' by Vickers, Supermarine's parent company, the new fighter entered service in August 1938. It was initially fitted with a two-

*A Mk XIV Spitfire with 'clipped' wings for better low-level performance.*

*This photograph shows the Spitfire's original elliptical wing shape to good advantage.*

bladed fixed wooden propeller, but a three-bladed variable-pitch metal prop was soon introduced. Later models would have four-, five- and, eventually, six-bladed (contra-rotating) propellers.

Development continued, focusing on more powerful versions of the Merlin, with superchargers and improved armament. The MK I's eight rifle-calibre machine guns were exchanged for a mixture of 50-calibre (12.7mm/0.5in) machine guns and 20mm (0.79in) cannon, and a limited bombing capability was introduced.

The introduction of the Focke-Wulf 190 and improved versions of the Messerschmitt 109 saw a seesawing of superiority for the remainder

## JULY

**17 July** The Bristol Beaufighter twin-engined fighter-bomber/night-fighter/torpedo bomber make its maiden flight.

## AUGUST

**August** RAF Bristol Blenheims become the first operational aircraft fitted with airborne interception (AI) radar.

**27 August** The Heinkel He178 becomes the first turbojet aircraft to fly, at Rostock in Germany.

## SEPTEMBER

**3 September** Hours after the declaration of war, RAF Whitleys drop propaganda leaflets.

of the war. Although the last Fw 190 versions were probably superior to the then current Spitfire XIV (which had a 1294kW/1735hp Rolls-Royce Griffon engine), German fighter development ended in 1945, while Vickers continued to extract every ounce of potential from the basic Spitfire design. The final production model, the Mk 24 was so different that a new name, the Vickers Valiant, was considered. The last RAF Spitfires, used in the weather reconnaissance role, were retired in 1957.

## Messerschmitt

The Spitfire and Hurricane's great fighter rivals in the early part of the war were both designed and built by the same firm, Messerschmitt AG of Augsburg, Germany. The Bf 109 was a match for the Spitfire for much of the war. The larger Bf 110 was the result of a flawed concept, and was soon withdrawn as a day fighter in high-threat areas, but went on to be a highly successful night-fighter.

Forbidden by the Treaty of Versailles to have a military air arm, Germany built up its Luftwaffe under the guise of civilian sport flying clubs and youth gliding organizations. When the Nazis came to power, they gave up the pretence. Even so, the most famous German fighter was initially developed as a 'fast courier' aircraft. Wilhelm 'Willi' Messerschmitt of the BFW aircraft company designed the four-seat Bf 108A monoplane in an international contest for touring aircraft. Although it won no prizes, the performance of this machine and its many advanced design features impressed the German Air Ministry, and as a result Messerschmitt was invited to design a fast 'single-seat courier' for a Luftwaffe competition.

*This Messerschmitt Bf 109G-2/Trop 'Black Six' was captured in North Africa and restored to flying condition. It crash-landed at an air show in 1997, before being restored again.*

## 1939

### OCTOBER

**16 October** Three Ju 88 bombers are shot down by Spitfires over Scotland.

**23 October** Mitsubishi introduces the twin-engine bomber, the Betty.

### DECEMBER

**14–18 December** A series of costly attacks on German shipping causes the RAF to abandon unescorted daylight bombing missions.

## 1940

The Flettner Fl 282 Kolibri is the first helicopter put into production.

The prototype featured the wings and tail of the Bf 108 (which itself was to become the Luftwaffe's main communications aircraft). A new fuselage was designed behind a Junkers Jumo 210 inverted-V 12-cylinder water-cooled engine of 680kW (507hp). The Jumo was not ready when the first prototype of the BF 109 was completed in May 1935, and it was fitted, ironically, with a Rolls-Royce engine (a Kestrel VI of 695kW/519hp), which was also used on the Hawker Fury.

Flying in May 1935, two months after the government announced the existence of the Luftwaffe, the Bf 109 was nearly a year ahead of the Spitfire. For the first time, many advanced features were included in one fighter airframe, including retractable undercarriage, an enclosed cockpit and stressed-skin monocoque construction. Early prototypes were dispatched to Spain in December 1936 for operational evaluation. They achieved no combat victories, but gathered much valuable data, which was applied to the Bf 109B. This made its first appearance in the Spanish Civil War in March 1937, and the Messerschmitts soon turned the tables on the nimble Polikarpovs flown by the

Republicans. This was as much due to their better tactical employment, though, as to any great technical superiority.

By 1939, the Luftwaffe's fighter arm was largely equipped with the Bf 109E variant, powered by a fuel-injected

....................................................

*Lineup of Messerschmitt Bf 109E-3 fighters in pre-war markings and camouflage.*

Daimler-Benz DB 601 engine. Superior to most French, Dutch and Polish fighters, it was closely matched to the Spitfire and Hurricane, but was somewhat hampered by its short endurance, which gave it only 20 minutes of combat time over England. In combat with RAF fighters, it scored slightly better than even, but could be said to have failed in its main task of protecting the bombers. (The failure was due, in part, to the employment of incompatible radios by the Luftwaffe's fighter and bomber arms.)

**JANUARY**

**31 January** RAF Coastal Command Hudson and Sunderland patrol planes enter service with ASV radar.

**FEBRUARY**

**1 February** First flight of the Bell P-39 Airacobra fighter.

**24 February** First flight of the Hawker Typhoon fighter.

Like the Spitfire, the Bf 109 was subject to constant development throughout the war years, but changed less in dimensions and overall weight. The Bf 109K of 1945 was less than a third heavier when fully loaded than the Bf 109E of 1938, but, like the Spitfire, gained about 160km/h (100mph) of speed from its more powerful engine. Handling suffered due to weight redistribution, and generally the mid-series Bf 109F aircraft (like the Spitfire Mk V) were regarded as the most enjoyable to fly. Nevertheless, most of the Luftwaffe's top aces preferred to fly the 109 until the end of the war, and amassed incredible victory tallies on the type. Erich Hartmann was the most successful ace of all, scoring 352 confirmed victories, most of them over the Eastern Front.

## Bf 110

Nazi propaganda sought, with some success, to convince the world that such aircraft as the twin-engine Focke-Wulf Fw 187 and the Heinkel He 112 (or the fictitious 'He 100') were in large-scale service. In fact, they were procured in only tiny numbers, and the Bf 109's only real partner was the Bf 110. This was probably the

*Messerschmitt Bf 110 fighters flying over Athens at the end of the Greek campaign of 1941. The heavily armed Bf 110 was designed as a long-range escort fighter.*

most successful result of a vogue for twin-engine multi-crew 'strategic' fighter designs, other examples including the US Bell Airacuda and the Dutch Fokker GI. A heavy fighter, it was intended to escort bombers into enemy territory, carry out ground-attack missions and intercept bombers at long range. In 1934, the Luftwaffe issued a specification for a strategic fighter (Zerstorer, or

destroyer) and Willi Messerschmitt set to work. Designed with tandem seating, twin tails and twin inline Daimler-Benz DB 600A engines, the sleek aircraft first flew in May 1936. The bombing requirement was ignored in favour of speed and range.

With long range and a powerful offensive armament of two cannon and four machine guns in the nose, the Bf 110s were very successful over Poland, France and the Low Countries.In the Battle of Britain, the Zerstorers were no match for the RAF's Spitfires and Hurricanes, and often had to be escorted by Bf 109s. The bombing capability was restored with the Bf 110C and several effective precision raids were made during the battle. Afterwards, the Bf 110 day-fighter was relegated to less

## 1940

APRIL

9 April Parachute troops are used for the first time in combat during the German invasion of Norway.

MAY

May Germany puts its Würzburg air defence radar into service.

13 May Sikorsky's VS-300, the first helicopter with a tail rotor, makes its first free flight.

29 May The Chance-Vought XF4U-1 Corsair first flies. Production of successive versions continues until 1952.

demanding theatres such as Sicily, and to roles such as fighter-bomber and convoy escort. On the other hand, the radar-equipped Bf 110G series proved the Luftwaffe's most effective night-fighter in the middle years of the war. The general shortage of combat aircraft and crews by 1943 meant that Bf 110s were employed against American day-bombers, often using air-to-air rockets. They suffered heavy losses to the escorting fighters.

*A Messerschmitt Bf 110G-4 fitted with airborne interception (AI) radar aerials.*

### French Fighters

As war loomed, many European nations scrambled to buy the best fighters they could afford. In practice, this often amounted to an order for a handful of Hurricanes or Curtiss 75 Hawks.

France had been a leader in monoplane fighter design. The Dewoitine company in particular had developed a series of parasol-winged fighters before adopting the low-winged format with open cockpits and fixed undercarriage. Several prototype designs with retractable gear and sliding canopies followed, then came the definitive Dewoitine D.520 of 1938. This compact fighter had all the best features of the day, including a hub-mounted cannon and four machine guns, and a powerful V-12 engine in a tight cowling. Unfortunately, French domestic

*The Dewoitine D.520 was France's finest fighter in 1940. It continued to serve with the Vichy French forces in North Africa and the Middle East.*

politics prevented timely production of the D.520 and other worthy designs such as the Morane-Saulnier MS.406. Several rearmament plans were drawn up, abandoned, then replaced with new plans. The aircraft industry was nationalized and reorganized, and aircraft were not ordered in sufficient quantity. Even when they were, the airframe, engine and component

JULY

**3 July** Northrop's N1M, the first true flying-wing aircraft, begins testing.

**6 July** The RAF makes the first use of aerial depth charges against submarines.

**8 July** The Boeing 307 Stratoliner, the first pressurized airliner, enters service with TWA.

**22 July** An RAF Blenheim night-fighter shoots down a German Dornier 17, guided by its own onboard airborne intercept (AI) radar.

*A Dewoitine D.520 flown by Capitaine Pierre le Gloan, a French air ace who fought the Germans in the Battle of France and the British during the Syrian campaign of July 1941.*

manufacturers could barely coordinate themselves to deliver armament, an engine and a propeller at the same time.

As war approached, orders for the D.520 were increased (and withdrawn) several times. Eventually, orders for 2250 were placed for the Armée de l'Air, plus another 120 for the Aéronavale, but the first unit was not equipped until November 1939, two months after the outbreak of war. Only 79 of the 246 D.520s built had been accepted for service by the end of the 'Phoney War' in May 1940, when Germany launched its assault on France and the Low Countries. The remainder were parked outside the Toulouse factory awaiting propellers and other components.

Tested against a captured Messerschmitt Bf 109E, the D.520 proved slightly slower, but more manoeuvrable. A 20mm (0.79in) cannon meant that the Dewoitine's armament was better than the early 109E's. In the Battle of France, the undertrained French pilots fought well, and the few D.520s in service were credited with 108 'kills' for the cost of 54 air combat losses. Nonetheless, the German blitzkrieg proved overwhelming.

## 1940

### AUGUST

**August** The twin-rotor Fa 223 Drache, the largest production helicopter of World War II, makes its first flight.

**10 August** Italy's Macchi MC.202 Folgore (Thunderbolt) makes its initial flight.

**28 August** Using a piston engine to drive a turbine inside the fuselage, the Italian Caproni-Campini N1 makes its first flight.

Despite the fall of France, D.520s served until 1945 – the Germans reinstating production for some of their own training units and for Vichy French forces and allies such as Bulgaria. Free French units also flew the D.520 and were active in the liberation of southern France. One pilot, Pierre Le Gloan, scored 18 victories in the war, becoming an ace against the Germans, Italians and British in turn.

To make up the shortfalls in indigenous fighters and bombers before the war, the French also turned to the United States. Large quantities of the Hawk 75 and later the P-40 were ordered from Curtiss, as were Douglas and Martin bombers.

The Curtiss Hawk monoplane series followed the successful P-1 to P-6E (Air Corps) and F6C (Navy) fighter series of the 1920s and early 1930s, but shared nothing beyond the name. By 1934, the Curtiss company realized that the future lay in monoplanes with retractable landing gear, and Don Berlin designed a modern cantilever monoplane with a 671kW (900hp) Wright R-1670 radial engine and an all-metal basic structure with fabric control surfaces. The Model 75 was ordered as the P-36 by the Air

*US production of the P-40, which included 1300 P-40Ks with increased fin area, 700 P-40Ls and 4219 P-40Ns (seen here), ended in December 1944 after 13,738 aircraft had been built.*

Corps in a series of increasingly powerful version, culminating in the P-36C with a 894kW (1200hp) Pratt & Whitney R-1830-17 radial. Armament increased from two machine guns above the engine to four in the outer wings.

France ordered 300 Hawk 75As, which were based mainly on the P-36A and the P-36C. In the Battle of France, the Hawks fared reasonably well, the ace Edmond Marin La Meslée claiming 20 kills against German aircraft. As was true for several aircraft types, the order was not complete when France fell and the undelivered aircraft were redirected to Britain – in this case, as the Mohawk. These were later passed to the South African Air Force or sent to India. In addition, Norway, the Netherlands, Thailand,

**OCTOBER**

**12 October** The Russian Ilyushin Il-2 Sturmovik flies, becoming the first aircraft to be armed with air-to-ground rockets.

**26 October** First flight of the North American NA73, later named the P-51 Mustang.

**NOVEMBER**

**11–12 November** Fairey Swordfish Torpedo bombers attack the Italian fleet at Taranto, causing severe damage. One battleship is sunk and two others severely damaged, for the loss of two aircraft.

**25 November** The DH.98, prototype of the de Havilland Mosquito, flies from Salisbury Hall, England.

Argentina and China all purchased Hawks of one model or another from Curtiss. America's P-36s were largely superseded by December 1941, but some were to be found in Hawaii during the Pearl Harbor attack. Two were able to get airborne and bring down a pair of Japanese dive-bombers, but most of the others were destroyed on the ground.

## USAAF Fighters

The fighter that replaced the P-36 was Curtiss's own P-40. It was known variously as the Tomahawk and Warhawk, both names that were bestowed by the British, as was usually the case. It is most commonly remembered, however, as Kittyhawk – a name that, strictly speaking, applied only to the later British Commonwealth variants.

The potential of the Hawk 75/P-36 was limited by the power of compatible radial engines. In July 1937, a P-36A was therefore tested, as the XP-37, with a turbocharged version of the new Allison V-1710 V-12 engine. A revised, non-turbocharged installation with an underwing radiator was flown as the XP-40 (Model 75P) on 14 October 1938, and the radiator was later moved to the chin position. The (then) US Army Air Corps ordered more than 500 P-40s (Model 81) in April 1939, and

......................................................

*The P-40E Kittyhawk was used by the Australian and New Zealand air forces.*

deliveries began in April 1940. From the firewall back, the P-40 was essentially the same as the earlier Hawk 75s, but had increased, if not stunning, performance and better handling. Armament was initially only two nose-mounted machine guns, which were soon supplemented by four wing guns. After the main early production P-40B and C, all armament was concentrated in the wings. British and Commonwealth air forces took all models of P-40 during the war, and some French orders were also delivered. The Royal Air Force's first aircraft were known as the Tomahawk IIA.

The American Volunteer Group (the 'Flying Tigers') famously fought the Japanese in Burma and China from late 1941 until mid-1942, using Hawk 81A-2s and, later, P-40Es. Nearly 40 AVG pilots were credited with five kills or more before the unit was absorbed into the USAAF's 23rd Fighter Group.

In all, 13,739 P-40s were built in three plants up to December 1944. Although pleasant to fly, the P-40 was obsolescent by the time it reached the front. And so Army orders for successive batches of only slightly improved P-40s became the subject of an inquiry by a committee led by

---

## 1940

### DECEMBER

**18 December** Flight-testing of one of the first guided missiles, the German Henschel Hs293A radio-controlled bomb.

**23 December** United Airlines introduces an all-cargo air service.

## 1941

### JANUARY

**29 January** The Tupolev Tu-2 twin-engined ground-attack aircraft flies in the USSR.

### FEBRUARY

**11 February** The RAF's first four-engined bomber, the Short Stirling, makes its combat debut in a raid on Rotterdam.

the future president Harry S. Truman. The Army was criticized for ordering too many P-40s, particularly after better competing designs came along, and for not insisting on greater performance improvements, but was cleared of favouritism towards the company.

*Lockheed P-38 Lightnings carrying out an attack on an enemy anchorage in the Pacific.*

Despite its obsolesence, the P-40 made a valuable contribution in theatres from North Africa to the South Pacific. It was also used as a trainer until more modern types became available.

Partnering the single-engine P-40 in the US Army's pre-war plans was the twin-engine, twin-boomed P-38 Lightning. The Lightning was a radical design for a single-seat fighter: it had twin tailbooms and a central nacelle containing the pilot and armament, which consisted of four machine guns and a 20mm (0.79in) cannon on most models. This arrangement reduced the need for careful harmonization of dispersed guns to concentrate fire at a single point, and did not require the costly and complex synchronization gear that kept bullets and propellers apart.

The P-38 was far more expensive and sophisticated than contemporary US fighters, and the Army initially bought it in only small numbers. In fact, the United Kingdom was the only customer for new-built aircraft. Only 50 P-38s were in US service by December 1941, but production quickly built up, and large numbers

*The P-38's long range made it ideal for operations in the Pacific theatre.*

were ferried to England from mid-1942 to act as escorts for the Eighth Air Force's growing fleets of heavy bombers.

The P-38F introduced the capability for external fuel (drop) tanks. In practical terms, this allowed the bombers to be protected for up to 720km (450 miles) from the home base, with allowance for combat and other manoeuvring.

## MARCH

**10–11 March** The Handley Page Halifax bomber flies its first mission with the RAF.

## APRIL

**2 April** Heinkel's He 280 becomes the world's first twin-engined jet aircraft and the first jet intended for combat, although it is not put into production.

**18 April** The Me 262V1 flies. Unlike production versions, it has a tailwheel undercarriage and a piston engine in the nose.

*The Nakajima Ki -43 'Oscar' was the principal fighter used by the Imperial Japanese Army Air Force in the early campaigns in the Pacific and Burma.*

There were numerous teething problems with the P-38, including inadequate heating, supercharger failures and parts falling off at high speed. As the range and performance of single-engine fighters improved, the P-38 was phased out of the European Theater of Operations (ETO).

The P-38 fared much better in the war against Japan. Richard (Dick) Bong of the 39th Fighter Squadron, based in New Guinea, became the top-scoring American ace of all time, destroying 40 Japanese aircraft while flying various models of P-38. The second-highest scorer, Thomas B. McGuire (38 victories), also flew P-38s. Both pilots received the Medal of Honor.

### Zero and Oscar

Development of advanced fighter aircraft was by no means the prerogative of the West, as the Allies found out in 1941. Only a few years previously, the Japanese seemed to be lagging behind in combat aircraft. In 1937 and 1938, respectively, the Army and Navy introduced the Nakajima Ki-27 and the Mitsubishi A5M fighters into service. These radial-engine monoplanes were similar in appearance, having fixed undercarriage units with large wheel spats. The Mitsubishis, later to be known to the Allies by the reporting name 'Claude', had open-topped cockpits, as did some of the Nakajima 'Nates'. Dismissed as copies of inferior American designs, they nonetheless included many advanced features. They were designed with manoeuvrability as the overriding concern, and during the war in China immediately won air superiority against the opposition, mainly Soviet-built biplanes.

**1941**

MAY

**6 May** First flight of the Republic XP-47B, prototype of the Thunderbolt, the heaviest single-engined aircraft of the war.

**10 May** Following gliding trials, the Messerschmitt Me 163A flies using rocket power.

**15 May** The Gloster E28/39, also called the Gloster Whittle, becomes the first British jet aircraft to fly.

**18 May** Saab's B 17 single-engined bomber flies.

Almost as soon as the nimble Ki-27 and A5M entered service, the Japanese Army and Navy issued specifications for their replacements. The Navy's performance requirements were extremely stringent, including better armament, a retractable landing gear, an enclosed cockpit and full radio equipment. Mitsubishi's Jiro Horikoshi set to work on the new carrier fighter, using the most modern technology available. His modern fighter design was optimized for range and manoeuvrability, its lightweight structure being built of a new aluminium alloy. The priority was to make it the best possible fighter, and to worry about its carrier landing equipment later. As such, it was the first naval fighter to be superior to its land-based contemporaries.

It first flew in March 1939, and a pre-series batch of the new fighters was rushed for combat evaluation in China in July 1940. Soon after, it entered service as the Type Zero Carrier, 'Zero' referring to the year of acceptance – 2600 in the traditional Japanese calendar. The Allied reporting system allocated 'Zeke' as the code name for the A6M. Americans who witnessed the war in China warned Washington about

*One of the finest aircraft of all time, the Mitsubishi A6M Reisen (Zero fighter) first flew on 1 April 1939 and was accepted for service with the Japanese Naval Air Force in July 1940.*

the capabilities of the new generation of Japanese fighters. Little notice appears to have been taken, however. When the Zero appeared over Pearl Harbor in December 1941, albeit in a supporting role, few in either the US Army or Navy had any idea that such a modern fighter existed in the previously little-regarded Japanese air services.

There were various forms of the Zero, differing mainly in armament, engine power and wingtips (folding or otherwise). They were a constant feature of the Pacific War, taking part in most of the major battles, from carriers or land bases. The attrition of carriers and trained pilots, as well as the failure to develop a reliable successor, saw the Zero's fearsome

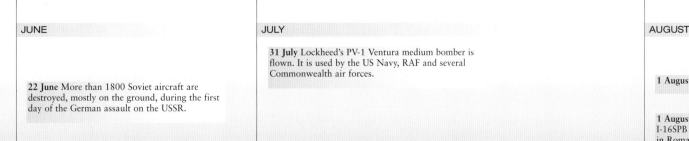

**JUNE**

**22 June** More than 1800 Soviet aircraft are destroyed, mostly on the ground, during the first day of the German assault on the USSR.

**JULY**

**31 July** Lockheed's PV-1 Ventura medium bomber is flown. It is used by the US Navy, RAF and several Commonwealth air forces.

**AUGUST**

**1 August** XTBF-1 Avenger torpedo-bomber makes first flight.

**1 August** A Soviet TB-3 bomber successfully employs Polikarpov I-16SPB 'parasite' dive-bombers in an attack on German forces in Romania.

reputation steadily slip. From 1944 onwards the aircraft were progressively expended in largely futile kamikaze attacks against the US and British fleets.

The reputation of the Zero owed much to its long range and high manoeuvrability (which was accomplished by omitting armour or fuel tank protection). And so fearsome was it that, for much of the war, every Japanese fighter was a 'Zero' to the average Allied soldier, sailor or airman.

Never as numerous, but just as important to the Imperial Japanese Army in the early part of the war, was the Nakajima Ki-43 Hayabusa (peregrine falcon). Unlike its naval counterpart, the Army's Ki-27 replacement progamme was not driven by a desire to push the technological boundaries, calling only for a small increase in speed. This was easily accomplished by fitting the specified retractable landing gear.

Hideo Itokawa and Yasumi Koyama of Nakajima took the best features of the Ki-27, designed a new fuselage with an enclosed cockpit, and applied the new 739kW (990hp) Nakajima Ha-25 14-cylinder radial. The lack of power in this engine was partly compensated for

by a very light structural design, no armour and only two machine guns for armament. Like the Zero, the Ki-43 was particularly nimble. Known as 'Oscar', it first flew in January 1939 and was particularly active in the China-Burma-India (CBI) theatre against RAF and USAAF squadrons. Its weaknesses included low speed and poor damage tolerance, and, once these were understood, the Allies were able to win superiority in 'Oscar'-patrolled areas. The Army did manage to develop better fighters, such as the Ki-84 Hayate ('Frank') and the Ki-61 Hien ('Tony'), but none was produced in large enough numbers to make an appreciable difference to Japan's fortunes.

### P-47 Thunderbolt

At the same time as Japan's main wartime fighters were emerging, the Republic Company in New York was developing the largest single-engine fighter of the war. Russian émigré Alexander Kartveli enlarged his earlier Seversky P-35 design into the P-43 Lancer, then into the P-47B Thunderbolt, which was first flown in May 1941. The US Army ordered nearly 800 examples before flight-testing even begun. With

*A Republic P-47 Thunderbolt being made ready for another sortie by its ground crew.*

---

**1941**

**SEPTEMBER**

**14 September** German heavy transport gliders are used for the first time in an assault role in an attack on Saaremaa island in the Baltic.

**OCTOBER**

**2 October** A prototype Me 163A exceeds 1000km/h (622mph), setting an unofficial world speed record.

**DECEMBER**

**7 December** Japanese carrier-based aircraft strike the American base at Pearl Harbor, Hawaii, sinking or disabling six battleships and bringing the United States into the war.

**1942**

**JANUARY**

**January** Troop and cargo gliders are used to resupply German troops cut off by Soviet forces at Kholm.

a 1491kW (2000hp) R-2800 radial engine and eight 12.7mm (0.50in) machine guns, the Thunderbolt was about the most powerful and best armed fighter seen to date. Its size and weight (nearly twice that of a Bf 109E) earned it the sobriquet 'Jug' – a name that stands for 'Juggernaut' and refers also to its resemblance to a milk container.

The P-47B entered service with the 56th Fighter Group in mid-1942. After a period of home defence duty, this unit headed off to Europe and the Eighth Air Force in early 1943. After initial problems with superchargers, and other troubles caused largely by the damp and cold of a British winter, the P-47s proved extremely durable. When fitted with reliable drop tanks, they were well able to escort bombers into Germany. After D-Day, the Eighth and Ninth Air

*The Republic Thunderbolt was designed around the 2000hp Pratt & Whitney Double Wasp radial engine.*

Force Thunderbolt groups proved particularly useful in ground-attack, tank-busting and close air support missions. When the escort part of their mission was over, the P-47s would often attack trains, convoys, airfields and other opportune targets. Their solid structure and armoured undersides usually allowed the Thunderbolts to take enormous punishment from anti-aircraft fire and still make it to a friendly airfield.

Also widely used in the Pacific and the CBI, the P-47 scored more than 3000 aerial victories and destroyed as many enemy aircraft on the ground. Francis Gabreski and Robert S. Johnson both scored 28 kills, putting them among the top five US aces of the war. Both flew with the 56th Fighter Group, which resisted trading in its Thunderbolts for Mustangs until after the war.

Total P-47 production was some 15,660 examples, more than any other American fighter. The most numerous model was the P-47D, which appeared in both 'razorback' and 'bubbletop' versions. The latter had a cut down rear fuselage and a transparent hood, giving much greater all-round visibility.

**13 January** The pilot of a Heinkel He 280 becomes the first to save his life with an ejection seat.

**14 January** Sikorsky's XR-4 helicopter makes its first flight. More than 400 were built by the end of the war.

**MARCH**

**5 March** The Gloster F.9/40, later called the Meteor and to become the Allies' first operational jet, flies using de Havilland H1 engines.

## P-51 Mustang

The P-51 Mustang came about as a result of British efforts to accelerate P-40 deliveries. Approaching North American Aviation (NAA) in late 1939, the British Government Purchasing Commission asked the California company to set up a production line to build some of the 2000 P-40s then on order for the RAF from Curtiss. 'Dutch' Kindelberger, the head of NAA, responded by claiming that his company could produce a better fighter – a bold claim, given that it had hitherto produced only bombers and trainers. Designers Raymond Rice and Edgar Schmued and aerodynamicist Ed Horkey got to work, and drew up plans for a highly advanced fighter. Given only 120 days by the British to produce and fly a prototype, the NA-73X was completed in time. However, the Allison engine was late and the first flight took place on 26 October 1940. The RAF ordered the first 340 as the Mustang Mk I in May that year, and received its first examples a year later.

Tested in Britain against the Spitfire V, the Mustang proved faster and had a longer range, although the Spitfire climbed faster and performed better at higher altitudes. The RAF

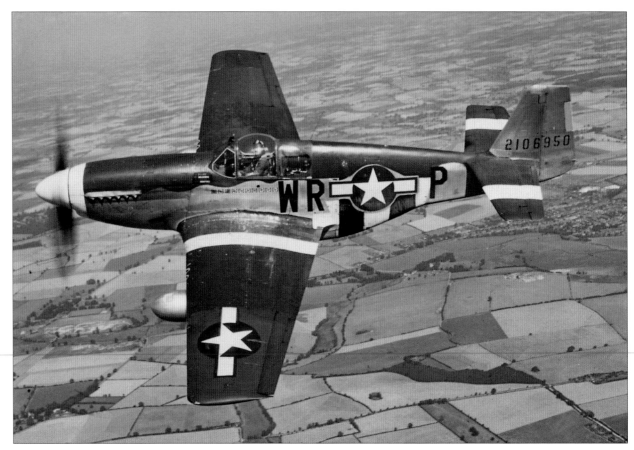

*A North American P-51C Mustang of the 354th Fighter Squadron, 355th Fighter Group, USAAF, which was based at Steeple Morden, near Cambridge, England, from the summer of 1943 to the end of the war.*

## 1942

### APRIL

**18 April** General Electric ground runs the first US jet engine, the GE I-A.

### MAY

**7–8 May** The Battle of the Coral Sea is the first major naval action conducted without the opposing surface units sighting one another. One carrier is lost by the United States and one by Japan.

**21 May** The Northrop XP-61 Black Widow flies; it is the first purpose-designed night-fighter.

*The North American Mustang served in every theatre of war.*

used the Mustang I mainly as a ground-attack and reconnaissance aircraft, so these were not important deficiencies. Mustang Is had six 7.7mm (0.303in) machine guns in the wings and two 12.7mm (0.50in) guns in the lower nose. The Mustang IA had four 20mm (0.79in) cannon in the wings, but no nose guns.

The USAAF eventually took notice of the Mustang, having retained several prototypes for their own testing. They ordered 150 cannon-armed P-51s and 310 P-51As armed with four 12.7mm (0.50in) machine guns. Other P-51s were aircraft originally intended for the RAF, but were held back after Pearl Harbor.

The secret to the Mustang's speed was its laminar flow wing. This had its maximum thickness at 50 per cent of the chord – not near the leading edge, as on most aircraft – and significant camber on the underside. Airflow stayed close to the wing and did not break up and cause drag. Maintaining the laminar flow required as smooth a surface as possible, so the P-51 was very precisely built using flush rivets and fasteners. The pilot was well protected with armour plate and the fuel tanks were self-sealing.

What transformed the Mustang from a low-altitude attacker and reconnaissance aircraft to a long-range high-altitude escort ship was the development of the Rolls-Royce Merlin 60 engine with its two-stage supercharger. This was installed by the British in April 1942, to create the Mustang X. Later that year, NAA made its own, more aesthetically pleasing installation of the same powerplant.

By November, NAA made a cleaner installation of the Packard-built version of the Merlin powerplant, leading to the first flight of the XP-51B. Deliveries of the production P-51B with an 1134kW (1520hp) Merlin V-1650-3 began in late 1943, and by March 1944 the first Mustangs appeared over Berlin, escorting B-17 heavy bombers.

The ultimate wartime model was the P-51D, which had six wing guns, greater external load capacity and a cut-down rear fuselage with a full bubble canopy. The new K-14 lead-computing gyro gunsight was the world's most advanced at the time. The P-51D made its combat debut just after D-Day in June 1944.

In the Pacific, Mustangs were able to escort the B-29s from their island bases all the way to the Japanese home islands. The air forces of South Africa, Canada, Australia, Nationalist China, Sweden and the Dutch East Indies all operated P-51s during the war, and more than 20 nations flew them in the postwar years.

The Mustang saw extensive action in the Korean War with US, South Korean and South African air forces. Used mostly in the ground-attack role, the P-51s suffered heavy losses to ground fire due to their exposed radiator and cooling system.

---

**JULY**

**30-31 May** The RAF despatches 1046 aircraft to Cologne in the first 'Thousand Bomber Raid'.

**10 July** The first Douglas A-26 Invader is flown. Later versions serve with the USAF up to 1972.

**19 July** The Messerschmitt Me 262 flies with Junkers Jumo 004 jet engines.

Due largely to the part it played in extending the safe range of the USAAF's bombers deep into Germany, the Mustang has sometimes been called the 'fighter that won the war'. This is probably overstating the case somewhat, although more than half of the Eighth Air Force's 'kills' were scored by Mustangs. Nonetheless, the type has become an enduring classic. Today, 60 years on, it is the most numerous 'warbird' fighter, with more than 100 still airworthy and in civilian hands.

## Grumman Wildcat and Hellcat

The US Navy fielded the most successful naval fighters and bombers of the war, new designs arriving periodically at the front. American industrial might, as well as the output of the many large training schools, ensured that large numbers of high-quality aircraft were increasingly available to fill the decks of the large carriers built after Pearl Harbor.

The Navy's first monoplane fighter was the Brewster F3A Buffalo. This entered service in 1940, but it was no longer on carrier decks by the end of 1941. The US Navy procured aircraft on behalf of the Marine Corps, and at least until the early war years it tended to hand down used and unwanted aircraft to the Marines; this is what happened with the Buffalo. Elsewhere, mainly in Asia, it served with British and Dutch squadrons, having a career that was nasty, brutish and short. In Finland, though, it proved exceptionally successful against the Soviets.

The pre-war Grumman biplane fighters, produced in series from the FF-1 ('Fifi') of 1931 to the F3F of 1935, were a mainstay of the US Navy's small carrier force in the last years of peace. Often known as 'flying barrels' due to their portly appearance, the Grummans introduced retractable undercarriages and enclosed canopies to the US Navy. The last of these aircraft were with the Marines by the time of Pearl Harbor, but their influence was felt long into the war.

By 1936, Grumman was working on a smaller biplane along the same lines called the

*The Grumman F4F Wildcat held the line in the Pacific theatre until better fighters became available.*

## 1942

### SEPTEMBER

**9 September** A Japanese Yokosuka 'Glen' floatplane is launched from a submarine and bombs a forest in Oregon. This and a subsequent mission on the 29th are the only attacks by aircraft on the US mainland.

**21 September** The Boeing XB-29, prototype of the Boeing Superfortress, makes its first test flight in Seattle, Washington.

### OCTOBER

**1 October** Bell's XP-59A Airacomet, the United States' first jet aircraft, flies at Muroc Dry Lake, California.

**3 October** The A4 (V-2) ballistic missile makes a successful test flight.

**3 October** The Grumman XF6F-1 Hellcat is flown for the first time.

XF4F-1. It was soon recognized that biplanes were on the way out, and the design was revised into the XF4F-2 monoplane. The two shared many features, including the undercarriage, which retracted into the lower fuselage by means of hand cranking. The XF4F-2 flew in September 1937, but lost out to the Buffalo for the US Navy's order. Revised yet again with a more powerful 895kW (1200hp) Pratt & Whitney Twin Wasp engine, it flew as the XF4F-3 in February 1939. An order for just more than 50 put the tubby little fighter into production as the Wildcat.

France and Britain again ordered large numbers of F4Fs, but only the United Kingdom's examples saw service, with the Fleet Air Arm, which initially named them Martlets. The name reverted to Wildcat for later versions.

Wing-folding was introduced on the F4F-4. This made a huge difference to carrier operations, allowing aircraft to be used on the small escort carriers then being produced for the US and British navies. The patented wing-folding system, also used on the TBF Avenger and later the F6F Hellcat, was developed with the help of bent paperclips and a pencil eraser,

and allowed the wings to pivot and lie backwards along the line of the fuselage. With the F4F-4's arrival, most US Navy F4F-3s were transferred to land-based Marine squadrons. Armament on the F4F-4 was increased to six 12.7mm (0.50in) machine guns, self-sealing fuel tanks were installed, and provision for drop-tanks was included.

The Wildcat was the only US carrier fighter in the great battles of 1942 at Coral Sea and Midway. Against unescorted bombers and dive-bombers, the F4F was quite effective, but no real match in combat with the A6M Zero, except in the hands of an expert pilot.

*Grumman Wildcats on patrol. The Wildcat distinguished itself during the battle for Guadalcanal in late 1942, operating from the airstrip called Henderson Field.*

**DECEMBER**

**24 December** The German V-1 pulse-jet pilotless aircraft is test-fired.

## 1943

**JANUARY**

**9 January** The Lockheed L-049 Constellation airliner flies for the first time. The US Army uses the first few as the C-69 transport.

Grumman was soon unable to build all the aircraft ordered by the United States and its allies. Production of the Wildcat was therefore switched to General Motors; its Eastern Aircraft Division built large numbers as the FM-1 and FM-2, the latter with a taller tailfin.

Using the abortive F4F-2 as a starting point, Grumman's engineers developed an all-new fighter to replace the Wildcat. While superficially similar, the F6F Hellcat was in a completely different league. First flying in October 1942, it had the largest wing area of any US single-seat fighter and could carry bombs and rockets as well as its six machine guns. Some versions carried a radar pod for night fighting on one wing.

The Hellcat scored three-quarters of all US Navy air-to-air victories in the war – a total of 4947 for carrier-based F6Fs. The US Navy's top ace (and the third-ranking American ace) was Hellcat pilot David McCampbell, who made 34 kills. In all, 307 American pilots became aces on the F6F.

*The Grumman F6F Hellcat was the fighter that turned the tide of the air war in the Pacific.*

## 1943

### MAY

**12 May** An acoustic homing torpedo dropped from an RAF Liberator sinks the German U-boat *U-456*.

**16-17 May** Using special 'bouncing bombs', Lancasters of the RAF's No. 617 Squadron destroy two dams in Germany's Ruhr Valley. The 'Dambusters Raid' is one of the most daring and famous of the war.

### JUNE

**15 June** The twin-engined Arado Ar 234 'Blitz' is the first jet bomber and reconnaissance aircraft to fly.

**28 June** The first flight of the Hawker Tempest Mk I, successor to the Typhoon.

The Vought F4U Corsair was designed around the huge new Pratt & Whitney R-2800 Double Wasp radial engine, which drove a large three-bladed propeller. To keep the propeller clear of the ground, the Corsair had an inverted gull wing, which contained six machine guns and had fabric-covered outer panels. The aircraft first flew in May 1940, but the original 'birdcage' canopy F4U-1 failed its carrier suitability trials in September 1942 due to the poor forward view on landing and the tendency for the undercarriage to bounce. It therefore entered combat with land-based Marine Corps units on Guadalcanal.

The most famous USMC unit was VMF-214 'Blacksheep', led by Gregory 'Pappy' Boyington, the top F4U ace, who scored 24 kills. US Navy Corsairs later went to sea and were credited with a kill ratio of more than 11 to one against Japanese aircraft. The growing demand for Corsairs saw production undertaken by three manufacturers, and more than 12,500 were built in a production run that did not end until 1952.

*Vought F4U Corsair fighter-bombers ranged on the flight deck of an American aircraft carrier.*

**24–25 July** Foil strips known as 'Window' are dropped from aircraft to confuse German radar during an RAF attack on Hamburg.

**29 July** The prototype Bell 47 helicopter makes its first untethered flight.

**17 August** Attacks by the US Eighth Air Force on Schweinfurt and Regensburg in Germany cost 60 B-17 bombers, the heaviest daily loss of the war.

## Bombers

Only the United States and Britain developed truly strategic bombing arms during the war and were capable of fielding increasingly large formations year by year. Allied bombers were usually categorized as 'medium' or 'heavy', the latter defined as having four engines, a long range and a large bomb load.

Japan, Italy and the Soviet Union never put heavy bombers into large-scale use, concentrating mainly on twin-engine or tri-motor designs. Germany's Heinkel He 177 was a four-engine aircraft, despite appearances: it mounted two Daimler-Benz DB 605 engines on a common shaft in each of its two nacelles. This arrangement was largely responsible for the 177's appalling record of engine fires. More than 1700 He 177s were built, but rarely did more than a dozen fly a mission together. They arrived to late in the war to have any strategic effect.

The United States was the first to produce a modern heavy bomber, although it required extensive modification before becoming suitable for combat. Boeing's Model 299 flew in 1935 and entered US Army service as the B-17B in

*A captured Heinkel He 177 Greif in RAF markings, being test-flown by the Enemy Aircraft Flight based at Farnborough. Heavy and experiencing continual engine problems, the He 177 was not a success.*

1938. The RAF bought 20 B-17Cs as its first four-engine bomber, but the aircraft it called the Fortress I had poor performance, weak armament and a failure-prone oxygen system. After a few daylight raids in 1941, the aircraft were withdrawn, but the experience gained allowed Boeing to improve the bomber. The B-17E had a larger fin and better turrets, and from August 1942, B-17s began raiding Germany from bases

in England. Combat experience led to further improvements. The definitive B-17G had 12.7mm (0.50in) calibre machine guns, including a chin turret to fend off head-on fighter attacks, and extensive armour plating.

The B-17 was partnered by the Consolidated B-24 Liberator, which flew later, in March 1939. Its slender high-mounted wing made it slightly faster and longer-ranged than the B-17, but its

## 1943

### SEPTEMBER

**9 September** Dropped by a Dornier Do 217, a German Fritz-X radio-guided bomb sinks the Italian battleship *Roma* before it can surrender to Allied forces.

**16 September** The 5440kg (12,000lb) Tallboy bomb is used in action for the first time, in an attack on the Dortmund-Ems canal.

**30 September** The first flight of de Havilland Vampire jet fighter, initially known as the 'Spidercrab'.

## 1944

### FEBRUARY

**28 February** Germany tests the Wasserfall (waterfall), the first guided surface-to-air missile.

### MARCH

**25 March** The first US guided bomb, named the VB1 Azon, is used in action by the 15th Air Force in Italy.

*The Boeing B-17D was the last variant to feature this type of tail configuration, and served mainly in the Pacific. The more familiar Fortress tail was introduced with the B-17E.*

*Consolidated B-24 Liberators attacking a target in Europe.*

bomb load was a little less. Wartime development saw armament improve along similar lines to the B-17s, later models having a powered nose and tail turrets. The Liberator became the most numerous US warplane ever built, with 18,188 produced. Its longer range saw it used more widely in the Pacific than the B-17, but the two types were the mainstay of the US Eighth Air Force's bomber campaign from 1942–45. On

**APRIL**

**25 April** US Army R-4 helicopters are used to rescue downed pilots in Burma.

**JUNE**

**5 June** The B-29 makes its operational debut from bases in India.

**5–6 June** In support of the Allied invasion of Normandy, nearly 14,000 sorties are flown in 24 hours, including air drops, bombing, fighter sweeps and maritime patrol.

**13 June** The first V-1 flying bombs are launched against England from sites in France.

some days, the Eighth Air Force alone dispatched more than 1000 bombers, and 1000 fighters were over Germany. The worst losses were around 60 bombers on one mission, a loss rate that was unsustainable in the long term. It took an equally heavy toll on the German fighter force, however, whose aircraft and crew losses were much harder to make up.

The programme to replace the B-17 and B-24 with a heavier, pressurized bomber began even before the war. It was a complex aircraft and production difficulties meant that the prototype Boeing B-29 Superfortress did not fly until September 1942, and only in May 1944 did it enter combat, against Japan. The B-29 fuselage was a very streamlined pressurized tube, its low-profile gun turrets being operated remotely. Its bomb load was nearly twice that of the B-17's and it was able to climb over the Himalayas from Indian bases and to fly from the Marianas

*A B-25 Mitchell pulls away from an attack on a Japanese torpedo boat.*

Islands to attack the Japanese mainland. Of course, the most famous missions of the B-29s were the August 1945 attacks on Hiroshima and Nagasaki, using the atomic bombs developed in great secrecy under the Manhattan Project. The

*The Boeing B-29 Superfortress, the aircraft that took the strategic bombing war to Japan.*

## 1944

### JULY

**5 July** Flight of the Northrop's MX-324, the first US purpose-built rocket-powered aircraft.

**12 July** The Gloster Meteor enters service with No. 616 Squadron, Royal Air Force.

**25 July** The first combat involving a jet aircraft takes place when a Messerschmitt Me 262 engages an RAF Mosquito.

B-29 was the only aircraft in the world capable of carrying these awesome weapons.

US medium bombers included the North American B-25 Mitchell, Douglas A-20 Havoc and Martin B-26 Marauder. These were mainly used tactically against transportation targets such as rail yards and bridges, and against airfields and shipping. The Mitchells were based almost everywhere except England, notably in North Africa, Italy, Burma and the Pacific. They first came to prominence with the so-called 'Doolittle Raid' of April 1942, when 16 B-25s were flown from the aircraft carrier *Hornet* to make a token but morale-boosting attack on Tokyo.

Many B-25s were later modified for strafing and anti-shipping attack by the addition of multiple fixed forward-firing guns. The B-25G and H versions were the ultimate expression of this, with a massive 75mm (2.9in) cannon in the nose. This hand-loaded gun had a terrific punch, but a low rate of fire, meaning that few shells could be fired during each attack run. B-25s were widely exported, and the RAF made

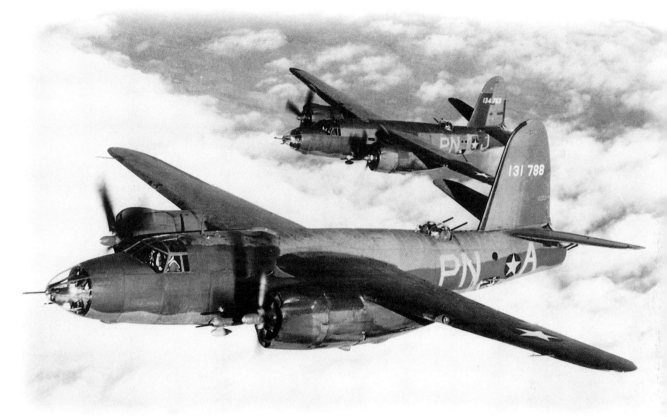

*Martin B-26 Marauders of the 449th Squadron, 322nd Bomb Group, USAAF.*

AUGUST

**4 August** An RAF Meteor becomes the first jet aircraft to score a 'kill' against another jet when it brings down a V-1 flying bomb by tipping it over with its wingtip.

**16 August** The Me 163B Komet rocket fighter is used to intercept USAAF B-17s for the first time.

SEPTEMBER

**8 September** The first V-2 to hit London falls on a street in Chiswick.

The USAAF converted some A-20s to radar-equipped P-70 night-fighters in the Pacific. The A-20 concept was revised by Douglas into the A-26 Invader, a sleeker, more powerful attack aircraft that saw some service in World War II, but which went on to important roles in the conflicts in Korea and Vietnam. It did not retire from US service until 1972.

Sometimes confused with the Douglas A-26, the Martin B-26 Marauder got off to a poor start, losing half the forced dispatched at Midway in June 1942. Many were lost while training crews in the United States, and it gained a terrible reputation. New models progressively enlarged the fin, wings and tailplane, and the safety record improved. Employed in a tactical role in Europe, they went on to achieve the lowest loss rate of any US bomber type; at least one example flew more than 200 missions.

*The Handley Page Hampden was highly manoeuvrable and took part in some spectacular attacks early in World War II, but it was vulnerable to fighter attack.*

extensive use of them, particularly in the period around the Normandy invasion in the summer of 1944.

The lighter A-20 was designated as an attack aircraft rather than a bomber, and it, too, was used as a strafer, particularly in the Pacific. The

RAF used some of its A-20s as night-fighters, including an experimental installation with a large searchlight in the nose. These 'Turbinlite' Havocs were intended to guide Hurricanes to the target, but this largely unsuccessful approach was quickly superseded by airborne radar.

### British Bombers

The RAF had several bomber types in service at the outbreak of war. All were twin-engine except the Fairey Battle, which suffered heavy losses in the Battle of France and was quickly withdrawn to support roles. The Handley Page

## 1944

### OCTOBER

**23 October** Kamikaze suicide attacks are used for the first time in the Battle of Leyte Gulf, sinking the US carrier *St Lo*.

### NOVEMBER

**3 November** The first Japanese balloon bombs are launched. They are intended to be carried by the jetstream winds and ignite American forests.

**12 November** RAF Lancasters with 'Tallboy' bombs sink the German battleship *Tirpitz* in a Norwegian fjord.

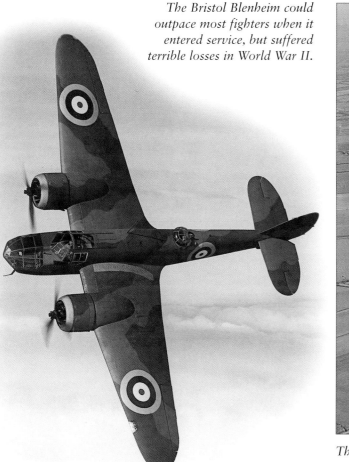

*The Bristol Blenheim could outpace most fighters when it entered service, but suffered terrible losses in World War II.*

*The Short Stirling was the first of the RAF's new four-engine bombers, but its wingspan was reduced to make it fit into existing hangars and it had a poor altitude performance.*

**DECEMBER**

**6 December** The first flight of the German Heinkel He 162 single-engined jet fighter, which sees limited service before the end of the war.

**18 December** The Bachem Ba 349 'Natter' rocket interceptor is test-launched.

**1945**

The Pitts S-1 Special is the first aircraft specially designed for aerobatics.

**JANUARY**

**8 January** The Lockheed XP-80 *Lulu Belle* flies in California. The P-80 Shooting Star becomes the first operational US jet aircraft.

Hampden, Gloster Whitley, Bristol Blenheim and Vickers Wellington were all employed on daylight raids in 1939–41. Heavy losses to German fighters, however, provoked a switch to night attacks and the withdrawal of most of these types from Bomber Command's main force.

The first of the RAF's 'heavies' was the Short Stirling, which entered operational service in April 1941. Well protected and with a heavy bomb load, the Stirling was hampered by its wingspan, arbitrarily restricted to under 31m (100ft) to fit in standard hangars. It could not fly very high with a full load. The Handley Page Halifax was a close contemporary and built in many variants, but again it suffered heavy losses in its early days.

The Avro Manchester was a later design, of similar dimensions to the Stirling and Halifax, but with only two engines – unreliable Rolls-Royce Vultures. The transformation of this failure into the Lancaster, mainly by substituting four Merlin engines, created the best British bomber of the war. The Lancaster's capacious bomb bay allowed for a heavier load of standard bombs (up to 6350kg/14,000lb) or huge specialized weapons such as the Tallboy

*The versatile de Havilland Mosquito filled many roles, from night fighter to anti-shipping. Pictured here is the B.Mk.IV bomber version, which had a glazed nose for the bomb-aimer.*

## 1945

### FEBRUARY

**28 February** The first manned flight of the Bachem 'Natter' ends in disaster with a crash and the death of the pilot.

### MARCH

**8 March** The US Navy tests the Gorgon air-to-air missile from a Catalina flying boat. It does not enter production.

**14 March** The first 9980kg (22,000lb) 'Grand Slam' bomb is dropped by Lancasters on Bielefeld railway viaduct. This is the largest conventional bomb of the war.

*Vickers Wellington bombers seen on the production line. The latticework of the 'geodetic' construction, designed by Barnes Wallis, is clearly visible.*

*The crew of this Halifax had every reason to be grateful. The aircraft brought them safely home after a 'friendly' bomb ripped through it during a night raid.*

and Grand Slam 'earthquake' bombs up to a weight of 9980kg (22,000lb).

One of the most memorable missions of World War II was the low-level attack on the Ruhr Dams in May 1943, in which 'bouncing bombs' designed by Barnes Wallis were successfully used by No. 617 Squadron to breach two dams and damage another.

Taking an entirely different approach was the de Havilland Mosquito, which had no defensive armament and only two crew members, rather than the seven in a 'heavy' and a bomber form. Constructed as a private venture, using wood rather than metal as its main construction material, the 'Mossie' was light and fast. Usual bomb load was only four 227kg (500lb) bombs,

but it could deliver them accurately and outrun Luftwaffe fighters. A version with a bulged bomb bay could carry an 1814kg (4000lb) 'cookie' thin-walled high-capacity bomb. Other variants had cannon and machine guns, or were filled with reconnaissance cameras. Many precision raids were made with Mosquitoes, including attacks on Gestapo headquarters in

**APRIL**

**10 April** Messerschmitt Me 262 fighters destroy 19 USAAF bombers and eight fighters in their most successful day of combat.

**21 March** A purpose-built Japanese rocket suicide aircraft, Yokosuka Ohka, makes its first attacks.

**JULY**

**28 July** A B-25 Mitchell crashes into the Empire State Building in New York, killing 19 people.

several occupied countries and at the prison in Amiens, France, where many resistance fighters escaped when the walls were breached.

## Luftwaffe

Like the RAF, Germany's Luftwaffe started the war with three different types of medium bomber in service. The Dornier Do 17, Heinkel 111 and Junkers Ju 88 were all used in the Battle of Britain as day-bombers and adapted for other roles as the war progressed. The Do 17 was the oldest of the three and, in defensive terms, the weakest. It was withdrawn in 1942. The Heinkel, with its distinctive glazed nose, was obsolete by late 1943, although it continued as a transport. It was the Ju 88 that proved the most adaptable of the three aircraft, seeing service as a day-bomber, night-bomber, torpedo-bomber, anti-ship attacker, long-range fighter and night-fighter. More than 15,000 Ju 88s were built.

Another Junkers, the Ju 87 Stuka (an abbreviation of the German for dive-bomber)

*An early production Heinkel He 111F with the type of nose used on all early He 111 variants.*

## 1945

### AUGUST

**6 August** The *Enola Gay*, a Boeing B-29 Superfortress of the 509th Composite Group, drops an atomic bomb on Hiroshima. More than 70,000 people are killed or die in the immediate aftermath.

**9 August** The B-29 *Bock's Car* drops a second atomic bomb on Nagasaki. More than 25,000 are killed.

### SEPTEMBER

**September** A Focke Achgelis Fa 223, flown to the United Kingdom for evaluation, makes the first helicopter crossing of the English Channel.

gained notoriety for its precision attacks in the blitzkreig campaign of 1939–40, its terror effect often aided by fitting air-driven screaming sirens. When faced with fighter opposition, as it was over Britain in 1940, it proved very vulnerable, but had more success in the conditions of local air superiority that usually prevailed over the Soviet Union. Specialized tank-busting versions with twin 37mm (1.5in) cannon proved especially effective, and one pilot, Erich Rüdel, was credited with destroying more than 500 Soviet armoured vehicles.

Germany's greatest innovation in bombing technology was the introduction of the first jet bomber and reconnaissance aircraft, the Arado Ar 234. The prototype first flew in June 1943, but did not make its operational debut until a year later, flying reconnaissance missions over the Normandy beachhead. Used as a bomber from December 1944, the twin-jet Ar 234 was never fielded in great numbers, largely because of disruption to airfields and fuel supplies caused by Allied bombing.

·····················································

*Junkers Ju 87D Stukas seen here in temporary camouflage.*

**OCTOBER**

**October** The Douglas DC-4 enters transatlantic service with American Overseas Airlines.

**20 September** The first turboprop engine, a Rolls-Royce Trent, is flown in a Meteor testbed.

## Jets

Jet aircraft are often seen as the main technological advance to come out of the war years. In reality, they predated World War II: the first jet engines were run in Britain and Germany in 1937 and the first jet aircraft, the Heinkel 178, was flown in August 1939. Britain's Frank Whittle and Germany's Hans Pabst von Ohain independently developed jet engines in the 1930s, but both suffered from bureaucracies that failed to understand the importance of this development. Initial German success against a weak opposition in the Soviet Union led to a diverting of funds away from new technology and a lack of priority to the jet programme.

The first jet fighter intended for production, the Heinkel He 280, did not fly until March 1941 and the first actual production fighter, the Messerschmitt Me 262, took to the air more than a year later. Continual engine troubles delayed the programme, as did Hitler's insistence that it be modified to carry bombs. The first test unit was set up in April 1944, but it was not until January 1945 that the jet fighters struck a significant blow against the daily USAAF bombing attacks, destroying

*An Arado Ar 234 jet-propelled reconnaissance aircraft, clearly showing the pilot's entry hatch. Both the bomber and reconnaissance versions of this jet aircraft were very active in the closing months of World War II.*

## 1945

### NOVEMBER

**6 November** A Ryan FR1 Fireball, which has both a piston engine and a jet, makes a carrier landing using only jet power.

**7 November** A Gloster Meteor IV sets a new speed record of 975km/h (606mph) over Herne Bay, England.

**7 November** Bell announces that a P-59 jet has been flown remotely, using a television camera to monitor the instruments.

*The Messerschmitt Me 262, although presenting a big threat to the American daylight bomber formations, came too late to have an effect on the outcome of the air war.*

*The Gloster Meteor, which is seen here in its F.Mk.3 version, was the world's first operational jet fighter.*

12 bombers for the loss of three Me 262s. Every attack cost several precious jets and experienced pilots. During takeoff and landing, the Me 262 was particularly vulnerable to attack by conventional fighters, which staked out the jet airfields with their distinctive concrete landing strips. In the end, the short life of the Me 262's Jumo 004 engines and the lack of fuel (for support vehicles rather than the aircraft

themselves) kept the jets on the ground and ensured that they had no effect on the war's inevitable final outcome.

The RAF's Gloster Meteor actually entered squadron slightly before the Me 262 in Germany. A more conservative design with thick, unswept wings, the Meteor was initially no faster than contemporary Spitfires, but developed engines that gave it a distinct speed

advantage. The two jet types never met in combat, but the Meteors destroyed a number of pulse-jet powered V1 flying-bombs over England before moving to the Continent for the final weeks of the war in Europe, where they were used mainly for ground attack. Later versions of the Meteor were the backbone of the RAF fighter force until the mid-1950s and were widely exported.

**29 November** A Sikorsky R-5 makes the first air-sea rescue by helicopter, when barge crewmen are saved in Long Island Sound.

DECEMBER

**22 December** The Beechcraft Bonanza, one of the first postwar touring aircraft, makes its first test flight.

# Breaking Records

*The last years of World War II brought with them many new advances in aeronautics and other fields, including that of atomic energy. It seemed that the next major war would be fought with jets, missiles and nuclear weapons, not propeller planes and free-fall bombs.*

As it happened, the Korean conflict of 1950–53 was more similar to World War II than later conflicts. However, the growing Cold War between the Soviet Union, with its various satellite and client states, and the United States and its allies provoked a rush to develop, exploit and field the new technologies. In civil aviation, the affluent 1950s encouraged a growth in air travel, which saw turbines replace piston engines and the era of mass international air travel begin.

*Left: Neil Armstrong, who became the first man to set foot on the moon in 1969, in the cockpit of a North American X-15 when he was a test pilot. Right: The Bell X-1, first aircraft to exceed the speed of sound.*

Both Western and Soviet aerospace industries benefited from German research, which generally led the field. The war situation from 1943 meant that little of this research progressed to the hardware stage, although the Luftwaffe did introduce into service three types of manned jet aircraft, two rocket-powered fighters, and ballistic, anti-ship and cruise missiles. It also tested surface-to-air and air-to-air guided missiles. In the spring of 1945, there was a race between the United States, Britain, France and the Soviet Union to gather up the most interesting of Germany's hardware for technical examination and its best scientists for interrogation. Under Operation Paperclip, a variety of German scientists were allowed to enter the United States, their past Nazi associations ignored. Much of their knowledge, as well as the information gleaned by Allied intelligence from captured aircraft and equipment, was soon tested by the US military. This led to one of the most exciting periods of aeronautical experimentation and development, exemplified by the series of 'X-planes' tested in the California desert from the late 1940s onwards.

The first of the X-planes was on the drawing board even before the end of the war, and flew in January 1946. The Bell XS-1 (where the S stood for 'sonic'), was usually known as the X-1, and its design was not particularly influenced by German research – other than that it was powered by a liquid-fuelled rocket engine, like the Me 163 Komet. The fuselage shape of the X-1 was based on that of a 0.50-calibre bullet because that was a shape known to go supersonic with ease. The design specifications

were provided by the National Advisory Committee for Aeronautics (NACA), the forerunner of NASA, and the funding came from the US Army Air Forces (which became the independent USAF in September 1947).

The X-1 could take off from a runway under its own power, but was usually carried aloft in the modified bomb bay of a B-29 'mothership', enabling it to carry enough fuel for high-speed runs. The X-1 made 50 flights – some powered and some just glides – in the hands of Bell, NACA and USAF pilots before entering the history books on 14 October 1947. Wartime fighter ace and

Air Force test pilot Charles E. 'Chuck' Yeager, who was then nursing cracked ribs from a horse-riding fall, climbed aboard the X-1 from inside the B-29. The craft was released like a large orange bomb above the Mojave Desert, and after a few seconds he ignited the rocket chambers – and roared away. The X-1 climbed to 13,716m (43,000ft) and past Mach 1.06, becoming the first manned vehicle officially to exceed the speed of sound.

Evidence suggests that another USAF pilot, George 'Wheaties' Welch, had exceeded Mach 1 in the prototype F-86 Sabre a week before Yeager's famous X-1 flight, albeit in a dive from 10,670m (35,000ft). At the time, these flight experiments were not widely known, and the X-1's achievements were kept secret for some months. When the supersonic flight was revealed, it was the X-1 and Yeager that received all the publicity. The USAF probably wanted to credit the X-1 to justify its investment in that programme,
.........................................................
*Charles E. 'Chuck' Yeager, the first pilot officially to exceed the speed of sound, in the Bell X-1.*

## 1946

| JANUARY | APRIL | MAY | JULY | SEPTEMBER |

**19 January** The first gliding flight of the Bell XS-1 (X-1) rocket-powered research aircraft.

**25 January** The Northrop XB-35, the first large flying wing, flies.

**26 January** A P-80 sets a new Los Angeles–New York speed record of 4 hours and 13 minutes.

**24 April** The Soviet Union's first jet fighter, the MiG-9, flies

**31 May** Heathrow Airport is opened, west of London.

**1 July** The first postwar atomic tests are conducted at Bikini Atoll in the Pacific Ocean.

**21 July** A McDonnell XFD-1 Phantom makes the first carrier takeoff and landing by a pure jet aircraft.

**7 September** The RAF raises the world speed record to 990km/h (615mph) with a Meteor IV.

**29 September** A Lockheed P2V Neptune flies from Columbus, Ohio, to Perth, Australia, a record straight-line distance of 18,081km (11,235 miles).

*The North American F-86 Sabre could exceed the speed of sound in a dive, thanks to its swept wings.*

and to conceal the more militarily significant fact that they had a practical warplane capable of (limited) supersonic flight.

The success of the X-1 spawned a whole series of aircraft, as well as some rockets which were designed entirely for research rather than as prototypes for production vehicles. Two further X-1s were built in a programme that continued until 1951, by which time even more impressive aircraft were flying.

The United Kingdom was nearly the first through the 'sound barrier' with a small research craft called the Miles M.52. Also a bullet-shaped air-launched aircraft, the M.52 was to be powered by an afterburning jet engine and housed the pilot in a nosecone ahead of the intake. The prototype was half-built at the end

of the war in August 1945, but overcautious bureaucrats decided it would not be safe for a pilot to undertake test flights, and cancelled the project. Most of the design data was then given to the United States, including the critical design element of an all-moving tailplane, which was promptly incorporated in the X-1. In October 1948, the same month that the X-1 entered the history books, the M.52 configuration was tested as a rocket-powered subscale model, and

## 1947

**NOVEMBER**

**13 November** The first experiments with aerial cloud seeding to alter the weather are carried out in Massachusetts.

**APRIL**

**4 April** The International Civil Aviation Organization (ICAO) is established to set and regulate international air navigation and transport development.

**27 April** The Douglas DC-6 enters service with American Airlines.

**AUGUST**

**31 August** The Antonov An-2 'Colt' utility biplane makes its maiden flight. More than 20,000 have been built, and production may continue in China.

**31 August** John 'Cat's-Eyes' Cunningham establishes a new 100km (62-mile) closed circuit speed record of 798km/h (496mph) in a de Havilland Vampire Mk 1.

**SEPTEMBER**

**18 September** The United States Air Force (USAF) becomes a separate military service.

**OCTOBER**

**1 October** First flight of the North American XP-86 (F-86), the first US swept-wing jet.

**1 October** George 'Wheaties' Welch breaks the sound barrier in the prototype F-86 Sabre, although his achievement is not officially recorded or recognized.

**14 October** Captain Charles 'Chuck' Yeager, flying a rocket-powered Bell X-1 aircraft, becomes the first pilot to officially exceed the speed of sound in level flight, reaching Mach 1.015 or 1078km/h (670mph).

**21 October** The YB-49, an all-jet version of the B-35 flying wing, is flown.

*The Lockheed F-80 Shooting Star was the United States' first operational jet fighter and performed excellent work as a fighter-bomber in the Korean War.*

*Conceived in 1945, the Douglas D-558 Skystreak was one of the United States' early transonic research aircraft. Three were built and tested.*

was last seen doing Mach 1.5 heading out over the Atlantic.

Other gifts of British jet technology included several Rolls-Royce Nene engines supplied to the Soviet Union. This was meant as a fraternal gesture to a wartime ally, but before long the engines were encountered in the skies over Korea in the form of the similar Klimov VK-1 used for the MiG-15 fighter. Like the F-86, this was a swept-wing jet with the air intake in the nose and the pilot seated under a bubble canopy. At a distance, it was hard to distinguish from a Sabre, apart from its high-mounted tailplane. The two aircraft had their strengths and weaknesses, but were closely matched in performance overall. By the 1953 ceasefire, better pilot training and management led the United States to enjoy an eventual victory-to-loss ratio of about twelve-to-one. Nonetheless, the war proved to the United States that their potential adversary in a third world war was by no means technologically backward, and constant research and development would be needed to stay ahead.

The business of building faster and faster combat aircraft was regarded not just as a military necessity, but as a matter of national

## 1947

### NOVEMBER

**2 November** The Hughes HK-1 flying boat, known as the 'Spruce Goose', makes its one and only flight, piloted by Howard Hughes. It remains the largest aircraft ever flown.

### DECEMBER

**17 December** The first flight of the Boeing XB-47 Stratojet, the first swept-wing jet bomber.

**30 December** The first flight of the Mikoyan-Guerevich MiG-15 swept-wing jet fighter.

## 1948

### JANUARY

**30 January** Orville Wright dies at Dayton, Ohio, aged 76.

### FEBRUARY

**6 February** A new 100km (62-mile) closed circuit speed record of 872km/h (542mph) is set with a Gloster Meteor IV.

### MARCH

**23 March** John Cunningham sets a new world altitude record of 18,119m (59,445ft) in a de Havilland Vampire.

prestige. Soon after hostilities were over, the Royal Air Force was keen to set the first official world speed record for a jet aircraft. On 7 November 1945, Group Captain H. J. Wilson flew a Meteor F.4 over a measured course at a fraction under 976km/h (606.25mph). Another RAF Group captain in another Meteor F.4 boosted the record to 990km/h (615mph).

A few hours later, the prototype XP-84 Thunderjet reached 983km/h (611mph) in California. This failed to take the record, but signalled the upcoming American dominance of the speed record for the next six years. Pilots of the US Air Force, flying from Muroc Dry Lake at Edwards Air Force Base, California, established new records. In June 1947, a modified P-80 Shooting Star took it, followed by a US Navy Douglas D-558-1 Skystreak, a pure research aircraft that broke the record twice in one week, raising it to 1048km/h (651mph) by the end of the year.

Versions of the USAF Sabre held the record until September 1953, when Britain recaptured it using a Hawker Hunter, flown along the south coast of England by legendary test pilot Neville Duke. A US Navy Skyray and an Air

*The Hawker Hunter briefly captured the world air speed record for Britain, flown by test pilot Neville Duke over a measured course off the south coast of England.*

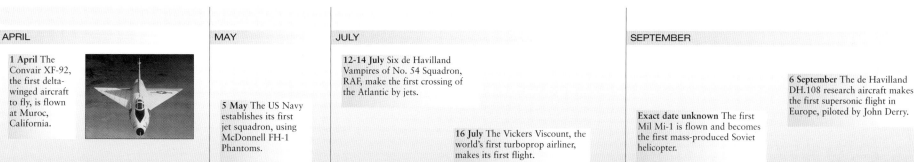

**APRIL**

**1 April** The Convair XF-92, the first delta-winged aircraft to fly, is flown at Muroc, California.

**MAY**

**5 May** The US Navy establishes its first jet squadron, using McDonnell FH-1 Phantoms.

**JULY**

**12-14 July** Six de Havilland Vampires of No. 54 Squadron, RAF, make the first crossing of the Atlantic by jets.

**16 July** The Vickers Viscount, the world's first turboprop airliner, makes its first flight.

**SEPTEMBER**

**Exact date unknown** The first Mil Mi-1 is flown and becomes the first mass-produced Soviet helicopter.

**6 September** The de Havilland DH.108 research aircraft makes the first supersonic flight in Europe, piloted by John Derry.

Force YF-100 Super Sabre took the record right back. This year, 1953, was to prove the high-water mark for speed records, and it changed hands five times.

At the time, the rules governing straight-line speed records were strict. A timed run was made in each direction along a straight course within a set time limit, to cancel out tailwind effects. It was also made at low level, not exceeding a height of 30m (100ft) – a requirement that called for precise flying. It was eventually dropped for safety reasons, allowing the first

*The aircraft that became known as the SR-71 was actually designated RS (Reconnaissance System) 71 to begin with.*

..................................................

*Below: The Lockheed YF-12 was the strategic interceptor version of the SR-71A. Two prototypes were built, but the project was abandoned.*

## 1949

| FEBRUARY | APRIL | MAY | JULY | AUGUST | SEPTEMBER |
|---|---|---|---|---|---|
| **26 February–2 March** The first nonstop round-the-world flight is made, by a Boeing B-50 named *Lucky Lady II*. The flight takes 94 hours 1 minute, and the aircraft is refuelled in the air four times. | **4 April** First tests of a probe-and-drogue refuelling system are conducted in the UK.<br><br>**26 April** Two pilots flying an Aeronca Chief light aircraft set a world flight endurance record of 1008 hours (six weeks), taking fuel and food by rope from a jeep on the runway. | **21 May** A Sikorsky S-52 helicopter establishes a new helicopter altitude of 6468m (21,220ft). | **27 July** John Cunningham flies the world's first jet airliner, the de Havilland DH.106 Comet. | **10 August** First flight of the Avro Canada C.102 Jetliner, the world's second jet transport aircraft. | **23 September** The USSR explodes an atomic bomb, becoming the second nation with nuclear weapons.<br><br>**29 September** First flight of the Douglas DC-6. |

*The North American X-15 rocket-powered research aircraft bridged the gap between manned flight within the atmosphere and manned flight beyond the atmosphere into space. Three X-15s were built.*

F-106. Another MiG, a twin-engined MiG-21 development called the E-166, snatched it back from a prototype McDonnell Phantom II in July 1962. Soviet pilot Georgii Mossolov flew both of the MiGs on their record flights.

The to-and-fro of speed records was brought to an end by the remarkable Lockheed Blackbirds, designed for speeds of more than three times the speed of sound. A YF-12 Blackbird, a version intended as an interceptor, was measured flying at 3331km/h (2070mph) in May 1965. Then an SR-71A, the production reconnaissance version, extended the record to 3529km/h (2193mph) on 28 July 1976. The crew of Eldon Joersz and George Morgan hold the record to this day for an aircraft that can take off under its own power.

In the postwar years, there was also hot competition for other records. These include time-to-climb records and various closed-circuit speed records (such as the 100km and 500km records). Most are held by versions of the MiG-25 'Foxbat'. Soviet and ex-Soviet aircraft types also dominate range and payload records.

Of all the US X-planes, two in particular stand out: the X-1 and the X-15. The latter

supersonic record to be set. In August 1955, Colonel Horace Hanes flew an F-100C Super Sabre to a new record of 1323km/h (822mph). This was a jump of 108km/h (67mph) above the previous record, but the next record involved the greatest increase ever, of 499km/h (310mph) to reach a speed 1822km/h (1132mph). This

was set by another research aircraft, the Fairey Delta 2, flown by Peter Twiss in March 1956.

In 1959, the Soviet Union entered the speed race with the Mikoyan E-66. A modified MiG-21 with an additional rocket engine, it reached 2388km/h (1484mph) in October, a record held for six weeks before it was retaken by a Convair

## 1950

### FEBRUARY

**1 February** The first night landings on an aircraft carrier are made by Grumman F9F Panthers on the USS *Valley Forge*.

### JUNE

**28 June** A Lockheed RF-80A flies the first operational US jet reconnaissance mission, over North Korea.

### SEPTEMBER

**22 September** The first nonstop jet flight across the Atlantic is flown by a Republic F-84E Thunderjet, using aerial refuelling. A second F-84 crashes in Newfoundland.

**28 September** The first USAF jet night-fighter delivered to the USAF is the Northrop F-89 Scorpion.

### NOVEMBER

**8 November** USAF Lieutenant Russell J. Brown, flying an F-80C, becomes the first pilot to win a jet-versus-jet air combat when he shoots down a North Korean MiG-15.

**30 September** The Berlin Airlift ends, after more than 2.25 million tons of supplies have been delivered to the people of Berlin over 15 months.

*The second North American X-15A was rebuilt after a landing accident to become the X-15A-2, and was the fastest aircraft ever flown. The third X-15 was destroyed during a test flight.*

controlled flight above the atmosphere. In this environment, the X-15 was controlled by puffer jets at the extremities – a method which was later adopted for the Space Shuttle.

On 3 October 1967, the X-15A-2 made its most significant flight when William 'Pete' Knight of the US Air Force reached 7274 km/h (11,702mph, or Mach 6.06) and a maximum altitude of 58,552m (192,100ft). Flight above Mach 5.0 is regarded as hypersonic, and NASA and the US Air Force's X-15 pilots certainly lived up to the Air Force Flight Test Center's motto: 'Toward the Unknown'.

plane had a career lasting nine years, the longest in the series, and took manned flight from the Mach 2 era through to Mach 6. Like the X-1, the X-15 was rocket-powered, and air-launched from a carrier aircraft – in this case, a modified B-52. It was unable to take off under its own power, however, and used a skid-type undercarriage for landings on a dry lakebed. First flying in 1959, the three X-15s were flown by a dozen pilots over 199 flights. Among them were the future moonwalker Neil Armstrong

and the Space Shuttle pilot Joe Engle. The purpose of the X-15 was to evaluate flight in the extreme upper atmosphere. The boundary between the atmosphere and space was defined as an altitude of 80km (50 miles), and the X-15 made 13 flights above that, for which the pilots were awarded astronaut wings.

While the X-15 flights were sometimes overshadowed by the achievements of the contemporary Mercury space missions, they often exceeded them in altitude and involved

### Airliners

Postwar civil aviation was not driven by the same imperatives as military aviation. Nonetheless, it benefited from advances in military transport aircraft, the construction of new airfields and navigation aids for the war effort, and the proving of equipment and routes over many thousands of flying hours clocked up carrying cargo and mail to the theatres of war. Most of the first generation of postwar airliners originated as military freighters, either by design or circumstance.

## 1951

### MAY

**18 May** The first of the RAF's trio of 'V-bombers', the Vickers Valiant, is flown.

**29 May** Charles Blair makes the first solo flight over the North Pole, flying from Norway to Alaska in a P-51C Mustang.

**25 May** The Canberra B2 enters service with No. 101 Squadron, RAF.

### JULY

**15–31 July** A pair of USAF H-19 Chickasaws makes the first helicopter crossing of the Atlantic, taking 42 hours 55 minutes in several stages.

### AUGUST

**7 August** A new airspeed record (for an air-launched vehicle) of 1992km/h (1245mph) is set in the Douglas D-558-II Skyrocket.

**15 August** The D-558-II sets a new altitude record of 22,706m (74,494ft).

### NOVEMBER

**2 November** A US Marine Corps F3D Skyknight shoots down a Yak-15 over North Korea in the first successful jet-versus-jet night combat.

**19 November** A new absolute speed record of 1123km/h (698mph) is set by an F-86D Sabre jet.

The Douglas DC-4 was one of the most important airliners of the late 1940s through to the 1960s. It served on most US domestic routes, as well as throughout Europe and elsewhere. It was developed from the DC-4E, a larger, pressurized prototype that was first flown in 1939, but which proved too complex and costly. By the time the simpler DC-4 flew in February 1942, the United States was at war, and production was diverted to military use

*The four-engined Douglas DC-4 was in widespread use as a civil airliner during the immediate postwar years.*

*The Douglas C-54 Skymaster was the mainstay of the United States Air Force Military Air Transport Service for many years, providing the USAF with a global airlift capability.*

## 1952

### APRIL

**15 April** The Boeing YB-52 Stratofortress eight-engined bomber flies. The B-52 remains in service over 50 years later.

**27 April** First flight of the Soviet Tupolev Tu-16 'Badger' strategic jet bomber.

### MAY

**2 May** BOAC's de Havilland Comets inaugurate the first commercial jet passenger service, from London to Johannesburg.

**29 May** The first combat mission using aerial refuelling is flown – a KB-29 refuels F-84 Thunderjets en route to North Korea.

### JULY

**15–31 July** A pair of USAF H-19 Chickasaws makes the first transatlantic crossing by helicopter.

### AUGUST

**August** The de Havilland Venom enters service with the RAF.

**30 August** Avro's Model 698 Vulcan delta-winged bomber flies. It remains in service until 1983.

### SEPTEMBER

**10 September** Using Constellations, TWA offers the first regular nonstop transcontinental service between Los Angeles and New York.

*Passengers making their way on board a Douglas DC-6 airliner of Pan American World Airways.*

*The prototype Douglas DC-7 in flight. The DC-7 was the outcome of an approach to Douglas by American Airlines to produce a stretched version of the DC-6B.*

as the C-54 Skymaster. More than 1160 C-54s were built to military contracts, and a further 78 DC-4s were ordered as airliners following World War II. The majority of surplus C-54s were converted to passenger configuration for civilian use. The US Army wanted an increased capacity version, which was developed as the YC-112, but military funding stopped after its first flight in 1946. Douglas modified the design as the DC-6, which became its most successful four-engined piston-powered airliner. The DC-6 entered airline service in 1947, and

## 1952

### OCTOBER

**2-3 October** The first British atomic bomb is exploded in the Monte Bello Islands in the Pacific.

**28 October** The Douglas XA3D-1, prototype of the Skywarrior, makes its inaugural flight. The Skywarrior is the heaviest aircraft to see regular service from aircraft carriers.

### NOVEMBER

**12 November** The Tupolev Tu-95 'Bear' turboprop strategic bomber flies in the USSR.

### DECEMBER

**24 December** The Handley Page Victor is the last of the 'V-bombers' to fly.

## 1953

### JANUARY

**3 January** European Airlines (BEA) receives Viscounts, the world's first turboprop airliner.

### APRIL

**9 April** The Convair XF2Y-1 Sea Dart supersonic flying-boat fighter is flown.

### MAY

**18 May** Jacqueline 'Jackie' Cochran becomes the first woman to break the sound barrier, flying a Canadair F-86 Sabre.

**25 May** The first flight of the North American YF-100A Super Sabre. The F-100 is the first USAF fighter in service capable of level supersonic flight.

was finally adopted by the US military as the C-118 during the Korean War. Like the DC-4, some DC-6s continue to operate as freighters in some parts of the world.

One innovation of the DC-4 was its constant-diameter circular-section fuselage, which allowed the basic design to be 'stretched'. The next development was the DC-7, with an even longer fuselage and Wright Turbo Compound engines, which recycled exhaust gases for extra power. Its extra fuel capacity made it one of the first airliners able to operate from New York to London without intervening stops in Newfoundland or Greenland. It flew most notably with Pan Am in its DC-7C 'Seven Seas' configuration, which could even make nonstop westbound flights against the prevailing winds. By the time the 7C was entering service in 1955, however, jets were on the horizon and its sales were limited compared to its predecessors.

## Constellation

Although Lockheed's own airliner plans were also affected by the war, the company was ready in 1945 with a tried and tested design, ready to

fly transcontinental and transatlantic routes. This was the L-049 Constellation, a four-engine machine with a pressurized cabin, an elegant humped fuselage and triple tail fins. The 'Connie' began life in 1937–38 as a smaller design called the Excalibur, but this was revised to meet specifications from TWA (then Transcontinental and Western Air).

*The Lockheed Constellation and its descendants gave excellent service on long-haul air routes.*

The company wanted an airliner able to fly coast-to-coast without multiple stops, such as were needed by aircraft such as the DC-3. TWA's major shareholder Howard Hughes had some input into the specification and cockpit layout, but it is not true that he designed the Constellation, as is sometimes claimed.

Like the DC-4, the Constellation was drafted into Army service as soon as it flew in January 1943, under the designation C-69. It saw limited wartime service and was not deployed overseas, being used mainly within the continental United States. The first 10 aircraft for TWA served as C-69s, and were returned at the end of World War II for airline use. Hughes and TWA cleverly used the data gathered during the wartime flights for route-proving purposes, giving the company a head start over some competitors when civil aviation was freed up after the war. Hughes himself sometimes flew the Connie,

| JUNE | JULY | AUGUST | OCTOBER | | NOVEMBER | DECEMBER |
|------|------|--------|---------|--|----------|----------|
| **18 June** A USAF Douglas C-124 Globemaster II crashes in Japan, the first air accident to take more than 100 lives. | **8 July** Belgian airline Sabena launches an international helicopter passenger service, with routes between Belgium, France and the Netherlands. | **31 August** The D-558-2 reaches an altitude of 25,380m (83,235ft). | **3 October** The air speed record is taken by a USN Douglas F4D-1 Skyray at 1211km/h (752mph).<br><br>**24 October** The Convair YF-102 is flown. It fails to go supersonic in testing and needs much redesign. | **29 October** The speed record changes hands for the fifth time in 12 months when a YF-100 Super Sabre exceeds 1215km/h (755mph). | **20 November** Scott Crossfield is the first person to exceed Mach 2 when he flies an air-launched Douglas D-558-2 Skyrocket to 2135km/h (1327mph).<br><br>**29 November** American Airlines puts the Douglas DC-7 into service. | **12 December** The air-launched Bell X-1A, flown by Charles 'Chuck' Yeager, reaches 2655km/h (1650mph/ Mach 2.44) at 21,340m (70,000ft). |

including a record-breaking Los Angeles–
Washington, DC, flight made in April 1944 with
a bevy of film stars aboard. The aircraft wore
TWA titles, and all this was good publicity for
both the airline and the Constellation.

Orville Wright made a rare public
appearance when the first C-69 was handed
to the Army at Dayton, Ohio, and he briefly
flew the aircraft during a 1944 publicity flight.
This was the last flight he made, and he was
clearly impressed by the progress made in just
over 40 years of powered flight.

Both US passenger services and European
service began in February 1946, and the aircraft
soon became very popular with passengers and
airlines alike. Operators from the Netherlands,
France, India, Australia and Brazil bought the
first model Constellations and soon came
demand for bigger versions. The L-049 was
followed by the L-649 and L-749. The definitive
L-1049 Super Constellation first flew in 1951.
It had true transatlantic range and could carry
up to 109 passengers. Its pressurized cabin and

*The Lockheed Super Constellation, seen here in
prototype form, was the finest airliner of its time.*

## 1954

| MARCH | APRIL | JUNE | | JULY | AUGUST | |
|---|---|---|---|---|---|---|
| **1 March** The USA explodes its first thermonuclear devices, or 'H-bombs'. | **1 April** The Supermarine Spitfire flies its last operational sortie with the RAF, a reconnaissance mission over Malaya. | **22 June** The Douglas X44D-1 Skyhawk flies at Edwards Air Force Base, California. It stays in production until 1979 and US service until 2003. | **29 June** The Boeing B-52 enters service with Strategic Air Command. | **15 July** The first flight of the Boeing 387-80, or 'Dash 80', the prototype for the 707 airliner and KC-135 tanker series. Production of 707-based airframes lasts into the 1990s. | **3 August** The Roll-Royce Thrust-Measuring Rig, or 'Flying Bedstead', makes an untethered vertical flight.<br><br>**20 August** A USAF F-100C raises the world speed record to 1323km/h (822mph). | **23 August** The first flight of the C-130 Hercules, which remains in production over 50 years later.<br><br>**26 August** An air-launched X-1A rocket plane is flown to an altitude of 27,432m (90,000ft). |

weather radar allowed it to fly over or around bad weather. Super Connies were also popular, with more than 500 built, many for military use as early-warning aircraft. The L-1649 Starliner was the final model, introduced to compete with the DC-7C. By the time this long-range version was in service in 1957, jets were beginning to take over and only 43 Starliners were sold, out of a total of 856 of all Constellation models sold.

Boeing's entry in the long-range market was the Model 377 Stratocruiser, which was also derived from an aircraft that began as a military freighter. The Model 367 (C-97) Stratofreighter shared the wings and tail fin of the B-50 bomber (itself an improved B-29), but had an all-new fuselage with twin decks. Too late for the war, the C-97 gave sterling postwar service as the KC-97 tanker aircraft, a few of which were used into the 1970s, and as a transport, despite lacking the loading ramps of many of its contemporaries.

*The Boeing Stratocruiser was a civil development of the C-97 military transport, which was itself a development of the B-29 bomber.*

With its 'double-bubble' fuselage, the Stratocruiser airliner was the epitome of space and luxury. Used for long overwater routes, mainly by Pan Am, the 'Strat' had large comfortable seats, sleeping berths and enough room for a bar and lounge in the downstairs section, leading to the nickname 'Stratoboozer'. The 377 was expensive and complex compared

to its contemporaries, and less suited to domestic services. Only 56 of the civil version were made.

### British Developments

In the United Kingdom, airlines initially made do with versions of wartime bombers, such as the Avro Lancastrian and York that were both derived from the Lancaster, and the Handley Page Hermes, which shared much with the Halifax. There were, however, big plans in the offing.

The Brabazon Report of 1943 looked forward to the postwar world, when Britain and its Empire would need a new generation of airliners in several classes. The report called for four new types to be built: a large transatlantic airliner, a small 'feederliner' to replace the DC-3, a medium-sized airliner for the Empire air routes, and a jet airliner capable of 800km/h (500mph). The committee's recommendations were carried out after the war, with varying degrees of success.

| SEPTEMBER | OCTOBER | NOVEMBER | DECEMBER | **1955** FEBRUARY | APRIL |
|---|---|---|---|---|---|

**29 August** An English Electric Canberra B2 sets a new world altitude record of 20,832m (65,890ft).

**29 September** The McDonnell F-101 Voodoo interceptor makes its maiden flight.

**17 October** A new helicopter altitude record is set at 7468m (24,500ft), by a Sikorsky XH-39.

**1 November** The Boeing B-29 Superfortress is retired from USAF service.

**19 December** The first flight of F-102A Delta Dagger, modified from the YF-102 to achieve Mach 1.

**14 February** The first flight of the Ye-2, prototype of the MiG-21 fighter. The MiG-21 'Fishbed' becomes the most widely used jet fighter.

**1 April** German national airline Lufthansa flies its first postwar service.

*The de Havilland Comet I jet airliner was potentially a world-beater, but was grounded after a series of fatal crashes, some of which were attributed to metal fatigue.*

the Britannia was another victim of the jet age, selling only 85 before production ended in 1960. The feederliner was the most successful of the group. The Vickers Viscount became the world's first airliner to use a turboprop (essentially a jet engine geared to drive a propeller), and it entered service in 1953. Unusually for a British aircraft, the Viscount sold well in the United States, as well as to countries as diverse as Pakistan and New Zealand. A total of 445 were built.

### The Comet – Dawn of the Jet Age

The most significant of the Brabazon Committee aircraft was the jetliner, built by de Havilland as the Comet. First flown by wartime night-fighter ace John 'Cat's-Eyes' Cunningham in July 1949, the Comet was the first jet transport aircraft, giving a significant lead over US industry, which was still devoted to piston engines – and would remain so for some time. Extensive testing followed before the Comet 1 entered service with BOAC in January 1952, and services soon expanded as far as Johannesburg. The Comet 1 was about the same size as a modern 737, but carried only 36–44 passengers.

The large airliner was built by the Bristol Aircraft Company, and named the Brabazon after the wartime committee's chairman. It was the biggest airliner of its age, not much smaller than a Boeing 747. Despite this, it had seating for only 80 passengers, albeit in considerable luxury. In the end, only a single prototype was built, flying in 1949 and being scrapped in 1953. The mid-sized airliner became the Bristol Britannia, which benefited from the research and technology derived from the Brabazon programme. Very fast and efficient at the time,

## 1955

**MAY**

**27 May**
The Sud-Est
Caravelle, the
first twin-
engined airliner,
flies in France.

**JUNE**

**28 June** A Bell 47 helicopter is landed on top of Mont Blanc, Europe's highest mountain, at an altitude of 4807m (15,772ft).

**17 June** The Tupolev Tu-104, the USSR's first jet airliner, flies. It is based on the Tu-16 'Badger'.

**OCTOBER**

**22 October** The YF-105, the prototype of the Republic Thunderchief tactical bomber, makes its first flight.

**NOVEMBER**

**24 November** The Dutch Fokker F27 Friendship turboprop airliner makes its maiden flight.

**DECEMBER**

**15 December** The last operational flight of the de Havilland Mosquito with the Royal Air Force.

## 1956

**MARCH**

**10 March** The delta-winged Fairey Delta 2 research aircraft sets a new speed record of 703km/h (1132mph).

**JUNE**

**1 June** The Douglas DC-7C 'Seven Seas' long-range airliner begins transatlantic service with Pan Am.

Things went well until late October 1952, when a Comet crashed while taking off at Rome – fortunately without loss of life. At Karachi in March 1953, however, a similar accident to a Canadian Pacific Comet cost the life of all 11 aboard. These two accidents were attributed to poor stall characteristics of the wing, and a programme to modify the leading edges was begun. A BOAC crash near Calcutta in May was more ominous: the aircraft broke up in a thunderstorm with the loss of 46 lives. Structural failure in bad weather was a rare but not unknown occurrence. The losses of two more Comets without warning over the Mediterranean in January and April 1954 could not be blamed on the weather, however, and all Comets were grounded until the cause could be established.

What was eventually discovered doomed the Comet, but was good for aviation safety in the long run. In the early 1950s, the effects of metal fatigue were poorly understood. The repeated flexing of the Comet's fuselage as it was put through cycles of pressurization and depressurization was causing cracks to propagate from the corners of aerials imbedded in the airframe and the cabin windows, which

*The Comet 4 was a much-improved 'stretched' version of earlier variants, but although it was popular with airlines it never recaptured the market from the Boeing 707.*

had sharp corners. Over time, these grew and joined up, aided by the outward pressure from the cabin, leading to a catastrophic structural failure. In one of the first exercises of its kind, the wreck of one of the Comets was raised from the sea for close study. A Comet airframe was

subjected to many simulated flights and pressurization cycles in a giant water tank until it, too, failed. As a result, the Comet 1 was withdrawn from airline service altogether.

The modified Comet 2 served only with the RAF, and the Comet 3 was never more than a

| JULY | SEPTEMBER | OCTOBER | NOVEMBER | | |
|---|---|---|---|---|---|
| **4 July** The U-2 makes its first flight over the USSR. | **7 September** The X-2 research aircraft reaches an altitude of 38,466m (126,200ft). | **20 October** The Bell XHU-1, later redesignated the UH-1 Iroquois, flies. More UH-1s are built than any other helicopter. | **November** The first of the Cessna 172 series flies. It becomes the most widely produced aircraft of all time, with more than 45,000 built. | **12 November** A USMC Sikorsky S-56 (CH-37) sets a helicopter speed record of 261km/h (162 mph). | **28 November** The Ryan X-13 Vertijet makes the first transition by a jet from vertical to horizontal flight. |
| | | **31 October** A Douglas R4D-5 Super Dakota named *Que Sera Sera* makes the first landing by an aircraft at the South Pole. | **11 November** First flight of the Convair B-58 Hustler supersonic bomber. | **18 November** The first flight of the Dassault Mirage III delta-winged fighter. | |

*The Soviet Union became the second nation to inaugurate regular jet passenger services, with the Tu-104.*

prototype, although it led to the larger, more powerful and generally improved Comet 4. This had rounded windows and aerial mounts, a larger wing and Rolls-Royce Avon engines that gave twice the thrust of the original Ghosts. It could carry up to 81 passengers. The Comet 4 flew and entered service in 1958, becoming the first airliner to operate a scheduled transatlantic jet service by a few weeks. Confidence in the Comet was never quite regained, though, and only 76 were built. By the time it was in service,

*The other pioneer commercial jet airliner was the Avro Canada C-102, which flew two weeks after the Comet prototype. It was abandoned because of Avro Canada's combat aircraft production commitments.*

| 1956 | 1957 | | | | | |
|------|------|--|--|--|--|--|
| DECEMBER | JANUARY | APRIL | MAY | JUNE | JULY | |
| **26 December** The first flight of the YF-106, prototype of the Delta Dart interceptor. | **18 January** Using aerial refuelling, three B-52s make the first nonstop aerial circumnavigation of the world by jet aircraft, taking 45 hours 19 minutes. | **4 April** The English Electric P.1B, precursor of the Mach 2 Lightning fighter, flies. | **15 May** An RAF Valiant drops Britain's first thermonuclear weapon over Christmas Island. | **28 June** The KC-135 Stratotanker enters service with the USAF. **4 July** The Ilyushin Il-18 four-engined turboprop airliner is flown in the USSR. | **July** An F8U-1 Crusader flown by John Glenn sets a new Los Angeles to New York speed record of 3 hours 23 minutes. **19 July** The first (and only) live nuclear air-to-air missile ever fired is launched by an F-89 Scorpion over Nevada. | **28 August** Boosted by a Double Scorpion rocket motor, an RAF Canberra sets an altitude record of 21,430m (70,308 ft). |

larger and longer-ranged American airliners were arriving on the scene, and these were to dominate the industry.

There were two other pioneering jet airliners. Missing out on the honour of being the first jet transport, the Avro Canada C.102 Jetliner first flew on 16 August 1949. It became the first jet transport to make an international flight when it embarked on a sales tour to the United States, and it was the first jet to carry airmail. Its niche would have been in fast regional services up and down the heavily populated US east coast, but in 1951 the Korean War intensified. The Canadian minister with responsibility for aircraft production now declared that the workshop space and expertise engaged in the Jetliner programme was needed for building CF-100 fighters. The programme was halted and the aircraft scrapped, only its nose-section being preserved for posterity.

The third jet airliner to fly, and the second to enter service, was the Soviet Union's Tupolev Tu-104, given the Nato code name 'Camel'. It was the first twinjet airliner, and like the Comet its engines were buried within the wing roots. The wings, tail and engines all came from the Tu-16 'Badger' bomber, but a new fuselage accommodated 50 passengers in its

*The Boeing B-47, which was a radical departure from conventional design, featured a thin, flexible wing – based on wartime research data – with 35 degrees of sweep and carrying six turbojets in underwing pods.*

| OCTOBER | NOVEMBER | DECEMBER | | 1958 |
| --- | --- | --- | --- | --- |
| | | | | APRIL |
| **4 October** The USSR launches *Sputnik 1*, the first artificial satellite. | **3 November** A Russian dog named Laika becomes the first living creature in space. | **6 December** The Lockheed Model 188 Electra flies. | **20 December** The first flight of a production Boeing 707. | **30 April** The Blackburn Buccaneer maritime strike aircraft makes its first flight. |
| | | **12 December** A new world speed record of 1943km/h (1207mph) is set by a McDonnell F101A Voodoo. | | |

standard configuration. First flying in November 1955, the Tu-104 entered service with state airline Aeroflot in September 1956. The Tu-104 suffered its share of accidents over the years, but without the glare of an open media. Without the usual commercial concerns faced by Western airlines, the Tu-104 was the subject of repeat orders by Aeroflot and CSA Czechoslovak Airlines. It had a production run of about 200 up to 1960, when newer types became available.

## 707 and DC-8

While the Comet was grounded, US planemakers were far from idle. Having accepted that jets were the way forward, Boeing began studies into a new jet transport. It was already receiving huge orders from Strategic Air Command for its B-47 Stratojet, a six-engine swept-wing bomber, and this was in need of a tanker aircraft somewhat faster than the current KC-97.

Two years from the project launch, the Model 367-80 demonstrator rolled out. Known as the 'Dash 80', it had nothing in common

*Passengers enjoying an in-flight meal inside the luxurious interior of a Douglas DC-8 jet airliner.*

## 1958

**MAY**

**7 May** A USAF F-104A sets a new altitude record of 27,811m (91,243ft).

**16 May** An F-104 sets the first speed record over 2000km/h when it is flown at 2259km/h (1404mph).

**23 May** The experimental Short SC.1 Vertical Take-Off and Landing (VTOL) aircraft makes a hovering flight.

**27 May** The XF4H-1, prototype of the McDonnell Douglas Phantom, is flown in St. Louis. The Phantom becomes the most-produced Western jet fighter.

**30 May** The first flight of the Douglas DC-8 four-engined airliner.

**AUGUST**

**31 August** The YA3J-1 Vigilante carrier-based nuclear bomber prototype makes its maiden flight.

**OCTOBER**

**4 October** A BOAC Comet 4 begins the first commercial transatlantic jet services.

**26 October** The Boeing 707 enters makes its first transatlantic service with Pan Am.

**DECEMBER**

**4 December** East Germany's only indigenous jet transport, the Baade VEB-152, is flown. It crashes on an early test flight.

By the time the airliner version was in the final design stage, Douglas was offering the DC-8 to airlines with a cabin that was a further 7.5cm (3in) wider. Boeing made the expensive decision to further widen its cabin to be just 2.5cm (1in) broader than the DC-8's, giving a much more spacious cabin overall. With that simple change, it won a major American Airlines order for the 707 and eventually the lion's share of the market. The Dash 80 can be said to be the ancestor of the C-135 and 707 families, but had a completely different fuselage to either of them.

The first actual 707 flew in December 1957, before the DC-8 but after the Convair CV-880. The 707 was the first to enter passenger service, however, in October 1958 with Pan Am on the New York–London route. The jets cost four times as much as the latest piston-engine airliners, but offered a much smoother and quieter ride, and cut journey times dramatically. A New York–Los Angeles flight was now possible in four and a half hours rather than seven and a half, and midatlantic refuelling stops became a thing of the past, at least when headwinds were light.

*In the early 1950s, Boeing took advantage of the expertise it had gained in its B-47 and B-52 jet bomber programmes to design what was to become a world-beating jet airliner, the Boeing 707. The prototype flew in July 1954.*

with the Model 367 Stratofreighter. The design featured a cylindrical fuselage and four engines on individual pods. Tested with passenger seats, freight doors and a refuelling boom, it proved appealing to both the US Air Force and the airlines. The USAF wanted a wider cabin to allow carriage of standard pallets, and the production C-135 aircraft had an interior width of 355cm (140in), an increase of 20cm (8in) over the Dash 80's cabin, which was based on that of the C-97.

## 1959

| MARCH | JUNE | SEPTEMBER | OCTOBER | DECEMBER | |
|---|---|---|---|---|---|
| **11 March** The first flight of the Sikorsky S-61, prototype of the YHSS-2 (later H-3) Sea King naval helicopter. | **17 June** The Dassault Mirage IV delta-winged supersonic bomber is flown. It remains in service until 2005. | **7 September** The Tupolev S-105, prototype of the Tu-22 'Blinder' supersonic bomber, flies in the USSR.<br><br>**18 September** The Douglas DC-8 enters service with Pan Am. | **31 October** Flying a Mikoyan Type Ye66, Colonel G. Mosolov establishes a new world speed record of 2681km/h (1665mph). | **6 December** A new world altitude record of 30,040m (98,556ft) is established by Commander L. Flint, flying a McDonnell F-4 Phantom II.<br><br>**14 December** The world altitude record is broken again by a Lockheed F104C Starfighter, flown by Captain J.B. Jordan to a height of 31,513m (103,389ft). | **9 December** A Kaman H-43B Husky sets a new helicopter altitude record of 9097m (29,846ft).<br><br>**15 December** An F-106A raises the speed record to 2455km/h (1525mph). |

In the late 1950s, air travel was still largely the preserve of the rich, and jet services charged a premium. Tourist-class fares to Europe were subject to arcane rules, requiring such things as 21-day minimum stays. Not for nothing were those who could afford to travel by this new mode of transport called the 'jet set'. When the first jets had passed through a couple of years of ownership, many were picked up by travel clubs, which were essentially charter airlines, which filled planes with package tour groups – beginning the era of jet travel for the masses.

Douglas entered the market slightly later with its four-engine jet, and did not benefit from massive orders for military tanker-transports based on a related design. Nevertheless, the DC-8 received the first order from a US carrier (American Airlines), and by the end of 1958 was nearly even with the 707 in terms of sales. The DC-8 was more expensive, however. In the end, there were only half as many DC-8s sold as 707s, although, in recent times, the DC-8 has benefited from re-engining. Receiving powerful high-bypass turbofans, it has proved popular in the freight market. There are more DC-8s in service today than 707s.

The third of the first-generation US airliners was Convair's CV-880. Howard Hughes was again involved in its creation, but in this case his influence was malign. He insisted on five-abreast seating and also demanded that the aircraft not be sold to TWA's direct competitors, which helped to ensure that the small, short-ranged CV-880 sold only 65 examples over the

*The Convair 880, announced in the spring of 1956, seated fewer passengers than its two rivals, the Boeing 707 and Douglas DC-8, but had the advantage of being faster. The Model 22 became the standard US domestic version.*

## 1960

**APRIL**

**19 April** Grumman flies the A2F-1, prototype of the A-6 Intruder carrier bomber.

**19 April** The Grumman E-2A Hawkeye carrier-based early-warning aircraft first flies.

**JUNE**

**24 June** The Avro (later Hawker Siddeley) 748 turboprop airliner first flies.

**AUGUST**

**12 August** The X-15 research aircraft is launched from a B-52 and flown to 41600m (136,500ft).

## 1961

**APRIL**

**12 April** Launched on a Vostok rocket, Major Yuri Gagarin becomes the first man to enter space and orbit the earth.

**28 April** The Mikoyan Ye66A, a MiG-21 derivative, reaches an altitude of 34,714m (118,898ft).

**MAY**

**5 May** A Mercury-Redstone rocket puts American Alan Shepard into space.

**JULY**

**9 July** The prototype Mil Mi-8, the Soviet Union's most successful helicopter, makes its first flight.

**SEPTEMBER**

**21 September** First flight of the YCH-47, prototype of the Chinook twin-rotor heavy-lift helicopter.

lifetime of its production run from 1959 to 1962. It was fast, however: the 880 designation referred to 880 feet per second, or 1006km/h (625mph). Convair threw good money after bad with the CV-990, a bigger, faster version that sold only 37 examples.

By 1962, jets were well and truly taking over for transcontinental and intercontinental flight. They were causing the decline of not only the piston-engined airliner, but also the ocean liner. The first year of jet service, 1958, was the first in which air passengers exceeded sea passengers on the transatlantic route. In 1965, Cunard retired the *Queen Mary* and redesigned its upcoming replacement, the *Queen Elizabeth 2*, for the luxury cruise market. Mass sea travel for other than short-distance and leisure journeys was at an end. Furthermore, short-range airliners such as the Boeing 727 were on the horizon, replacing the last of the piston-engined airliners. By the end of the decade, the 747 and the Concorde would again revolutionize the world of air travel.

*The first Convair Type 990 flight was made on 24 January 1961, but there was no prototype.*

| OCTOBER | NOVEMBER | **1962** JANUARY | APRIL | JUNE | JULY | DECEMBER |
|---|---|---|---|---|---|---|
| **30 October** A modified Tu-95 'Bear A' bomber drops a 50-megaton hydrogen bomb over Novaya Zemlya Island. This is the most powerful weapon ever tested. | **22 November** A modified F4H-1F Phantom II is flown at a record speed of 2585km/h (1606mph). | **9 January** The first flight of the Hawker Siddeley Trident, the first 'tri-jet'. | **24 April** The first flight of the Lockheed A-12 Mach 3 reconnaissance aircraft at Groom Lake, Nevada. | **27 June** The Mikoyan Ye-152 recaptures the speed record for the USSR with a flight of 2681km/h (1666mph).<br><br>**29 June** The Vickers VC10 airliner makes its first flight. A number remain as service as tankers with the RAF. | **17 July** An X-15A sets a new air-launched altitude record of 95,936m (314,750ft). | **31 December** The US Navy retires its last airship. |

# Cold War Conflict

*By the 1960s, the Cold War had the world in its icy grip. Since mid-1961, West Berlin had been sealed off from the East by the Berlin Wall. In October 1962 came the Missile Crisis, when Soviet nuclear missiles were revealed to be stationed on the island of Cuba.*

In June 1963, President John F. Kennedy visited Berlin, declaring the West's solidarity with the city's people. Nuclear bombers flew on round-the-clock airborne alert. Meanwhile, the French had left Indochina, which became divided into North and South Vietnam. And incursions from the North meant that US 'advisers' were increasingly involved in the military affairs of the South.

The United States armed forces had rationalized their aircraft designation system in September 1962. The standard chosen was the Air Force pattern, which had role identifiers, vehicle types and numbers and series letters. This mainly affected US Navy types, previously designated with a system based on their manufacturer. For example, the Douglas A4D-2N Skyhawk (the second model of the fourth Douglas attack aircraft, modified for night/all-weather missions)

*Left: A Douglas A4 Skyhawk from Naval Air Weapons Station China Lake, the high desert home of the Naval Air Warfare Center Weapons Division, test-firing a Shrike anti-radar missile. Right: A Douglas A4C.*

*The MiG-17 was a much-refined successor to the MiG-15 and served in huge numbers with the Soviet-bloc air forces. It was a deadly opponent over North Vietnam.*

*A North-American F-86 Sabre taking off for a mission.*

became the A-4C (the third model of the fourth attack aircraft in the current inventory). This caused grumblings among some, who preferred the more descriptive older system. It simplified matters, however, particularly over time as fewer new types entered service and manufacturers merged.

## Soviet Air Power

Ranged against the United States and its NATO allies were the enormous air forces of the Union of Soviet Socialist Republics. Air forces plural because the Soviet Union maintained several independent air arms, including PVO Strany, or air defence forces (with missiles, radars and interceptor fighters); VVS (Voenno-Vozdushnye Sily), the main air force, divided into Strategic Aviation, Frontal (tactical) Aviation and Transport Aviation; and Aviatsiya Voenno-Morskogo Flota, or Naval Aviation, which was mostly land-based.

The Soviet Union was often accused of copying Western designs. Critics often pointed to the outward resemblance between, among others, the MiG-15 and F-86 and the Su-27 and F-15 fighters, the Su-24 and F-111 bombers, the Il-76 and C-141 transports, and several airliner

## 1963

| JANUARY | | FEBRUARY | | APRIL | MAY |
|---|---|---|---|---|---|
| | **17 January** The X-15 is flown to 82600m (271,000ft). This is considered beyond the atmosphere, and pilot Joe Walker wins astronaut wings. | **February** The RAF puts the Blue Steel stand-off nuclear missile into service. | **9 February** The Boeing 727 tri-jet flies. Production continues until 1984, with more than 1800 built. | **20 April** The first supersonic VTOL aircraft, the EWR VJ 101, flies in Germany. | **1 May** Flying an F-104, Jacqueline Cochran sets a women's speed record of 1937km/h (1203mph). |
| **9 January** the Yakovlev Yak-36 experimental VTOL aircraft flies in the USSR. | | | **25 February** The first flight of the Franco-German Transall C.160 transport. | | |

*The Sukhoi Su-27UB 'Flanker C' is a two-seat trainer version, retaining full combat capability.*

*Originally designated FX, the F-15 Eagle flew for the first time on 27 July 1972.*

designs. These superficial similarities mask a quite different approach to most aspects of aircraft construction, maintenance and operation practised by the Soviet Union and its successors.

Not all Soviet aircraft were related to their Western equivalents. One aircraft that was totally unique was the Tupolev Tu-95/142

'Bear', the world's only turboprop strategic bomber. Entering series production in 1956, the Bear was a considerable technological accomplishment – and one not even attempted in the West. A few turboprop attack aircraft had already been built, such as the unsuccessful Douglas Skyshark and the slightly better

Westland Wyvern, and most maritime patrol aircraft were also turboprops because this type of powerplant offered high fuel efficiency, but the Western powers assumed that jets were more practical for bombers because of their greater speed and altitude capabilities. Moreover, combining a swept wing with turboprops was

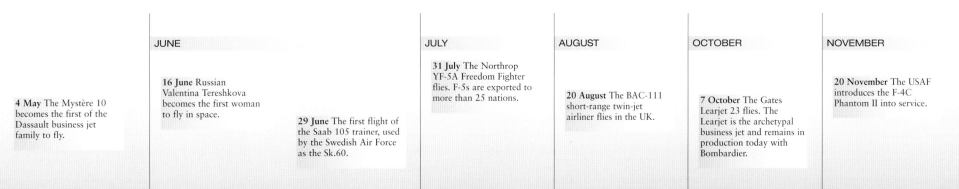

| | JUNE | | JULY | AUGUST | OCTOBER | NOVEMBER |
|---|---|---|---|---|---|---|
| | **16 June** Russian Valentina Tereshkova becomes the first woman to fly in space. | | **31 July** The Northrop YF-5A Freedom Fighter flies. F-5s are exported to more than 25 nations. | **20 August** The BAC-111 short-range twin-jet airliner flies in the UK. | **7 October** The Gates Learjet 23 flies. The Learjet is the archetypal business jet and remains in production today with Bombardier. | **20 November** The USAF introduces the F-4C Phantom II into service. |
| **4 May** The Mystère 10 becomes the first of the Dassault business jet family to fly. | | **29 June** The first flight of the Saab 105 trainer, used by the Swedish Air Force as the Sk.60. | | | | |

considered too difficult. The Bear, though, used four enormously powerful Kuznetsov NK-12MV turboprops, which had an output of 11,033kW (14,795hp) each. These drove large contra-rotating propellers and gave a top speed of 925km/h (575mph), not significantly less than contemporary jet bombers such as the B-47 and faster than some, such as the Vickers

*The prototype F-111A variable geometry interdictor/strike aircraft flew for the first time on 21 December 1964, the initial variant being followed into service by the F-111E.*

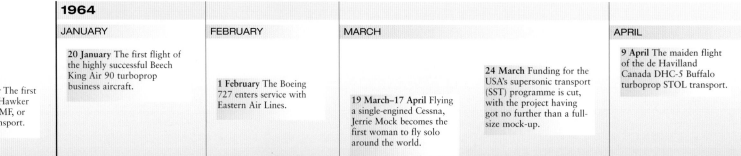

*The Su-24 Fencer made its first flight in 1970 and deliveries of the first production version, the Fencer-A, began in 1974.*

Valiant. The Bear was built in many versions, as bomber, cruise missile carrier, electronic warfare platform and reconnaissance aircraft. The Soviet Air Force versions were the Tu-95s (sometimes mistakenly called Tu-20s in the West), and the naval maritime patrol, anti-submarine and communications relay versions were the Tu-142.

Bears were frequently encountered by Royal Air Force and NATO fighters over the Baltic and the North Sea. Sometimes these were

## 1963

### DECEMBER

**17 December** The first flight of the C-141 Starlifter, the USAF's first large turbojet transport.

**21 December** The first flight of the Hawker Siddeley 748MF, or Andover, transport.

## 1964

### JANUARY

**20 January** The first flight of the highly successful Beech King Air 90 turboprop business aircraft.

### FEBRUARY

**1 February** The Boeing 727 enters service with Eastern Air Lines.

### MARCH

**19 March–17 April** Flying a single-engined Cessna, Jerrie Mock becomes the first woman to fly solo around the world.

**24 March** Funding for the USA's supersonic transport (SST) programme is cut, with the project having got no further than a full-size mock-up.

### APRIL

**9 April** The maiden flight of the de Havilland Canada DHC-5 Buffalo turboprop STOL transport.

*A satisfied-looking Russian crew pictured after making a test flight in an Ilyushin Il-76 Candid.*

probing missions to evaluate the defensive response and sometimes they involved mock cruise missile launches at the United Kingdom. On occasion, Bears flew from northern Russia all the way to Cuba. Western pilots reported the extraordinary noise generated by the turboprops and propellers, heard even through their pressurized cockpits and helmets. Despite the old-fashioned appearance of the Bear, and the development of jet bombers such as the Tu-22 'Backfire' and Tu-160 'Blackjack', it continued in production into the 1990s and still serves in considerable numbers with Russian forces.

*The C-141A StarLifter was first flown on 17 December 1963.*

| MAY | SEPTEMBER | OCTOBER | NOVEMBER | DECEMBER |
|---|---|---|---|---|

**6 May** The Royal Air Force aerobatic team the Red Arrows flies its first display.

**21 September** The Mach 3-capable North American XB-70 Valkyrie bomber prototype flies.

**27 September** The British Aircraft Corporation (BAC) TSR2 strike aircraft makes its first flight.

**14 October** The Sikorsky YCH-53 (S-65), prototype of the Sea Stallion flies. CH-53s are the heaviest US helicopters.

**16 October** Test of the first Chinese nuclear weapon.

**18 November** The Grumman C-2 Greyhound, a carrier onboard delivery (COD) derivative of the E-2 Hawkeye, is flown.

**21 December** The first flight of the General Dynamics F-111A variable-geometry ('swing wing') bomber.

**22 December** The first flight of the SR-71 Mach 3 reconnaissance aircraft takes place in secret at Groom Lake, Nevada.

*Above: The Tupolev Tu-22 Blinder was first seen publicly at the Tushino air display in 1961.*

*Above: The Tu-95 Bear saw service as a maritime reconnaissance aircraft and cruise missile launcher.*

*Right: The Tu-160 supersonic bomber first flew on 19 December 1981.*

## 1965

| FEBRUARY | MARCH | APRIL | MAY | JUNE |
|---|---|---|---|---|
| **25 February** First flight of the Douglas DC-9. Production continues into the twenty-first century as the MD-80/90 series and later the Boeing 717. | **6 March** A SH-3A Sea King crosses the USA from an aircraft carrier on the West Coast to one on the East Coast.<br><br>**18 March** Cosmonaut Alexei Leonov makes the first 'spacewalk'. | **15 April** The Aérospatiale SA.330, prototype of the Puma transport helicopter, is flown in France. | **1 May** A YF-12A establishes a new world speed record of 3331km/h (2070mph). | **4 June** The Nanchang Q-5 'Fantan', an improved and much revised derivative of the MiG-19, flies in China. |

## British Bombers

In 1963, the Royal Air Force had no fewer than three heavy bombers in service: the Vickers Valiant, Handley Page Victor and Avro Vulcan, all built to a specification issued in 1947.

The first of these 'V-bombers', the Valiant, was the most conservative of the designs and was ordered as a form of insurance against failure of the two more advanced types. Although largely forgotten today in comparison with the other V-bombers, the Valiant was the first RAF aircraft to see combat and the first to drop an atomic weapon. (Both events took place in October 1956, when Egyptian airfields were attacked as part of the Suez Campaign, and the South Australian desert was the scene of nuclear tests.) When the Victor and Vulcan reached full operational status, the Valiant was switched to low-level tactical missions. Training for these was much more stressful on the airframe,

*The Vickers Valiant was the first of the Royal Air Force's trio of V-bombers.*

however, and, after a series of accidents, the wing spars of most aircraft were found to be suffering the effects of fatigue. The Valiant was grounded in late 1964 and withdrawn a few months later.

The Handley Page Victor was aerodynamically more advanced. With a crescent wing and tail planform, it had a tapered nose, and the windscreen was flush with its upper service.

The Victor was initially employed as a high-level bomber, then as a carrier of the Blue Steel stand-off nuclear missile. The threat from Soviet surface-to-air missiles and their associated radars forced a change of tactics to low-level penetration and a change of colour scheme from 'anti-flash' white to grey and green camouflage. Only once did the Victor drop bombs in anger, against Communist guerrillas in Malaya in the early 1960s. The RAF saw the use of strategic bombers against small forces hiding in the jungle as an ineffective way to fight insurgents, even if the aircraft were able to drop 35 conventional 454kg (1000lb) bombs at a time – a contrast to the approach the United States was to take in the conflict in Vietnam just a few years later.

With the formation of Victor squadrons, some Valiants were converted to air refuelling tankers. After the Valiants were prematurely retired, some Victors were converted to take their

JULY

**23 July** The first aircraft (a USAF F-4C Phantom II) is shot down by a surface-to-air missile in combat.

**10 June** A Trident airliner makes an automatic landing at Heathrow using the Smiths Autoland system.

**12 June** First flight of the Britten-Norman Islander light transport aircraft.

**SEPTEMBER**

**7 September** The prototype of the AH-1 Cobra series flies. This is the first purpose-designed attack helicopter.

**27 September** First flight of the A-7 Corsair II carrier-based attack aircraft.

**NOVEMBER**

**15 November** A Flying Tiger Line 707 makes the first circumnavigation of the world crossing the North and South poles.

*The last in a long line of Handley Page bombers, the prototype HP80 Victor, seen here cruising at altitude, made its first flight on 24 December 1952.*

place, acting as tankers for Victor and Vulcan bombers and for interceptor fighters and attack aircraft. The Victor B.2 served in the nuclear strike role until 1975; the K.2 tanker continued until 1993, after playing a vital role in the 'Black Buck' raids on the Falklands in 1982, and in the 1991 Gulf War.

The Vulcan was the last of the V-bombers to fly, the second to enter service, and the most charismatic and famous of the trio. The Vulcan was a tailless delta, with four engines buried in the wingroots – a feature of all the V-bombers. Deliveries to the RAF began in 1956. The Vulcan, like the Victor, went through a variety

of incarnations, from high-level bomber to missile carrier to low-level bomber; late in its career, some were converted to tankers.

Originally, the Vulcan was to carry the American Skybolt, the replacement for the Blue Steel missile. This had a longer range and did not require the same careful handling; the Blue Steel was powered by volatile hydrogen peroxide-based fuel. Unfortunately, however, the US government cancelled Skybolt, and the United Kingdom's strategic deterrent passed to the Navy's Polaris submarines.

Again the Vulcan saw action as a bomber in only one brief campaign, over the Falkland Islands in May 1982. Flying from Ascension Island, a tiny British outpost in the Atlantic between Brazil and West Africa, Vulcans made raids on the airfield and radar installations around Stanley Airfield. As planned, each Vulcan sortie required 11 Victors, passing fuel in a chain to get one bomber to the target and back. Even more, though, were needed as airborne spares and to help get thirsty tankers safely back to base. The 'Black Buck' raids did relatively little material damage, but effectively denied the airfield to the Argentine jets and

## 1965

### DECEMBER

**2 December** The USS *Enterprise* becomes the first nuclear-powered warship to see combat when it launches air strikes on North Vietnam.

**17 December** The USAF tests air-to-air refuelling of helicopters using a CH-3 and a KC-130 tanker.

## 1966

### JANUARY

**7 January** The SR-71 Blackbird enters USAF service.

**10 January** The first flight of the Bell 206A, civil version of the H-58 Kiowa. As the Jet Ranger, it becomes one of the most successful light helicopters.

**17 January** A B-52 and a KC-135 collide over Spain, dropping several nuclear weapons over land and sea.

### FEBRUARY

**23 February** The first flight of the Dornier Do 28 light transport.

### JULY

**12 July** The first gliding flight of the Northrop/NASA M2F2 lifting-body research aircraft.

forced them to keep fighters out of the combat zone to defend Buenos Aires: the Stanley raids proved that the Argentine capital was well within Vulcan range.

### Medium Bombers

The V-bombers were partnered by the English Electric Canberra, which had first flown in May 1949 as the first European jet bomber. A fairly conservative twin-engine design, the Canberra replaced the Avro Lincoln, a derivative of the Lancaster, in Bomber Command from 1951. Versions were equipped for tactical nuclear missions from bases in West Germany, but the Canberra was used principally as a conventional medium day-bomber and saw action with the RAF at Suez, in Malaya and Borneo.

The Canberra also proved an export success, selling to many countries, including India, Argentina, Chile, Venezuela, Peru, Australia, New Zealand and South Africa. Even the US Air Force bought the design, licensing it to Martin, which built it as the B-57 and developed it for new roles, including night-attack variants that served effectively in operations over Vietnam. Several different photo-reconnaissance (PR)

*The Avro Vulcan B.2 was intended to carry the American Skybolt intermediate-range air-launched ballistic missile, which in the event was cancelled. Some carried the Blue Steel stand-off missile.*

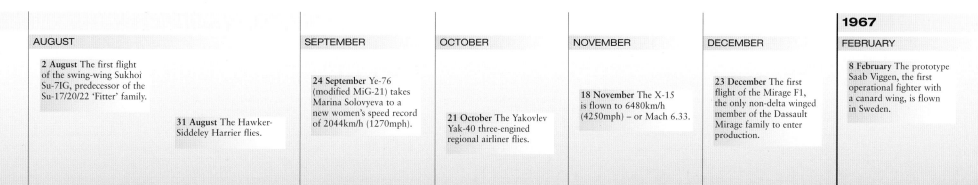

**AUGUST**

**2 August** The first flight of the swing-wing Sukhoï Su-7IG, predecessor of the Su-17/20/22 'Fitter' family.

**31 August** The Hawker-Siddeley Harrier flies.

**SEPTEMBER**

**24 September** Ye-76 (modified MiG-21) takes Marina Solovyeva to a new women's speed record of 2044km/h (1270mph).

**OCTOBER**

**21 October** The Yakovlev Yak-40 three-engined regional airliner flies.

**NOVEMBER**

**18 November** The X-15 is flown to 6480km/h (4250mph) – or Mach 6.33.

**DECEMBER**

**23 December** The first flight of the Mirage F1, the only non-delta winged member of the Dassault Mirage family to enter production.

**1967**

**FEBRUARY**

**8 February** The prototype Saab Viggen, the first operational fighter with a canard wing, is flown in Sweden.

versions were built by Shorts in Northern Ireland, including the PR.9, which served the Royal Air Force for more than 40 years. The PR.9 was particularly active in its latter years, seeing service over Iraq, Afghanistan and the Horn of Africa before it was finally retired in July 2006.

The Canberra's Soviet equivalent was the Ilyushin Il-28 'Beagle', which first flew in 1948. Again, this was not a giant leap forward from

*Ilyushin's Il-28 formed the mainstay of the Soviet bloc's tactical striking forces during the 1950s.*

*Originally designed for the radar bombing role as a replacement for the de Havilland Mosquito, the English Electric Canberra was the greatest success story of Britain's postwar aviation industry and was retired only in 2006.*

## 1967

### APRIL

**7 April** The first flight of the Aérospatiale SA.340 Gazelle, a successful light helicopter using the 'fenestron' tail rotor system.

**9 April** The first Boeing 737 flies. The 'Baby Boeing' goes on to be the most successful jetliner ever, with more than 5000 built to date.

**23 April** Cosmonaut Vladimir Komarov is killed in the landing of *Soyuz 1*, the first person to die during a space flight.

### MAY

**9 May** The Fokker F28 Fellowship twin-engined jetliner flies in the Netherlands.

**23 May** The Hawker Siddeley Nimrod jet maritime patrol aircraft prototype, based on the de Havilland Comet, makes its first flight.

### JUNE

**10 June** The Mikoyan-Gurevich 23-11/1, prototype of the MiG-23 'Flogger', flies in the USSR.

**17 June** The first Chinese thermonuclear device is detonated.

wartime bombers, apart from its jet powerplants. The three crewmembers included a pilot, bomb aimer and rear gunner, whereas the Canberra relied on speed for its defence. The Il-28 was widely used by the Soviet Union and exported to many Communist nations. It saw action in various small conflicts, but perhaps it was most effective in North Korea, Cuba and Vietnam. In each theatre, its mere presence (actual or otherwise) was enough to force the deployment of considerable numbers of US interceptors, in case the bombers took an active offensive role, which they rarely did.

During the Six-Day War in 1967, the Egyptian Air Force's Il-28s were the first target of Israel's ground-attack aircraft, and were destroyed in their dispersals. China built several thousand Il-28s as the Harbin H-6, and continues to use the type today. Chinese versions were also exported, with the last users outside China being Romania and North Korea.

*A Convair F-102A Delta Dagger test-firing a Hughes AIM-4 Falcon, the first guided air-to-air missile in the world to enter operational service.*

### Missile Age

Probably the most important postwar development in military aviation was the guided missile. This soon appeared in many forms for use from many types of platform and for many uses, such as surface-to-air, surface-to-surface and air-to-surface. Tests with air-to-air guided missiles were made by the Luftwaffe before the end of World War II, but the first successful such weapon was the US Air Force's Hughes GAR-1 (later AIM-4 Falcon), first tested in 1949. It was a short-range radar-homing missile optimized for attacking slow-moving unmanoeuvrable targets such as large bombers, and it required a direct hit to score a kill. An infrared version was also created, and both became operational in 1956.

A version of the AIM-4 with a nuclear warhead was developed. This might seem like overkill, but its purpose was to destroy formations of enemy bombers before they could drop their own atomic payloads. Its tactical limitations included a short range of about 8–16km (5–10 miles), and it could not be used over friendly territory. The AIM-4 was followed by the AIM-7 Sparrow,

| JULY | SEPTEMBER | OCTOBER | | |
|---|---|---|---|---|
| **4 July** RAF Lightnings begin making random sonic booms over the UK in secret experiments to judge the effect of a future supersonic transport (SST). | **9 September** The Tupolev Tu-134 commences services with Aeroflot. | **October** The General Dynamics F-111 enters service with the USAF. | **23 October** The Canadair CL-215, the only aircraft designed specific for aerial firefighting, makes its maiden flight in Quebec. | **24 October** The first successful interception directed by an airborne control aircraft is made when a US Air Force EC-121 directs an F-4C to shoot down a North Vietnamese MiG-21. |
| | **21 September** The first flight of the Lockheed YAH-56 Cheyenne attack helicopter. | **3 October** The X-15A-2 is flown to its final record speed of 7297km/h (4534mph) or Mach 6.72 by Bill Knight. | **20 October** An F-111 crew makes the first use of an escape capsule to abandon an aircraft. | |

which had many limitations in its original form and a reputation for unreliability in the combat conditions it encountered over Vietnam. Improved versions and derivatives remain in service today.

*An SH-2 SeaSprite helicopter of the US Navy armed with an AIM-7 missile.*

The most successful air-to-air missile (AAM) has been the AIM-9 Sidewinder series, developed by the US Navy's labs at China Lake, California. A simple infrared-guided weapon, the Sidewinder needed little specialized equipment to integrate with the launch platform and no assistance from it after launch, making it a 'fire-and-forget' weapon. The first combat use came in September 1958, when Nationalist Chinese (Taiwanese) F-86F Sabres fought People's Republic of China (PRC) MiGs over the Taiwan Straits. The Sabres easily defeated the MiGs and the conflict ended in stalemate. One side effect, however, was that a

*Two F-16 Falcons from Hill Air Force Base, Utah, armed with AIM-9 Sidewinder air-to-air missiles.*

damaged MiG returned to its base with the majority of an AIM-9 stuck in its tailpipe. The parts were analysed, giving the Soviet Union's missile programme an enormous boost and leading to the K-13 (or AA-2 Atoll), initially a direct copy of the AIM-9B.

The Sidewinder has become the most widely produced air-to-air missile of all time, with many tens of thousands built, including unlicensed copies in Russia and China.

## 1967

### NOVEMBER

**18 November** The Dassault Mirage G, Europe's first swing-wing aircraft, flies in France.

## 1968

### FEBRUARY

**10 February** The Boeing 737-100 enters airline service with Lufthansa.

**21 February** A US airliner is hijacked and flown to Cuba. This is the first of a series of hijackings.

### MARCH

**17 March** The F-111A enters combat in Vietnam, soon suffering a series of mysterious losses.

### MAY

**25 May** The first flight of the Grumman EA-6B Prowler, an electronic warfare derivative of the A-6 Intruder.

**5 May** A Grumman Gulfstream II becomes the first business jet to make a nonstop transatlantic flight.

*An F-106 Delta Dart all-weather interceptor approaching to land.*

## Fighters as Weapons Systems

With the advent of air-to-air missiles, fighter aircraft moved from being gun platforms to becoming part of a weapons system, which often comprised the radar, fire-control system, the missiles and ground stations, as well as the aircraft itself. The USAF Convair F-102 and F-106 fighters were prime examples of this, being designed for semi-autonomous control to the point of interception. The pilot made the takeoff and set an initial course, but his aircraft was then given steering commands from the

*The Convair XF-92A was the world's first turbojet-powered aircraft to fly with a delta-wing configuration.*

| JUNE | SEPTEMBER | DECEMBER | **1969** FEBRUARY | MARCH |
|---|---|---|---|---|
| | **8 September** The Anglo-French SEPECAT Jaguar fighter-bomber flies. | **31 December** Maiden flight of the Tupolev Tu-144, the world's first supersonic transport. | **12 February** The Mil Mi-12, the world's largest helicopter, also known as the V-12, flies in Russia. | **2 March** The first flight of the prototype Anglo-French Concorde SST is made in Toulouse. |
| **30 June** The world's largest production aircraft, the Lockheed C-5A Galaxy makes its first flight. | **30 September** Roll-out of the Boeing 747 prototype in Seattle, Washington. | | **9 February** The Boeing 747 prototype makes its maiden flight. The 747 remains the largest airliner to fly until 2005. | |

182    C H A P T E R   S E V E N

ground, feeding through the autopilot until reaching the point at which the missiles were fired at the oncoming bombers. The pilot held the weapons' release trigger until the missiles or rockets launched automatically, then the system turned the aircraft onto a safe course, avoiding the resulting explosion.

The F-102's origins were in a request for a weapons system designated WS-210A. The original airframe was designated XP-92 by the old system, P standing for 'pursuit'. Largely based on a German design by Dr Alexander Lippisch, the XF-92A became the first pure delta-winged aircraft to fly, in September 1948. The XF-92A was too small to be much more than a research craft, but it led to the YF-102, which was intended as a prototype for the new interceptor.

The limits of aeronautical knowledge were tested by the YF-102, which resolutely failed to go supersonic in flight trials, despite a sleek design and plenty of power. Actually, wind tunnel testing had pointed to problems with potential excessive drag, but it was too late to

*An F102A Delta Dagger in mid-air, this popular name was chosen for the aircraft in 1957.*

*The Avro Canada CF-105 was one of the most advanced interceptors in the world.*

do anything before the programme reached the hardware stage. A solution was found by scientist Richard Whitcomb, who called for the YF-102's fuselage to be modified by the addition of bulges at the rear, making it conform to his 'area rule'. Broadly speaking, this states that the cross-section of the fuselage where it joins the

## 1969

| APRIL | | JULY | AUGUST | | SEPTEMBER |
|---|---|---|---|---|---|
| **1 April** The Harrier GR.1 enters service with the RAF, which becomes the first air arm to field a VTOL fighter. | **2 April** The British-built second Concorde flies. | **21 July** The *Apollo 11* Lunar Module lands on the Moon. Neil Armstrong and Edwin Aldrin become the first humans to walk on its surface. | **6 August** The Mi-12 lifts lifts a world record 40,204kg (88,636lb) to a height of 2255m (7398ft). | **16 August** Darryl Greenamyer sets the first piston-engined air speed record since before World War II, flying a Grumman Bearcat to 769km/h (477mph). | **19 September** The first flight of the prototype of the Soviet Mil Mi-24 'Hind-A' assault helicopter. |
| | | | | **30 August** The Tu-22M-0, prototype of the swing–wing 'Backfire' strategic bomber, makes its first flight. | |

wing should be 'pinched' to reduce drag. Bulges achieved the same effect less elegantly, but the production model F-102A was built with the correct 'wasp waist' and easily exceeded Mach 1.

By the late 1950s, the guided missiles had an influence beyond their use as weapons. In the late 1950s, they seemed to be about to replace certain types of manned aircraft altogether. In Britain, the Defence Minister was Duncan Sandys, who had led a committee for defence against German

flying bombs and rockets during World War II. Now he was sure that surface-to-air missiles and air-launched stand-off attack missiles would make fighter aircraft and conventional bombers obsolete. He cancelled all current fighter and attack aircraft programmes in his 1957 Defence White Paper. Only the English Electric Lightning

interceptor survived because its development was too far advanced.

In Canada, the United States managed to persuade the government that its air defence could be accomplished by nuclear-tipped BOMARC missiles, rather than the Avro Canada Arrow interceptor. This advanced delta-winged aircraft was cancelled in February 1959, causing great damage to the Canadian aerospace industry. The BOMARCs entered service in 1963, by which time a change of government had led to the purchase of US-built CF-101 Voodoo interceptors. The Voodoos lasted in frontline Canadian service until 1984, outlasting the BOMARCs, which were retired in 1971.

### Spies in the Skies

The Cold War was largely fought through a series of proxy wars in Southeast Asia, Africa and Latin America. In most of these theatres, conventional fighters and bombers played only a limited part. Rarely did forces of the Soviet Union and the United States or NATO come into direct conflict. One exception is when reconnaissance and intelligence aircraft crossed into disputed territory.

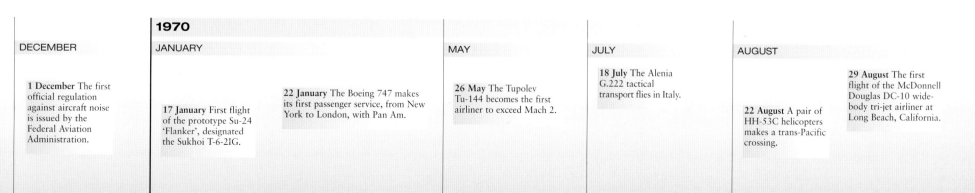

*The English Electric Lightning was constantly improved during its career.*

**1970**

**DECEMBER**

**1 December** The first official regulation against aircraft noise is issued by the Federal Aviation Administration.

**JANUARY**

**17 January** First flight of the prototype Su-24 'Flanker', designated the Sukhoi T-6-2IG.

**22 January** The Boeing 747 makes its first passenger service, from New York to London, with Pan Am.

**MAY**

**26 May** The Tupolev Tu-144 becomes the first airliner to exceed Mach 2.

**JULY**

**18 July** The Alenia G.222 tactical transport flies in Italy.

**AUGUST**

**22 August** A pair of HH-53C helicopters makes a trans-Pacific crossing.

**29 August** The first flight of the McDonnell Douglas DC-10 wide-body tri-jet airliner at Long Beach, California.

The first incidents between Soviet and US aircraft took place soon after the end of the war in the Pacific, over Manchuria and Korea. As relations between East and West cooled, there were an increasing number of incidents in Europe, particularly around its fringes – over the Baltic Sea, and around Yugoslavia and Turkey. A number of transport planes, maritime patrol aircraft and even civilian airliners were attacked by Eastern Bloc fighters for actual or alleged airspace violations. The air corridor between West Germany and West Berlin provided many opportunities for East German and Soviet MiGs to shoot down straying aircraft on the pretext that that they were spy planes. In 1964, a USAF T-39 Sabreliner and an RB-66 Destroyer were shot down by MiGs in separate incidents. The T-39 crew were killed, but the RB-66 crew parachuted to safety and were released by the authorities after a

few days. The T-39 was ostensibly on a training mission, but the RB-66 was a dedicated Elint (electronic intelligence) platform, and it is probable that it was listening to military communications or radar emissions.

In the Far East, the Republic of China (Taiwan) flew many clandestine missions on behalf of the United States, with equipment such as the RB-69, a reconnaissance version of the P-2 Neptune, and the U-2 spyplane. The US Navy

*One of the most controversial and politically explosive aircraft of all time, the Lockheed U-2 high-altitude reconnaissance aircraft made its first flight in August 1955.*

lost four Neptunes in the 1950s to Soviet or Chinese anti-aircraft fire or MiGs. Beginning surveillance flights in the early 1960s, the RB-69s did not restrict themselves to skirting the Chinese coast and roamed some way inland, where four were shot down between 1961 and 1964. Meanwhile, the CIA was training Taiwanese pilots to fly the much more sophisticated and higher-flying U-2C 'Dragon Lady'.

From 1962 to 1974, ROC Air Force 'Black Cat' pilots flew the U-2C on missions over the Chinese mainland, photographing nuclear test sites, Chinese supply routes to North Vietnam and other targets of strategic interest. Again, this was a risky business, and five U-2s were lost, four of them to SA-2 surface-to-air missiles. As had been proved in May 1960, when Francis Gary Powers was shot down near Sverdlosk by an SA-2, U-2s were vulnerable to SAMs despite flying at a high altitude (more than 21,000m/70,000ft).

The U-2 was a glider-like craft with a maximum speed of only about 810km/h (510mph), and there was a narrow operating margin between its safe top speed and its stalling speed at high altitude. Developed in secret by

## 1970

**SEPTEMBER**

**Exact date unknown** New anti-hijacking measures are announced in the USA, including air marshals on flights and passenger screening at airports.

**6 September** Three jetliners are hijacked by Palestinian terrorists and flown to Dawson's Field in Jordan, where they are blown up on the 12th.

**NOVEMBER**

**16 November** The Lockheed L-1011 TriStar flies at Palmdale, California.

**DECEMBER**

**21 December** The Grumman YF-14A Tomcat is flown. It is lost in a crash on its second flight.

## 1971

**JANUARY**

**6 January** The first AV-8A Harriers are delivered to the US Marine Corps.

**MARCH**

**21 March** The first flight of the Westland Lynx military utility helicopter.

**25 March** The first flight of the Ilyushin Il-76 'Candid' four-engined jet freighter.

*The A-1 version of the Douglas Skyraider was developed specifically for ground-support operations in Vietnam.*

Lockheed's so-called 'Skunk Works' advanced development department, a successor to the U-2 was planned even before its vulnerability to surface-to-air missiles was proven.

The new single-seat high-speed aircraft was commissioned by the Central Intelligence Agency as the A-12, and produced under the code name 'Oxcart'. The A-12 and its successors were large twin-engine jets of advanced design and construction, capable of speeds around Mach 3.35 (3500km/h; 2200mph) at 23,000m (75,000ft). Flight tests began in 1962 at a secret location in Nevada known as 'The Ranch', better known today as Groom Lake, heart of the so-called 'Area 51'.

Thirteen A-12s were built, as were three YF-12 interceptors. These two-seaters tested the AIM-47A missile as a counter to Soviet bombers, which could be dealt with long before they reached populated areas of Canada or the United States. The US Air Force ordered more than 90 F-12s, but in 1965 the programme was cancelled, largely due to its high cost. The logic used to support the decision was that the Soviet Union did not at the time possess bombers fast enough to make the interceptor's extraordinary performance necessary.

The YF-12 proved that a two-seater would make a better reconnaissance machine, and a successor was built under the designation R-12. A proposed bomber version was the B-71. During the 1964 election campaign, President Johnson announced the programme's existence to demonstrate that the United States was not falling behind technologically. For reasons that remain obscure, he referred to it as the 'SR-71'. President Johnson's word was translated as an order and the two-seat reconnaissance model became the SR-71 from then on, with the popular name 'Blackbird'.

The first SR-71 flew in December 1964 and the type entered service in January 1966. A total of 32 SR-71s was built and operated from California, the United Kingdom and Okinawa. The Powers U-2 incident had led to a ban on overflights of the Soviet Union, and satellites made them less necessary for observation of fixed installations. Satellites, though, used up valuable fuel to manoeuvre and could often not react to changing events such as troop deployments. The Blackbird was the answer. With its powerful side-looking radar, oblique cameras and other sensors, it could collect imagery while over international waters or a friendly country, meaning that it was immune from defences – in theory, at least. SR-71s were used over Vietnam, the Middle East, Cuba and around the periphery of the Soviet Union,

| MAY | JUNE | | JULY | AUGUST | SEPTEMBER |
|---|---|---|---|---|---|
| **26 May** Cessna completes its 100,000th aircraft. | **4 June–11 August** Briton Sheila Scott makes the first circumnavigation of the Earth via the poles in a light aircraft, a Piper Aztec. | **18 June** Southwest Airlines is founded in Texas. It becomes the first 'no frills' airline. | **23 July** The Australian GAF Nomad light transport/airliner is flown. **5 August** American Airlines introduces the DC-10 into passenger service. | | **12 September** The Bede BD-5, at the time the world's smallest aircraft, is flown in the USA. **26 September** Concorde makes its first Atlantic crossing. |

providing timely intelligence during a number of conflicts and crises. The SR-71 was expensive to build (its cost perhaps exceeding its weight in gold) and operate, requiring much dedicated ground and life-support equipment. It also required its own specialized tankers to supply the special fuel it used, which itself was said to cost more than fine whisky.

## Vietnam

From 1964, significant numbers of US aircraft became involved in the conflict between the Democratic Republic of Vietnam (DRV, or North Vietnam) and the Republic of Vietnam (RVN, or South Vietnam). The DRV received the support of the Soviet Union and China, receiving materiel, training and advisers; the RVN received the support of the United States and its allies, including South Korea and Australia, and large numbers of troops were poured into the theatre.

The air war saw almost every type of US combat aircraft used against North Vietnam or its army and Viet Cong insurgents operating in the South, and later in the neighbouring countries of Laos and Cambodia. From

*US troops embarking in a Bell UH-1 in Vietnam. The 'Huey' had a heavy rotor that enabled it to cut through tree branches when operating from jungle clearings.*

the piston-engine A-1 Skyraider to the eight-jet B-52, US aircraft dropped more than 5.4 million tonnes (6 million tons) of bombs during the war. Naval and land-based fighter and attack aircraft faced increasingly sophisticated defences, in the form of an integrated air defence system built along Soviet lines. From 1965, in addition to anti-aircraft guns of all calibres, the North Vietnamese fielded SA-2 surface-to-air missiles. This forced many changes in US tactics and the

## 1972

| JANUARY | FEBRUARY | APRIL | MAY | JUNE | JULY |
|---|---|---|---|---|---|
| **21 January** The first flight of Grumman's YS-3A, prototype of the S-3 Viking carrier-based anti-submarine aircraft. | **5 February** The first flight of the first of two EC-137D testbeds for the E-3 AWACS surveillance aircraft. | **16 April** The Lockheed L-1011 TriStar enters service with Eastern Airlines. | **10 May** The YA-10, prototype of the Republic A-10 Thunderbolt II close-support aircraft, makes its first flight.  **25 May** A modified NASA F-8C Crusader becomes the first digital fly-by-wire aircraft to fly. | **2 June** Aérospatiale's SA.360 Dauphin makes its first flight.  **21 June** An Aérospatiale Lama helicopter sets a new record altitude at 12,441m (40,820ft). | **27 July** The first flight of the McDonnell Douglas F-15 Eagle air superiority fighter at St Louis, Missouri. |

development of 'Wild Weasel' platforms for suppressing the missiles and radars, using sophisticated electronics and anti-radiation missiles such as the AGM-45 Shrike.

Helicopters played a greater role in Vietnam than in any previous conflict. The ubiquitous Bell UH-1 'Huey' was used as a 'battle taxi' by the Air Cavalry and other units to deliver forces to areas of enemy concentration, then to remove them, along with the dead and wounded, when the fighting was done. This was a new form of warfare, and probably fundamentally flawed. Although the US forces won all its major engagements with North Vietnamese Army (NVA) units, the 'airmobile' tactic of withdrawing after the battle and not holding ground allowed the enemy to return and, eventually, to control much of South Vietnam's countryside. The helicopters were vulnerable to small-arms fire and later to hand-held missiles such as the SA-7 'Grail'. More than 4000 helicopters were lost in the conflict, not including the badly damaged ones that were rebuilt only by replacing almost every part.

Armed gunship versions of the UH-1 were employed as escorts, and later as attack aircraft, armed with door-mounted machine guns, rocket pods and multi-barrelled mini-guns. With all the extra weight and drag, the Huey 'Hog' gunships had trouble keeping up with their 'slick' transport counterparts. This spurred the development of the AH-1 Hueycobra, a purpose-built attack helicopter with the same engine, rotors and tail of the UH-1, but a new slim fuselage containing two crew in tandem. A nose turret held a mini-gun or a grenade launcher, sometimes partnered with a machine gun, and rocket pods or additional guns could be carried on the stub wings. The Cobra entered combat in Vietnam in late 1967 and proved twice as fast as the UH-1C Huey, able to scout ahead and clear landing zones before the transports arrived. The AH-1 also proved effective against the relatively rare appearance of NVA armoured vehicles, but a number were lost to SA-7s. The Cobra was the first attack helicopter and was adopted by the US Marines and many foreign users, including Israel and Japan.

Heavy-lift helicopters, such as the CH-47 Chinook and the CH-53 Sea Stallion (or 'Jolly Green Giant'), came into their own in Vietnam for roles such as setting up and supporting

*The Sikorsky CH-53 Sea Stallion saved many American airmen from the jungle during the war in Vietnam.*

remote bases, moving artillery and recovering downed Hueys. The Chinook was used briefly as a gunship and the CH-53 was widely used by the US Air Force for search-and-rescue missions for downed aircrews.

The full range of carrier-based airpower was employed in Vietnam, with the exception of nuclear weapons. That said, and despite US denials at the time, such weapons were aboard the

| SEPTEMBER | OCTOBER | **1973** JANUARY | APRIL | MAY | JUNE |
|---|---|---|---|---|---|
| **September** The Grumman F-14 begins to enter US Navy service. | **28 October** The A300, the first Airbus aircraft, takes to the air in France. | **18 January** The A-10 is announced as the winner of the competitive fly-off with the Northrop YA-9. | **16 April** The EMBRAER EMB-110 Bandeirante turboprop transport for the Brazilian Air Force flies. It goes on to be a successful commuter airliner. | **30 May** The first flight of the Polish WSK-Mielec M-15 Belphegor, the world's only jet-powered agricultural biplane. | **3 June** A Tu-144 breaks up in flight during the Paris Air Show, killing 14 people.  **4 June** The IAI Kfir, an unlicensed derivative of the Dassault Mirage III, flies in Israel. |

carriers operating on Yankee Station off the coast of North Vietnam and Dixie Station in the south.

Although the mix of aircraft varied by carrier type and date, light attack missions were flown by the A-1 Skyraider and A-4 Skyhawk, and later the A-7 Corsair II. Medium all-weather attack was the speciality of the A-6 Intruder, and the heavy attack mission was briefly carried out by the A-3 Skywarrior before the type was modified into tankers and electronic warfare platforms. Reconnaissance photography was mainly gathered by the RA-5C Vigilante. Early warning and control was the job of the E-1 Tracer and E-2 Hawkeye. Fleet defence and fighter escort was provided by the F-8 Crusader and the F-4 Phantom II. Various aircraft, including the A-4, A-6 and A-7, could refuel their brethren in flight using a 'buddy pod' system.

In addition to the guns and surface-to-air missiles arranged in ever increasing numbers around key targets, the North Vietnamese People's Air Force (VPAF) maintained a fleet of Soviet-designed fighters from the MiG family. In late 1964, it declared its first MiG-17 unit operational and during 1965 added supersonic MiG-21s. In 1969 came the formation of a unit

of Shenyang J-6s (Chinese-built MiG-19s). The VPAF fighter force never exceeded about 100 aircraft at a time, but gave its enemy considerable headaches, despite the much more sophisticated warplanes of the US Air Force, with its powerful radars and modern missiles. The MiG-17s and J-6s were armed with cannon only, and the MiG-21s with R-3S 'Atoll' missiles equivalent to the earliest model Sidewinders. The MiGs had the advantages of good manoeuvrability and small size, which made them hard to acquire visually and on radar.

The Americans were hindered by rules of engagement that required positive visual identification, which negated their radar-guided beyond-visual-range AIM-7 Sparrows. The AIM-9s were rear-aspect launch only, so US pilots had to position themselves behind the tighter-turning MiGs to be sure of a hit. The AIM-4 Falcon required a direct hit to be effective and scored only five kills during the war. The AIM-7 proved susceptible to damage from humidity and rough handling, particularly when repeatedly loaded and unloaded from aircraft. It had a high failure rate; problems of rocket motors failing to ignite and weapons failing to guide led to a kill

*The Grumman E-2 Hawkeye was the US Navy's main electronic surveillance aircraft in the 1991 Gulf War.*

probability of only about 10 per cent for each Sparrow fired. In 1969, the USAF adopted the Navy's missile, the AIM-9, and slowly improved its success rate, scoring seven kills in all.

In the skies over Vietnam, US pilots found themselves in turning dogfights, a form of combat that had been thought to belong to history. And many kills were missed for the want of a gun. The USAF and US Navy's main fighter, the F-4 Phantom II, had up to eight missiles, but no internal gun. USAF F-4Cs and Ds could carry an external 20mm (0.79in)

## 1973

### OCTOBER

**21 October** The Austrian Militky MBE1 becomes the first successful electric-powered piloted aeroplane.

**26 October** The Dassault-Breguet/Dornier Alpha Jet advanced jet trainer makes its first flight.

## 1974

### JANUARY

**20 January** The General Dynamics YF-16 lightweight fighter prototype flies.

### MAY

**23 May** The Airbus A300 begins passenger duty with Air France, flying its inaugural service from Paris to London.

### JUNE

**9 June** The YF-17, Northrop's contender for the USAF's light fighter contest, is flown.

### AUGUST

**14 August** The prototype Panavia Tornado IDS (Interdictor Strike) aircraft is flown in Germany.

cannon pod, but this was not really accurate enough for air-to-air shooting, although it did account for nine MiGs. The F-105, which was not really a fighter, was built with an internal gun, and knocked down 28 enemy fighters with gunfire and two or three with Sidewinders. The US Air Force remedied the Phantom's gun problems by developing the F-4E, which had a reprofiled nose containing a fixed M61 20mm (0.79in) Vulcan cannon. The F-4E flew in 1969, but did not score in Vietnam until 23 May 1972, the first of only five kills by this aircraft and weapons combination before the air war effectively ended in early 1973.

May 1972 saw one of the busiest periods of air combat of the whole war. On 10 May, the most furious air battles of the war were fought over Hanoi and Haiphong. The US Navy crew of Randall Cunningham and Willy Driscoll shot down three MiGs with AIM-9s from their F-4J, becoming the first US Navy aces of the war, and a USAF team of Richard S. Ritchie and Charles DeBellvue scored the first of an eventual five. In all, US crews claimed 12 victories this day and the North Vietnamese five. Other US losses included Cunningham and Driscoll's Phantom, which was brought down by a surface-to-air missile as it was returning to the USS *Constellation*, although the crew ejected and were rescued.

At one point during the war, the US Navy in particular was almost at parity with the VPAF, losing an average of almost one aircraft for every enemy one destroyed in aerial combat. This led to the establishment in March 1969 of the Naval Fighter Weapons School, commonly known as 'Top Gun'. This taught the skills of visual dogfighting, which had been lost due to

*An RF-4C Phantom flanked by a pair of F-15 Eagles from Kadena Air Base, Japan.*

**1975**

| SEPTEMBER | OCTOBER | NOVEMBER | DECEMBER | JANUARY |
|-----------|---------|----------|----------|---------|

**21 August** The first flight of the Hawker-Siddeley HS.1123 Hawk jet trainer, which serves with the RAF and is widely exported.

**1 September** Flying from Beale, California, to Farnborough, UK, an SR-71 Blackbird flies 5617km (3490 miles) in 1 hour 55 minutes.

**17 October** The Sikorsky YUH-60 helicopter, which is developed into many Blackhawk and Seahawk variants, is flown.

**28 October** France's carrier-based strike aircraft, the Dassault Super Étendard, makes its first flight.

**14 November** The US Air Force introduces the F-15A Eagle into service.

**23 December** The Rockwell B-1A swing-wing bomber prototype flies. The programme is cancelled in 1977, but revived in 1981 as the B-1B Lancer.

**14 January** The General Dynamics YF-16 is announced as the winner of the USAF Light Weight Fighter contest.

an emphasis on radar and long-range missile shooting. Selected US Navy fighter crews flew missions against smaller, more manoeuvrable aircraft such as stripped-down A-4s and F-5s, flown by instructors in the 'adversary' role. The return of Top Gun graduates (including Cunningham and Driscoll) to the combat zone helped the US Navy achieve a high kill ratio by the war's end.

During the Korean War, the USAF's Strategic Air Command (SAC) had deployed its biggest or newest bombers, such as the B-36 or B-47. In Vietnam, the B-52 was used in combat from June 1965. The prototype B-52 had flown in 1952 and the eight-engine bomber had become the mainstay of SAC, flying 24-hour airborne alerts armed with nuclear weapons, ready to retaliate against a Soviet first strike. In Vietnam, the B-52 was initially tasked with missions under the name 'Arc Light'. These were daylight bombing raids against suspected troop concentrations and jungle camps within South Vietnam. Although it was hard to judge the results of these sorties, which certainly destroyed large areas of forest, Viet Cong prisoners reportedly said that it was the only US aircraft they feared. B-52s dropped

their bombs from an altitude so high that they could not be seen, so there was no warning before their bombs exploded.

Urban targets were off limits to the B-52s until December 1972, when peace talks broke down and President Nixon ordered attacks on Hanoi and other industrial centres. In the Linebacker II campaign from 18–29 December, more than 700 sorties were flown and 136,000 tonnes (150,000 tons) of bombs dropped on

power stations, rail yards, airfields and other targets. By now, Hanoi was one of the most heavily defended cities in the world, and hundreds of surface-to-air missiles were fired at the B-52s, bringing down 12 of them during this period. Flying at night meant that the threat from the MiG was greatly reduced, but radar-equipped and ground-controlled MiG-21s shot down three B-52s. In turn, gunners on B-52s destroyed two MiG-21s. The bombing brought

*A Lockheed AC-130 'Spectre' gunship in action. The AC-130 was used to interdict the Ho Chi Minh Trail in Vietnam.*

## 1975

| FEBRUARY | | MARCH | JUNE | | AUGUST | SEPTEMBER |
|---|---|---|---|---|---|---|
| **1 February** A modified F-15 called the 'Streak Eagle' completes a run of time-to-height records by reaching 30,000m (98,425ft) in 3 minutes 27 seconds. | **22 February** Sukhoi's T-8-1, prototype of the Su-25 'Frogfoot' attack aircraft, flies. | **5 March** The Shin Meiwa US-1 patrol amphibian enters service with the Japanese Maritime Self-Defence Force. | **3 June** The Japanese Mitsubishi F-1 maritime attack aircraft is flown. | **22 June** Russian Svetlana Savitskaya sets a new women's speed record when she flies a Mikoyan Ye-133 (modified MiG-25) to 2683km/h (1667mph). | **28 August** The first Robinson R22 light two-seat helicopter flies. | **30 September** The Hughes YAH-64, prototype of the Apache attack helicopter, makes its first flight. |

the North Vietnamese back to the negotiating table, and a peace agreement was signed in January, beginning the final withdrawal of US combat forces from Vietnam.

*The B-52 was the mainstay of the West's airborne nuclear deterrent forces for three decades.*

## Transports and Tankers

No less important than bombers and fighters in modern war are the logistical support aircraft that bring 'bombs, beans and bullets' to the battlefield, supply fuel to keep fighters on patrol, and give bombers the means to reach and return to distant targets. The most successful postwar military transport has been the Lockheed C-130 Hercules, which first flew in 1954 and is still in production, in its revised C-130J form, more than 50 years later. The turboprop-powered 'Herc' has changed little in appearance in all this time, apart from the addition of a weather radar, eliminating the 'Roman nose' profile of the prototypes.

As well as being the USAF's standard tactical airlifter, able to operate from rough strips due to its strong undercarriage, the C-130 has been modified for search-and-rescue, weather reconnaissance, special forces duties, electronic intelligence, psychological warfare broadcasting, and a myriad of other special roles. The most warlike of these is the AC-130 'Spooky' gunship, armed with a battery of machine guns and even a 105mm (4.1in) cannon, as well as a variety of sensors for finding, tracking and destroying targets at night. Entering USAF service in the latter part of the Vietnam War, AC-130s have been used in almost all subsequent US military operations, from Grenada through Panama, Somalia, Afghanistan and both Iraq wars.

Nearly 70 air forces use the C-130 today, including those of Iran, an adversary of the United States since the 1979 Islamic Revolution, and Iraq, whose military aviation is slowly being rebuilt following the US-led invasion of 2003.

So far, more than 2200 C-130s have been built, with a few examples having served for more than 40 years with the same air forces and even the same squadrons.

## B-52

Already mentioned in the context of the Vietnam War, the Boeing B-52 Stratofortress became one of the symbols of the Cold War

---

### 1976

| DECEMBER | JANUARY | MARCH | APRIL | MAY | JULY | AUGUST |
|---|---|---|---|---|---|---|
| **26 December** The Tu-144 becomes the first supersonic commercial aircraft to enter service when it commences mail flights between Moscow and Alma Ata. | **21 January** Concordes of British Airways and Air France make flights to Bahrain and Rio de Janeiro, respectively, inaugurating the world's first supersonic passenger services. | **24 March** A Boeing 747SP flies nonstop from Everett, Washington, to Cape Town, South Africa, setting a distance record for a commercial aircraft of 16,560km (10,290 miles). | **1 April** Piper delivers its 100,000th aircraft. | **24 May** Transatlantic Concorde services are launched with flights from Paris and London to Washington Dulles International Airport. | **28 July** An SR-71 sets a new speed record of 3529km/h (2193mph). | **12 August** The first flight of the Italian Aermacchi MB-339 advanced jet trainer. |

years. Replacing the Convair B-36, which had six piston and four jet engines, and the Boeing B-47, with six jets in three underslung pods, the B-52 had eight jets in four pods. It was faster than the Convair and longer-ranged than its Boeing forebear.

The USAF's Strategic Air Command (SAC) stood up its first B-52 wing in 1955, armed initially with free-fall nuclear bombs and later with stand-off missiles such as Hound Dog and air-launched cruise missiles (ALCMs). Once the Soviet Forces had fielded their own strategic ballistic missiles, the great fear was that US bombers would be caught and destroyed on their airfields. As well as aircraft on ground alert, armed and ready to take off within minutes, the SAC maintained airborne alerts of bombers from the 1950s to mid-1960s, ready to attack from over the North Pole or Mediterranean on receipt of the correct war codes from SAC headquarters.

It was on one of these airborne alerts that a B-52 collided with a supporting KC-135

*The Dassault Mirage III was one of the great military success stories of the jet age.*

tanker over Palomares in southern Spain, scattering four nuclear bombs over land and sea. All were recovered, but one came very close to detonating, and radiation was dispersed over an area of countryside. After this incident in January 1966, SAC discontinued the armed airborne alerts.

A total of 744 B-52s was built in several versions. The B-52G was the most numerous, with 193 produced. It and the turbofan-powered B-52H were the versions retained throughout the 1970s and 1980s, with ever more sophisticated defensive and offensive electronics and countermeasures. The B-52s saw

| 1976 | | | | 1977 | |
|---|---|---|---|---|---|
| SEPTEMBER | OCTOBER | NOVEMBER | DECEMBER | MARCH | |
| **6 September** A Soviet pilot flying a MiG-25 'Foxbat' defects to Japan, providing an intelligence bonus to the West. | **1 October** A Thorp T-18 becomes the first homebuilt aircraft to circumnavigate the world, starting and ending at Oshkosh, Wisconsin. | **November** The Hawker-Siddeley Hawk T1 trainer enters service with the RAF. | **22 December** The USSR's first wide-body airliner, the Ilyushin Il-86, makes its first flight. | **24 March** The first E-3A AWACS (Airborne Warning and Control System) aircraft is delivered to the USAF. | **27 March** The largest loss of life to date in an air accident occurs when KLM and Pan Am 747s collide on the runway at Santa Cruz airport, Tenerife. |

*In 1956, the French Air Ministry issued a draft specification for a new supersonic bomber to carry France's first atomic bomb. The result was the Mirage IV.*

France left the military part of the NATO Alliance in stages from 1958 to 1966, but by then it was building its own jet fighters, transports and other aircraft. Pre-war designer Marcel Bloch changed his name to Dassault and set up a company under that name in 1947. The

*The Mirage F1 has equipped several air forces throughout the world, in addition to France's own.*

action over Iraq in 1991, shortly after which the G models were retired.

B-52s were to see further action over the Balkans, Iraq and Afghanistan, where they were used for close air support of friendly troops, a role that their designers could never have envisaged in the early 1950s. The B-52H continues in service with two wings of the USAF's Air Combat Command (which replaced SAC in 1991). With further upgrades and possibly new engines, it may stay in service as late as 2040, by which time the individual aircraft will be 80 years old.

## France

While most NATO nations were soon equipped with mostly US-designed combat aircraft, France rebuilt its air force and naval air arm by initially continuing production of some German aircraft that had been produced for the Nazi occupiers. It then licensed the building of some aircraft such as de Havilland Vampires to serve alongside American types such as the F-86.

| MAY | JUNE | AUGUST | | SEPTEMBER | DECEMBER |
|---|---|---|---|---|---|
| **17 May** The Sukhoi T-10, prototype of the Sukhoi Su-27 'Flanker', is flown in Russia. | **10 June** The A-10 Thunderbolt II begins service with the USAF. | **13 August** The first gliding test of the Space Shuttle Orbiter *Enterprise*, dropped from a modified 747. | **23 August** The MacCready *Gossamer Condor* is the first human-powered aircraft to demonstrate sustained controlled flight.<br><br>**31 August** A MiG-25 is flown to a record altitude for a non-rocket craft of 37,650m (123,534ft). | **26 September** Entrepreneur Freddie Laker introduces his low-cost 'Skytrain' service on the London–New York route. | **14 December** The Mil Mi-26 'Halo' flies. It is the world's heaviest helicopter and the largest single-rotor helicopter. |

This was a supersonic radar-equipped fighter armed with air-to-air missiles and cannon. It was widely exported and saw combat with Israel, Argentina and Pakistan.

The Mirage IV was a nuclear bomber, essentially the Mirage III design doubled in size. It lacked the range to hit most important targets in the Soviet Union and return to base, so its role was dubbed 'pre-strategic', meaning that it would bomb Soviet forces as they crossed into West Germany in the event of all-out war. The addition of the ASMP cruise missile gave extra reach to the Mirage IV late in its career, which began in 1960 with the Armée de l'Air. When it finally retired in 2005, the remaining aircraft were serving only in the reconnaissance role. Like the previous Dassault fighters, the Mirage F1 was a popular export; however, uniquely among production Mirage models, it was not a delta-wing design.

The Mirage 2000 first flew in 1978 and bore a superficial resemblance to the Mirage III, but offered fly-by-wire controls, a sophisticated multi-mode radar and Mach 2 performance. The Étendard and Super Étendard carrier-based attack aircraft were designed for the French

*The Mirage 2000, the first of the Mirage family to take advantage of fly-by-wire technology, was designed as an interceptor to replace the Mirage F1. The first single-seater flew for the first time at Istres on 10 March 1978.*

French aircraft industry was mainly organized in regional groups, but Dassault eventually came to dominate the manufacture of fixed-wing aircraft in France, building fighters, bombers, airliners and executive aircraft. Its first aircraft were the straight-winged Ouragan of 1951 and several varieties of swept-wing Mystère, both of which saw action with Israel, as well as extensive French service.

Dassault achieved true international success with the Mirage series of tailless deltas. The first production model was the Mirage III of 1956.

## 1978

**JANUARY**

**26 January** The naval version of the Westland Lynx begins service with the UK Fleet Air Arm.

**MARCH**

**3 March** The prototype of the Dassault Mirage 2000 fighter flies.

**MAY**

**5 May** The US airline industry is deregulated.

**9 May** The first crossing of the English Channel in a powered hang-glider is achieved.

**20 May** The 5000th McDonnell Douglas F-4 Phantom II is delivered.

**JUNE**

**1 June** The Tu-144 flies its last service, having been retired for economic and safety reasons.

**28 June** The Dassault Super Étendard enters service with the Aéronavale.

*The Dassault Étendard was originally designed to meet the needs of a mid-1950s tactical strike fighter.*

naval air arm, or Aéronavale. Both saw combat over Lebanon and the Balkans in the 1980s and 1990s with France, while the 'Super E' fought with Argentina in 1982 and Iraq during the Iran–Iraq War.

Dassault's combat aircraft were popular with countries that could not afford US equipment or

*The Dassault Super Étendard was intended for the low-level attack role, primarily against shipping.*

| JULY | AUGUST | SEPTEMBER | NOVEMBER |
|---|---|---|---|
| **1–19 July** Two Beech Bonanzas make the first round-the-world flight in formation. | **20 August** The BAe Sea Harrier enters service with the UK Fleet Air Arm. | **3 September** An Air Rhodesia Viscount is shot down by a hand-held Sa-7 surface-to-air missile, the first confirmed instance of a portable SAM destroying an airliner. | **8 November** The Canadair CL-600, first of the Challenger business aircraft series, flies. |
| | **12 August** The Pilatus PC-7 turboprop trainer flies in Switzerland. | **13 September** The first flight of the Aérospatiale Super Puma. | **18 November** The first pre-production McDonnell Douglas F/A-18 Hornet flies. The design is derived from the YF-17 Cobra. |

*The Saab Lansen equipped seven fighter-bomber squadrons at its peak, and served in many other roles, including target tug and trials aircraft, well into the 1990s.*

*At the time of its service debut, the Saab J-35 Draken was a component of the finest fully integrated air defence system in western Europe.*

which were subject to arms sanctions or which wished to mix Western and Soviet equipment for political reasons. On occasion, notably with Iraq and Argentina, they wound up fighting against NATO nations.

## Sweden

Neutral Sweden was another nation that adopted a policy of supplying its military with indigenous equipment. This policy began during World War II, when fighting raged in neighbouring countries and foreign aircraft frequently violated Swedish airspace. Given its neutral status, Sweden could not acquire replacements for its pre-war American, British, Italian and German aircraft. The state aircraft company SAAB therefore built the B 17, a dive bomber influenced by the Curtiss SB2C Helldiver and the twin-engine B 18 level bomber. The J 21 was SAAB's first fighter, of unusual twin-boomed configuration with a pusher propeller and one of the first ejection seats.

After the war, the J 21R was developed, with a jet engine in the rear. The J 29 was a swept-wing jet, only the third such design in the world when it flew in 1948. Its shape led to the nickname 'flying barrel' and it saw action in the ground-attack role during UN operations in the Congo in the early 1960s. More than 660 were built, with a few sold to Austria.

| 1978 | 1979 | | | | | |
|---|---|---|---|---|---|---|
| DECEMBER | JANUARY | FEBRUARY | APRIL | MAY | JUNE | |
| **29 December** In Britain, Freddie To makes the first flight of the *Solar One*, the first solar-powered aircraft. | **6 January** Delivery of the first General Dynamics F-16A to the USAF. | **27 February** The last of 2960 A-4 Skyhawks are delivered, ending a record production run of 26 years. | **20 April** The last of 16 production Concordes makes its first flight. | **25 May** An American Airlines DC-10 crashes at Chicago, killing 273 people. Shortly afterwards, all DC-10s are grounded for safety checks, severely affecting many airlines. | **12 June** The MacCready *Gossamer Albatross* becomes the first human-powered aircraft to cross the English Channel, winning a £100,000 prize. | **27 June** The F-15 Eagle sees its first combat use. Israeli F-15s shoot down five Syrian MiG-21s. |

The next indigenous fighter was the J 32 Lansen (Lance), which was much larger and in some ways similar to the Hawker Hunter, although it had an afterburning engine and was mainly built as a two-seat attack aircraft. In 1955, Saab introduced the J 35 Draken (Dragon), with a 'double delta' wing planform and supersonic performance. Swedish arms sales policies of the time meant that Saab did not actively seek export customers, but the Draken was sold to Denmark, Finland and Austria. The Austrian Drakens remained in service until 2005, when replaced by Northrop F-5Es, pending delivery of Eurofighter Typhoons.

Continuing the company's tradition of innovative designs was the Saab 37 Viggen (Thunderbolt), built in several versions for air combat, attack and reconnaissance. First flying in 1967, the Viggen was the first production jet with canard foreplanes. Among other advantages, this helped to give a very short takeoff and landing run, which suited Sweden's strategy of dispersing operations to 'bare bases' and strips of prepared highway. It was supersonic at both high and low level, and carried a range of air-to-air or anti-shipping

*The Saab 37 Viggen (Thunderbolt) was designed to carry out the four roles of attack, interception, reconnaissance and training. The first of seven prototypes flew for the first time on 8 February 1967.*

missiles. The Viggen was the backbone of the Swedish Air Force (Flygvapnet) throughout the 1970s and 1980s, until it was gradually replaced by the smaller Gripen.

The Cold War came to a close from 1989–1991, when the Soviet Union lost its grip on its client states in Eastern Europe and eventually itself. Many aircraft and aircraft types were soon retired as tensions eased, but warplanes built in those years, or designed for missions that will now never be flown, are still in widespread service around the world.

## JULY

**13 July** The grounding order on the DC-10 is lifted.

**24 July** The Bell XV-15 experimental tilt-rotor is flown.

**24 July** A NASA KC-135 is test flown with winglets, which reduce drag and improve fuel efficiency.

## AUGUST

**14 August** A new piston-engined air speed record of 803km/h (499mph) is set by Steve Hinton in the modified P-51 Mustang Red Baron.

## DECEMBER

**2 December** The Gruman Gulfstream III flies. The GIII begins the trend of drag-reducing winglets on business aircraft.

**12 December** The Sikorsky SH-60 Seahawk anti-submarine helicopter is flown.

# Superfighters and Giants

*The past 25 years have seen many changes in aviation markets. The number of major civil planemakers has declined as several of the former industry giants have merged or have withdrawn from the civil marketplace. Others are hanging on, but have failed to sell large numbers of their recent designs.*

In the past decade, the main sales battle has been between Boeing and Airbus. On annual sales figures, the two aerospace giants are now about even, but competition for new customers is fierce. A rare new entrant in the in the field has been Brazil's Embraer, founded in 1969 but entering the jet airliner market in the 1990s with a series of regional jets. The present 'E-Jets' series (EMB-170, -175, -190 and -195) now rivals the dominant Boeing 737 and Airbus A320 families.

*Left: A Boeing 747 of KLM, the Royal Dutch Airline, lifts away from an airport in the Far East. Right: This photograph shows the relative sizes of the Boeing 747 and its predecessor, the Boeing 707.*

New technologies have increased the power and fuel efficiency of jet engines, which on large commercial aircraft are invariably high-bypass turbofans. These have a large front fan that directs most of the airflow around, rather than through, the central core. They are quieter and less polluting than the turbojets or low-bypass turbofans that are used on first-generation jetliners and on

*The largest transport aircraft in the world at the time of its appearance, the Lockheed C-5A Galaxy was first flown on 30 June 1968.*

35 years has been the Boeing 747. The 'Jumbo Jet' revolutionized air transport by lowering seat-mile costs and allowing airliners to use business and first class to subsidize economy- or tourist-class fares, meaning that many people were able to experience international air travel. The 747 had its origins in a USAF Military Airlift Command requirement for a new airlifter to supplement the Lockheed C-141 Starlifter.

The C-141 first flew in 1963 and was the first military jet transport designed and built as such from the start. Although faster and longer-ranged than its predecessors, it could not lift the outsize loads of aircraft such as the piston-engined C-124 Globemaster.

Lockheed, Boeing and Douglas all submitted bids for the 1964 CX-HLS (Cargo Experimental-Heavy Logistics System) for a much larger jet airlifter – in fact, the winner would be the largest aircraft in the world. Boeing's design was deemed the most aerodynamically efficient of the three, but the contract was awarded to Lockheed in 1965. The resultant C-5 Galaxy became the first production aircraft with high-bypass turbofans, an innovation that was to have a big impact on the 747 and all subsequent jetliners. Boeing did not waste the work it had done on the CX-HLS, and Pan Am became interested in a super-large airliner based on some of ideas that had been developed on the airlifter. Pan Am had previously called for a stretched 707 able to carry 520 passengers, but this was taking the design beyond its practical limits.

In March 1965, Boeing decided to launch the 747 programme. Its aim was to create an all-new 'wide-body' with more than a single aisle in the cabin and, at 366 passengers, a greater capacity than any previous airliner. In April 1966, Pan Am made a launch order for 25 aircraft at $525 million – at the time, the

most combat aircraft. The increased thrust and better fuel economy has allowed twin-engine aircraft to take over many routes that were once the preserve of three- and four-engine airliners.

The most significant airliner of the past

## 1980

| MARCH | JULY | AUGUST | NOVEMBER | DECEMBER |
|-------|------|--------|----------|----------|
| **12–14 March** A pair of B-52s makes a nonstop circumnavigation of the world, taking 42 hours 30 minutes. | **12 July** The KC-10 Extender, an aerial refuelling derivative of the McDonnell Douglas DC-10, flies. | **7 August** Janice Brown pilots Paul MacCready's *Gossamer Penguin*, the first solar-powered aircraft without battery-stored energy, in a 15-minute test flight in California.  **16 August** The first flight of the EMBRAER Tucano turboprop trainer. | **9 November** The last passenger flight of the de Havilland Comet when a Dan-Air Comet 4C makes a flight for enthusiasts.  **13 November** Service entry of the F/A-18 Hornet with the US Navy. | **6 December** The MacCready *Solar Challenger* makes a flight of 29km (18 miles). |

largest value order ever made. A new factory north of Seattle had to be built at a cost of $200 million. This was a huge gamble for both airline and manufacturer at a time when supersonic airliners seemed to be the next coming thing. Boeing's competitors did not believe that such a high-capacity airliner was justified at the time, and failed to develop rival designs. Boeing hedged its bets by ensuring that the 747 was easily convertible to a freighter if the passenger market failed to meet expectations.

The company studied a double-deck design, but the requirement to evacuate all passengers in an emergency proved too difficult to meet. The cockpit was mounted above the main cabin to allow an uninterrupted floor and hinged nose for freight. The roofline of a high-mounted cockpit required fairing back to the main spine, and consideration was given to using the space behind the pilots to house air-conditioning systems and other machinery. In fact, it was used initially for lounges and bars, but more often as first- or business-class seating.

The first 747 was rolled out in September 1968, and flown in February 1969. There were problems with the Pratt & Whitney engines throughout the test programme, and many replacement engines were required. Even after 747 services began in January 1970, the delivery of reliable engines was delayed, and completed airframes waited at the factory with concrete weights on their pylons. For this and other reasons, including a general economic recession, the programme itself was delayed. The company was in crisis and had to lay off a large part of its workforce, having built up debts of $1 billion. The cutbacks helped the financial position, the engine situation improved, and soon alternatives from General Electric and Rolls-Royce were offered for the 747. Orders for 747s from US and foreign airlines grew, reaching 150 in 1970.

*The Boeing 747 has been an important asset to QANTAS, the Australian airline. The introduction of the Boeing 747, with its high capacity and very long range, enabled the airline to drop some routes between Australia and Europe.*

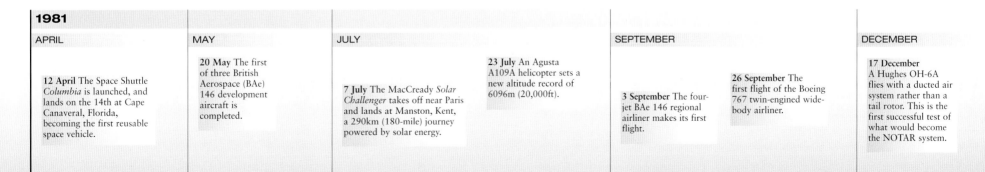

**1981**

| APRIL | MAY | JULY | | SEPTEMBER | DECEMBER |
|---|---|---|---|---|---|
| **12 April** The Space Shuttle *Columbia* is launched, and lands on the 14th at Cape Canaveral, Florida, becoming the first reusable space vehicle. | **20 May** The first of three British Aerospace (BAe) 146 development aircraft is completed. | **7 July** The MacCready *Solar Challenger* takes off near Paris and lands at Manston, Kent, a 290km (180-mile) journey powered by solar energy. | **23 July** An Agusta A109A helicopter sets a new altitude record of 6096m (20,000ft). | **3 September** The four-jet BAe 146 regional airliner makes its first flight.  **26 September** The first flight of the Boeing 767 twin-engined wide-body airliner. | **17 December** A Hughes OH-6A flies with a ducted air system rather than a tail rotor. This is the first successful test of what would become the NOTAR system. |

*Stretching the upper deck of the 747 produced the 747-300, adding more seats and improving aerodynamics.*

*Four 747-200s were bought by the US Air Force to serve as National Emergency Airborne Command Posts for the US president and his battle staff in the event of a nuclear attack.*

By the early 1980s, the 747 was well established around the world. The 500th example built was delivered to Scandinavian Airlines System (SAS) in 1981. Almost all the national flag-carriers operated 747s at one time or another. And for many years, Australia's QANTAS billed itself as 'the world's only all-747 airline'. A short fuselage, long-range version, the 747SP, was also introduced, and was used by QANTAS, South African Air Lines, United Air Lines and a few other operators.

In 1983, the first major redesign of the basic 747 appeared as the 747-300. Its extended 'hump', which was 7m (23ft) longer, meant that it was initially marketed as the 747 SUD (Stretched Upper Deck). Then the point was made that this abbreviation was used in hospitals for 'Sudden Unexplained Death'. A change to EUD, for Extended Upper Deck, was not widely used either, and the -300 was only a moderate success. It led, however, to the 747-400, which has become the standard 'Jumbo' since its introduction in 1989. The -400 has the larger upper deck, but also a revised wing, with 1.8m (6ft) high drag-reducing winglets on the tips. These and new technology engines helped to give the 747-400 the longest range of any airliner to that time, and this new performance allowed airlines to cut out refuelling stops on the longest routes – bad news for some cities and, in particular, some Pacific islands. The -400

| 1982 | | | | | 1983 |
|---|---|---|---|---|---|
| FEBRUARY | APRIL | AUGUST | SEPTEMBER | DECEMBER | JANUARY |

**4 February** A Mil Mi-26 helicopter lifts a record 20,000kg (44,092lb) to 4600m (15,092ft), one of a series of weight-lifting records set at this time.

**19 February** First flight of the Boeing 757 narrow-body twin-jet airliner.

**20 April** A converted Victor tanker makes the longest ever operational reconnaissance mission, flying for 14 hours 45 minutes from Ascension Island to search for Argentine forces near South Georgia.

**30 April–1 May** An RAF Vulcan bombs Port Stanley Airport on the Falkland Islands in the longest bombing mission flown to date, taking 15 hours 45 minutes.

**19 August** The first Boeing 767 is delivered to United Airlines.

**30 September** The first round-the-world helicopter flight is completed in a Bell Model 206L LongRanger II flown by H. Ross Perot Jr. and J.W. Coburn.

**26 December** The An-124 'Condor' becomes the largest aircraft in the world.

**1 January** The Boeing 757 enters service with Eastern Airlines.

could accommodate 416 to 524 passengers – again, a record – apart from some SR (short-range) versions used on internal flights in Japan, which had up to 550 seats. The loss of one of these in an August 1985 crash cost 520 lives, the worst airline accident involving a single aircraft.

### European Rival

In 1965, when the decision was taken to proceed with the 747, other moves were afoot that would change the airline industry. At the time, the most significant seemed to be the development of supersonic transport (SST) designs – by both the main US manufacturers and an Anglo-French partnership. It was easy enough to overlook the formation of the Airbus Study Group, a collection of German aircraft makers that soon grew into a consortium of German, French and British companies. At the 1969 Paris Air Show, an agreement was signed by the French and German governments and the main manufacturers to create a wide-body twinjet to be called the Airbus A300B. The specifications were tailored to the US domestic market as a higher-capacity 727 replacement. Airbus Industrie was set up in December 1970 and the

first A300B1 was ready for flight in late October 1972. By this point, the British government had pulled out, but Hawker Siddeley stayed on to design and build the wings. This they would continue to do for all subsequent Airbus jets, first as British Aerospace, then as BAE Systems.

The A300 entered commercial service with Air France in 1974. At first, Air France and Lufthansa took the bulk of production, partly for political reasons. The issue of government support at the start-up of Airbus was not controversial at the time, when there were three major American airliner manufacturers. In recent times, though, Airbus and Boeing (and to a much lesser extent, Ilyushin) have become the only players in the wide-body market, meaning that subsidies for Airbus have become a major political issue between the United States and Europe.

*The Airbus has been a huge success story, and much of it has been due to the short-haul A300. It is estimated that an Airbus-built airliner takes off somewhere in the world every 20 seconds.*

| MARCH | JUNE | JULY | AUGUST | SEPTEMBER | NOVEMBER | **1984** JANUARY |
|---|---|---|---|---|---|---|
| **29 March** The first Airbus A310s are delivered to Swissair and Lufthansa. | **20 June** The de Havilland Canada DHC-8 (Dash 8) airliner makes its maiden flight. | **22 July** Australian Dick Smith completes the first solo helicopter flight around the world, in a Bell Jet Ranger. | **29 August** The Beech Starship I prototype flies. It is one of the first aircraft to be constructed almost entirely of composite (carbon fibre). | **11 September** The first flight of the Agusta A129 Mangusta attack helicopter in Italy. **15 September** The F-117A, which remains secret, reaches operational status with the USAF. | **11 November** The Spanish-Indonesian CASA-IPTN CN-235 military transport/airliner prototype flies. | **12 January** The US Marine Corps receives its first McDonnell Douglas/British Aerospace (BAe) AV8B Harrier II. |

A300s did gain Airbus a significant toehold in the US domestic market with sales to Eastern, Continental and American Air Lines. The A300 proved more fuel-efficient than the tri-jet TriStars and DC-10s then in service, an important consideration following the oil crises that began in 1973. They also proved popular with Asian airlines, including Air India and Thai International. At the time, US rules prevented long flights over water by twin-engine aircraft because the failure of one engine could lead to a ditching due to the high fuel consumption of the remaining powerplant. In Asia, these rules did not apply, and the A300 was popular on routes over the Bay of Bengal. More than 850 A300s have been built, including many freighter models, for the likes of freight operators Federal Express and UPS.

The success of the A300 inspired Boeing to build its own wide-body twins, beginning with the 767. At the same time, it developed the 757, mainly for domestic routes, with the same cabin diameter of the 707, 727 and 737. The first model of the 767, the -200 entered service with United Air Lines in 1982, and was followed by the -200ER (Extended Range) and the stretched -300 and -400 models.

*An Airbus A300-600F in the colours of UPS, the United Parcel Service. The A300-600 development of the earlier A300B4 incorporated a number of improvements.*

*The Boeing 757 was developed as a successor to the very successful 727. The 757 had little in common with its predecessor, but kept the Boeing sales challenge alive.*

| 1984 | | | | | 1985 | 1986 |
|---|---|---|---|---|---|---|
| FEBRUARY | MAY | JULY | AUGUST | DECEMBER | JULY | JANUARY |
| **22 February** The first Airbus A320, the first airliner with 'fly-by-wire' controls, is flown. | **12 May** The Airbus A310 enters commercial service with Air France. | **2 July** The Armée de l'Air declares the Mirage 2000 operational. | **16 August** Franco-Italian company Avion de Transport Régional flies the ATR-42 50-seat turboprop airliner. | **14 December** The Grumman X-29 flies. Using new composite materials allows supersonic flight with forward-swept wings. | **29 July** The Kawasaki XT-4, prototype jet trainer for the Japanese Air Self Defence Force, is flown. | **28 January** The space shuttle *Challenger* explodes shortly after takeoff, killing the crew of seven. |

The 767 forced the issue of long-range operations by twin-engine aircraft over oceans, desert and polar regions. A stringent set of standards was established under the acronym ETOPS (Extended-range Twin-engine Operational Performance Standards). Essentially, the old requirement that twin-engine aircraft never fly further than 60 minutes from a suitable diversion airport was replaced by rules that allowed newer jets to fly 90 minutes, then 120 minutes, from a diversion field at cruising speed on a single engine. This allowed for a worst-case scenario of an engine failure two hours from an airport and a diversion at the lower altitudes and higher fuel consumption caused while flying on one engine. This allowed more direct routes to be flown without doglegs to stay within range of diversion airports. Each airline must satisfy the authorities that each of its twin-engine types (including subtypes with different engines) can always reach safety in the event of engine failure. If diversion airports are closed or restricted due to weather, the route must change to stay within ETOPS limits.

Many millions of hours of operation have proved that modern high-bypass engines have an extremely low in-flight shut-down or failure

*The Airbus A310 has achieved excellent sales, mainly thanks to its excellent economy and range performance. The design incorporates numerous high-lift devices.*

rate, but it does happen. Airlines and aircraft makers are powerful lobbyists and have achieved ETOPS extensions for particular routes of 180 minutes, even 207 minutes. Although no modern airliner has crashed because it ran out of fuel too far away to reach a safe airfield, many safety experts are wary of extending ETOPS further or allowing operations without limits.

## Baby Buses

Airbus followed up the A300 with the shorter A310, then the narrow-body A320 series, which has grown to include the A318, A319 and A321. These differ mainly in passenger capacity. The A320 series was the first to offer fly-by-wire control systems, where there is no direct mechanical connection, hydraulically boosted or

*The A318, also known as the 'Mini-Airbus', is the smallest member of the A320 family. During development, it was known as the A319M3, indicating its history as a direct derivative of the A319.*

training. The same philosophy was used for the next series of Airbus jets, the A330 twinjet and the four-engine A340, which were developed simultaneously and flew in 1992 and 1991, respectively. The A330 was designed to compete with the 767 on ETOPS routes across the North Atlantic and Pacific. Its cockpit is basically the same as the A320 and the fuselage diameter is inherited from the A300. The A340 is a four-engine version of the same design, and as such is immune from ETOPS regulations, so it has proved popular on longer over-water routes.

*The A321 is a lengthened version of the A320.*

otherwise, between the pilots and the control surfaces. A flight control system (FCS) computer interprets control inputs and transfers them to the moveable surfaces on the wings and tail. The A320 also replaced the traditional control yoke with a side-stick controller.

Commonality between versions is an important part of the Airbus system. A pilot qualified to fly the A320 can fly the others in the series with only a minimum of extra

*The Airbus A340 has four engines and is long-ranged.*

## 1987

### MARCH

**9 March** The Yakovlev Yak-141 VTOL aircraft flies. Two prototypes are tested, but the type does not enter production.

### APRIL

**April** The Tu-160 'Blackjack' supersonic swing-wing bomber enters service with the Russian air force.

### MAY

**29 May** A young German pilot lands a Cessna 172 light aircraft in Moscow's Red Square. The head of the USSR's air defence forces is sacked.

### OCTOBER

**9 October** European Helicopter Industries (EHI), a collaboration between the UK's Westland and Italy's Agusta, flies the prototype EH101.

## 1988

### FEBRUARY

**29 February** A Gulfstream GIV flies eastbound from Houston to Houston to set a round-the-world record of 36 hours 8 minutes.

### APRIL

**15 April** A Tu-154, modified as the Tu-155, is the first aircraft powered by liquid hydrogen–fuelled engines.

**28 April** Air France accepts the first A320s to enter service.

**29 April** The largest member of the Boeing 747 series, the 747-400, makes its first flight.

### 777

Boeing's counter to the A330 and 340 was the 777. Although resembling a scaled-up 767, it had an all-new design with a much wider fuselage and the first fly-by-wire system on a Boeing airliner. The 777 was the first commercial aircraft designed entirely by computer-aided design (CAD) software, without using any conventional paper drawings. The 777 made extensive use of non-metallic composite materials such as carbon fibre, which comprised nearly 10 per cent of airframe weight.

The engines on the 777 are the largest and most powerful turbofans ever fitted to a commercial airliner. The General Electric GE-90-115s fitted to the 777-300ER version have a front fan with a diameter of 3.3m (128in) and can put out 513kN (115,300lb) of thrust.

The first 777 flew in June 1994 and the type has been sold in large numbers to airlines such as United, British Airways, Japan Air Lines and Emirates. Many have used it to replace the 747 on routes that do not require the full capacity of the 'Jumbo'.

### Boeing vs Airbus

By the late 1990s, the product lines of the two major remaining airliner constructors were roughly equivalent. The various 737 models competed with the A320 and its relatives; the 767 and 757 matched the A300 and A310; and the larger 767s and the 777 shared the market with the A330 and A340. Since then, the two companies' market philosophies have diverged.

The Airbus range lacked only a competitor for the 747, a design more than 30 years old. In 1994, the first studies began into a super-large airliner. Initially called the A3XX, but renamed the A380 in 2000, the design emerged with a full upper deck.

Boeing made studies into larger, modernized 747s under the designation 747X, but abandoned them at the point when Airbus had 66 A380 orders and it had none. It had already

*The Boeing 777, seen here in the livery of United Airlines, was the first commercial aircraft in the world to be designed entirely by computer.*

Relaxation in ETOPS rules have favoured the A330 and other twins, hurting A340 sales. Later models of the A340, such as the A340-500, currently fly the longest scheduled routes in the world, including Singapore Airlines's Newark–Singapore service, an 18-hour nonstop flight, covering 15,345km (9535 miles). Although an A340-500 can carry 313 passengers, the extremely long-range services are flown with a 181-passenger layout.

**1989**

**NOVEMBER**

**15 November** The Soviet space shuttle *Buran* (snowstorm) makes its one-and-only unmanned flight.

**22 November** The first B-2 bomber is revealed, some months before its first flight.

**DECEMBER**

**9 December** The first Saab JAS 39 Gripen is flown in Sweden. It is lost in an accident in March 1989.

**21 December** The Antonov An-225 'Cossack' heavy freighter flies in the Ukraine. It is the heaviest aircraft ever to fly.

**JANUARY**

**2 January** The first flight of the Tupolev Tu-204 twin-engined airliner with fly-by-wire control system.

**FEBRUARY**

**9 February** The Boeing 747-400 enters service with Northwest Airlines.

*The Boeing Sonic Cruiser project was abandoned by December 2002, in favour of the slower but fuel-efficient Boeing 787 Dreamliner. However, much of the research from the Sonic Cruiser was applied to the 787.*

announced the beginning of development on the Sonic Cruiser, a long-range airliner with up to 300 seats and the ability to cruise close to the speed of sound at up to Mach 0.98. (A 777 cruises at about Mach 0.82.) This signalled the beginning of a major divergence in philosophy between the two major planemakers.

Boeing's new rationale was that passengers wanted to fly point-to-point between cities, rather than travelling to a national capital or regional hub, flying to a second hub, then taking another aircraft to the final destination. The Sonic Cruiser was a radical design compared to every other subsonic airliner since the DC-3: its wing was at the rear, joined to the forward fuselage by a long, highly swept section. The engines were buried in the wing with the intakes on the underside. A canard foreplane was mounted behind the cockpit.

The Sonic Cruiser attracted a lot of attention, but there were doubts that it could reach its stated performance targets, which were revised several times. Its speed advantage over conventional types could be realized only if it climbed and descended to and from cruising altitude much faster. In the end, not enough

## 1989

### MARCH

**19 March** The first example of the V-22 Osprey tilt-rotor flies. It makes its first transition from vertical to forward flight in September.

**22 March** Carrying the *Buran* orbiter on its back, the An-225 sets a series of records, including a maximum takeoff weight of 508,200kg (1,129,370lb).

### MAY

**28 May** The AIDC Ching-Kuo, Taiwan's indigenous fighter (IDF), flies. A total of 130 is eventually built.

### JULY

**17 July** The Northrop B-2 Spirit 'Stealth Bomber' makes its first flight from Palmdale to Edwards AFB, California. At $2.25 billion each, the production B-2 is the most expensive aircraft ever built.

### AUGUST

**18 August** A QANTAS Airways Boeing 747-400 makes the first unrefuelled nonstop UK–Australia flight, taking 19 hours 10 minutes.

## 1990

### JANUARY

**2 January** The first flight of the South African Atlas XH-2 attack helicopter, which enters service as the Atlas Rooivalk.

**10 January** The MD-11, a much-improved derivative of the DC-10, makes its maiden flight at Long Beach.

*The Airbus A380 is an ambitious project and has attracted much airline interest.*

*The A380's upper deck extends along the entire length of the fuselage. This allows for a spacious cabin with 50 per cent more floor space than the next largest airliner, providing seating for 555 people in standard three-class configuration.*

airlines showed an interest and the project was cancelled, soon to be replaced by a more conventional design, featuring some of the new technology planned for the Sonic Cruiser.

The A380 prototype was unveiled in January 2005 and made its first flight on 27 April of that year. The first version, the A380-800, has a capacity of 555 seats and is 73m (240ft) long with a 79.8m (262ft) wingspan. By comparison, a 747-400 is 70m (230ft) by 66.4m (218ft). Future A380 versions will be stretched to take 656 passengers initially, then up to 800. The advantage of the double-deck layout is that stretching the fuselage gives twice as many

additional seats for the same overall length. This is particularly important given that Airbus and the major airport authorities have agreed that the A380 and its future variants should be able to fit within a 'box' 80m (262ft) square to allow for loading, unloading and servicing without major reconstruction of existing

terminals. As it is, the arrival of the A380 has required modifications at many airports, notably to terminal gates, air bridges and taxiways.

The A380's weight (up to 620 tonnes/ 683 tons) fully loaded is spread over a 20-wheel undercarriage, but the wider track puts more load outboard onto some areas such as the

| MARCH | APRIL | AUGUST | SEPTEMBER | OCTOBER | **1991** |
|---|---|---|---|---|---|
| | | | | | APRIL |
| **29 March** The Ilyushin Il-114 64-passenger twin turboprop airliner makes its maiden flight. | **13 April** First flight of the Sukhoi Su-27IB prototype, a side-by-side seating trainer/attack variant of the Su-27 fighter. | **23 August** The first of two VC-25A 'Air Force One' presidential transports based on the 747-200 are delivered.<br><br>**27 August** The Northrop/McDonnell Douglas YF-23 flies. It is a contender for the USAF's ATF (Advanced Tactical Fighter) contest. | **29 September** The Lockheed/Boeing/General Dynamics YF-22 is flown. It is written off in an accident in April 1992. | **11 October** The Rockwell/MBB X-31, a super-manoeuvrable aircraft with thrust-vectoring control, is flown. | April The Lockheed/Boeing F-22 is announced the winner of the competition for the USAF's new 'Air Dominance' fighter.<br><br>**27 April** First flight of the Eurocopter Tiger combat helicopter, designed to French and German army requirements. |

*The Boeing 7E7 Dreamliner is a wide body, twin engine passenger airliner currently under development.*

fillets where taxiways turn on and off runways, and these have needed enlarging or strengthening at many airports.

The A380 also requires revised air traffic procedures because of the wake vortexes generated at its wingtips. These swirls of air have the power to flip over lighter following aircraft. Test flying has proved that smaller jets should stay a minimum of several miles behind an A380 for safety.

Airbus set a break-even point of 250 orders for the A380. Initial interest came from established long-haul operators such as Singapore Airlines and QANTAS, but also from relative newcomers in the Middle East and Asia such as the UAE's Emirates, Abu Dhabi's Etihad, and India's Kingfisher. The only American customers to date are freight operators such as FedEx.

The size and complexity of the A380, particularly the vast amount of wiring needed to power the aircraft's functions and the in-flight entertainment systems for every seat, caused production delays, and deliveries to the first operator slipped by several months. The A380 has many critics, particularly from the United States, where slow sales and technical problems feed the belief that the A380 is a 'white elephant'. Few have memories long enough to recall the early days of Boeing's 747 programme, when problems came close to sinking the company.

### 7E7 to 787

The work done on the Sonic Cruiser was not wasted. Boeing still believed in the point-to-point philosophy versus hub-and-spoke operations. A new twin-engine design was revealed in April 2004 as the 7E7, with E standing for efficiency. This had an elegant tapered wing, a long nose and a highly swept 'shark's fin' vertical tail. The design incorporates an unprecedented amount of composite construction, including entire fuselage sections. In all, the 787 will incorporate 50 per cent composites by weight and 80 per cent by volume.

Large parts of the airframe will be built outside the United States, including in Japan and Italy, and will then be transported by air for final assembly in Seattle. To this end, Boeing has created four Large Commercial Freighters (LCF), which are 747s fitted with an outsize, unpressurized centre section for carrying parts of the 787 from the foreign factories to the final assembly line. Airbus Industrie uses a modified A300 named the Beluga for similar purposes.

A year after it was announced, the 787 design was frozen, and by now had lost its shark's fin and pointed nose, although its wing design remained. By October 2006, Boeing had just over 400 firm orders for the 787, and airlines were planning new point-to-point routes that suited its long range and capacity of up to 296 passengers.

| 1991 | | | 1992 | | |
|---|---|---|---|---|---|
| MAY | SEPTEMBER | OCTOBER | MARCH | MAY | AUGUST |
| **10 May** The Canadair Regional Jet (CRJ), an airliner derivative of the Challenger 601 business jet, is flown. | **15 September** The McDonnell Douglas C-17 Globemaster III heavy four-engined jet freighter is flown. | **25 October** The first four-engined Airbus, the A340, makes its first flight. The prototype is a 375-seat A340-300 model. | **26 March** The Saab 2000, an improved version of the Saab 340, flies in Sweden. | **12 May** The last of 1013 707 airframes, an E-3D Sentry for the RAF, is delivered. | |
| | **September** American Patty Wagstaff becomes the first woman to win the US National Aerobatic Championship. | | | | **30 August** The ALH (Advanced Light Helicopter), developed jointly by Hindustani Aeronautics and Messerschmitt Bolkow-Blohm, is flown in India. |

## The A350

Announced in November 2004, the A350 began as a derivative of the A330 with new engines and greater use of composite materials, particularly in the wings. Airbus was reluctant to use composite fuselage sections (as on the 787) because it is less tolerant to minor damage. Bumps from ground-handling vehicles and equipment ('ramp rash') may cause damage under the surface, which is not obvious from the outside.

The A350 design was revised with a new larger windscreen, giving a different appearance to all previous Airbus designs. Many other parts, including the wing and tail, will be composite or other high-technology material. The largely cosmetic changes over the A330 did not win over airline executives, who wondered why a new fuselage was not part of the package. A major rethink resulted in a relaunch of the project at the 2006 Farnborough Air Show as the A350XWB (for eXtra Wide Body), with an extra row of seats and a total diameter 13cm (5in) greater than that of the 787. As of October 2006, just over 120 firm orders had been received for the A350XWB. The redesign has put initial deliveries back to 2012.

*The Airbus A350 is a long-range mid-sized wide-body family of airliners currently under development, designed to compete with the Boeing 777 and 787. The aircraft will have a cruising speed of about Mach 0.85.*

The 787 will incorporate a number of design features that will be noticeable to the passengers. One is improved cabin air quality, with higher humidity and better circulation than currently found. Cabin lighting will come from light-emitting diodes (LEDs), which can be adjusted to create different moods, depending on the time of day or night. Certain to be popular with many passengers are new, larger windows with a liquid crystal display (LCD)–based auto-dimming system rather than the traditional moving blinds. In extensive surveys taken during the design phase, bigger windows were the feature requested more than any other.

| | | **1993** | | | | |
|---|---|---|---|---|---|---|
| NOVEMBER | DECEMBER | JANUARY | MARCH | JUNE | SEPTEMBER | OCTOBER |
| **2 November** The first flight of the Airbus A330 long-range twinjet airliner. | **18 December** The McDonnell Douglas MD 900, the first production NOTAR (No Tail Rotor) helicopter, flies in Arizona. | **February** the Bolivian Air Force (Fuerza Aérea Boliviana) retires the last F-86 Sabre in military service. | **11 March** The Airbus A321, a stretched version of the A320 and able to carry up to 220 passengers, is flown. | **8 June** Handover of the first Saab JAS 39A Gripen to the Swedish Air Force (Flygvapnet). | **30 September** The RAF retires the Buccaneer strike aircraft, which saw combat in the 1991 Gulf War. | **15 October** The Handley Page Victor, last of the RAF's V-bombers, is retired from the tanker role with the RAF. |

After abandoning the idea of larger 747 derivatives in the period when the A380 was still the A3XX, Boeing has returned to the concept with the 747-8. This has also benefited from the design work put into the Sonic Cruiser and 787. It will not be greatly enlarged, having only 450 passengers in its initial 747-8 Intercontinental version, but will have new wings. The initial engines offered will be the new General Electric GEnx, as developed for the 787 and available for the A350XWB. As of late 2006, 40 747-8s had been ordered, all but two of them the freighter version.

## Superfighters

Today, only a few nations can afford the 'superfighters' offered by the last remaining manufacturers of state-of-the-art combat aircraft. The cost of jet fighters has grown exponentially to the point where some have exceeded the $100 million 'sticker price', including the Lockheed Martin F-22 and Japanese Mitsubishi F-2. Some nations, including New Zealand and the Philippines, have disbanded their air combat arms or let them wither, ostensibly for budgetary reasons.

*After some delay, Eurofighter has broken into the export market with orders from Austria and Saudi Arabia.*

Others make do with 'legacy' aircraft such as the MiG-21, Northrop F-5 or the F-16A.

In the future, unmanned air vehicles (UAVs) will take over more of the roles of fighter, attack and electronic warfare aircraft, as well as reconnaissance. For most of the world's governments, however, manned combat aircraft are fielded as much for domestic and external political reasons as they are for their military utility in time of war. Conventional fighters and attack jets, and their associated trainers and transports, will continue to have a place for the foreseeable future.

The cost of developing combat aircraft is too great for many nations, which has prompted several instances of international cooperation, mainly in Europe. Examples include the Anglo-French SEPECAT Jaguar, the Franco-German Dornier-Breguet Alpha Jet, the Anglo-Italian-German Panavia Tornado and the Italian-Brazilian AMX. The most complex and long-running of these arrangements has been the Eurofighter partnership between the United Kingdom, Germany, Italy and Spain, set up in 1986 to produce a fighter and attack aircraft for those four nations and for export. The

| **1993** | **1994** | | | | |
| --- | --- | --- | --- | --- | --- |
| DECEMBER | FEBRUARY | MARCH | APRIL | JUNE | AUGUST |
| **17 December** The first of 21 B-2 Spirit bombers to be built is delivered to the USAF. | | **27 March** The first Eurofighter EFA 2000, later named Typhoon, flies in Germany. | **21 April** Jackie Parker becomes the first qualified female USAF F-16 fighter pilot. | **12 June** The first flight of the Boeing 777 heavy twinjet. It is the first aircraft to be designed entirely on computers rather than on paper. | **August** The RAF accepts its first female combat pilot, Flight Lieutenant Jo Salter, who flies Tornado GR1s. |
| **21 December** The Cessna Citation X flies. It is the world's fastest business jet with a top speed of Mach 0.92. | **15 February** The Eurocopter (formerly Aérospatiale) EC 135 twin-engined utility helicopter makes its first flight. | | | | |

Eurofighter design drew heavily on BAe's Experimental Aircraft Programme (EAP), and a number of other technology demonstrator programmes. The EAP technology demonstrator first flew in August 1986 and amassed invaluable data before retirement in May 1991.

The Eurofighter copied EAP's unstable canard delta layout, adding active digital fly-by-wire flight controls, advanced avionics, multifunction cockpit displays, carbon-fibre composite construction and extensive use of aluminium-lithium alloys and titanium. At first known as the EFA (European Fighter Aircraft), then as the Eurofighter 2000, the production fighter has become the Typhoon in RAF service, but is usually known as the Eurofighter in the other countries. Of the partner countries, only Spain, with its F/A-18 Hornets, has previously had a modern highly manoeuvrable fighter in its inventory, and the Eurofighter offers a great leap in capability. Although some export sales contests have been lost, the Eurofighter has sold to Austria and Saudi Arabia.

*The Dassault Rafale (squall) is produced in three different versions.*

Two European nations historically independent in arms procurement have gone their own way in developing fighter aircraft for their militaries. France showed initial interest in the Eurofighter project, but pulled out in 1985 to develop its own fighter, which eventually became the Dassault Rafale (squall). Like the Eurofighter, its gestation has been protracted, but it entered initial service with the French Aéronavale in 2001 and equips a unit aboard the nuclear-powered carrier *Charles de Gaulle*. The first operational Armée de l'Air squadron did not form until 2006. Although both the Rafale and Eurofighter have their own strengths and weaknesses, each is a highly manoeuvrable twin-engine fly-by-wire aircraft with canard foreplanes and a wide range of weapons options. The Rafale has yet to win an export order, although prospects for sales in North Africa and the Middle East are strong.

### Sweden's Gripen

Following in a long tradition of innovative combat aircraft, Sweden's Saab Gripen (griffon) was the first of the 'Euro canards' to enter service. Developments in computers and

| | | **1995** | | | **1996** |
|---|---|---|---|---|---|
| **SEPTEMBER** | **DECEMBER** | **APRIL** | **JUNE** | **NOVEMBER** | **JANUARY** |
| **13 September** Airbus flies the A300-600ST (Super Transporter) or Beluga, a specially modified freighter for outsized loads such as Ariane rocket parts. | **16 December** The Antonov An-70 four-engined freighter flies, the first large aircraft with propfan engines. It is lost in a collision in February 1995. | **26 April** The USAF reactivates the first of two SR-71s, having put them in storage in 1990. | **7 June** The Boeing 777 is put into service by United Airlines, initially on the Washington–London route. | **28 November** An MD-11 is successfully landed in tests to prove that a large transport aircraft can be controlled by engine power alone. | **4 January** The Boeing-Sikorsky YRAH-66 Comanche prototype flies. It is intended as a stealthy reconnaissance platform, but is cancelled in early 2004. |
| | | | | **29 November** The first flight of the McDonnell Douglas Super Hornet, an enlarged derivative of the Hornet. The first Super Hornet is an F/A-18E single-seater. | |

electronics have allowed the performance and capabilities of several versions of the Viggen to be exceeded by a much smaller package in the JAS 39 Gripen. The designation comes from Saab's 39th military design and the Swedish words *jakt* (fighter), *attack* (attack) and *spaning* (reconnaissance). The single-engine Gripen first flew in 1988 and entered squadron service with *Flygvapnet* in 1997.

A shift towards international and coalition operations has seen the JAS 39C and D versions equipped to NATO standards and declared as part of Sweden's Rapid Reaction Force for out-of-area operations. In contrast to previous Swedish fighters, the export of which was restricted by political considerations, Gripen has been sold or leased to the Czech Republic, Hungary and South Africa, with other customers in prospect.

The main competition for Europe's top-of-the-line fighters comes from the US F-15, which

*The Saab JAS-39 Gripen (Griffon) lightweight multi-role fighter was conceived in the 1970s.*

remains in production more than 30 years after its first flight, and the Super Hornet, a derivative of the F/A-18 Hornet that is enlarged and more capable, and which first entered US Navy service in the early 1980s. Both were originally McDonnell Douglas aircraft, and are now made under the Boeing banner following the 1997 merger of the two companies.

Boeing's only domestic challenger is Lockheed Martin. This is itself the result of a merger between Lockheed, the aircraft-maker, and Martin, the electronics and weapons firm that stopped building aircraft in the 1960s. Lockheed Martin builds the F-16, which continues to sell in ever-improved versions, but is approaching the end of its development life, and the F-22

## 1996

**MARCH**

**21 March** A modified Tu-144 SST (the Tu-144LL) begins test flights in Russia for NASA as part of research into future SSTs.

**APRIL**

**5 April** The first flight of the Lockheed-Martin C-130J, an advanced C-130 development with a two-crew cockpit and new engines.

**25 April** The first flight of the Yakovlev Yak-130 advanced trainer. It is later developed and marketed in association with Aermacchi of Italy.

## 1997

**SEPTEMBER**

**7 September** The first F-22 Raptor is flown.

**18 September** The revived Zeppelin company flies the New Technology Zeppelin NT airship at Friedrichshafen, Germany.

**25 September** The first flight of the Sukhoi S-32 (later the S-37) forward-swept-wing fighter demonstrator.

**OCTOBER**

**16 October** The stretched 777-300 is first flown. With a length of 73m (242ft), it is the longest airliner built to date.

## 1998

**FEBRUARY**

**28 February** The very large Ryan (later Northrop Grumman) RQ4A Global Hawk UAV (unmanned air vehicle) is flown.

*Above: The F/A-18 Hornet is the current mount of the Blue Angels, the aerobatic team of the US Navy.*

*Left: The F-15E Strike Eagle, seen here breaking away after taking on fuel, is the strike/attack variant of this well-proven design.*

Raptor, a highly sophisticated 'air dominance' fighter developed jointly with Boeing in the late 1980s and the winner of a competition with the YF-23 design of (then) Northrop and McDonnell Douglas.

The Raptor is a second-generation 'stealth' design. Advances in computer technology and materials allow smooth and curved surfaces to deflect and disperse hostile radar beams in the way that the angular and faceted F-117

## 1999

### AUGUST

**Summer** Cirrus Aircraft successfully flight-tests the CAPS (Cirrus Aircraft Parachute System) ballistic emergency aircraft parachute.

### SEPTEMBER

**4 September** The first flight of the Boeing Business Jet (BBJ), a dedicated executive/private version of the 737-700.

### JANUARY

**January** The Boeing Super Hornet enters service with the first US Navy training squadron.

**14 January** The first flight of the Sikorsky S-92 Helibus medium helicopter.

### FEBRUARY

**8 February** The Tupolev Tu-334 short-range turbojet flies in Russia. The Tu-334 is intended as a replacement for the 1963-vintage Tu-134.

### MARCH

**21 March** The Breitling Orbiter 3 makes the first nonstop round-the-world balloon flight, travelling 30,804km (25,360 miles).

*The F-22 is designed for a high sortie rate, with a turnaround time of less than 20 minutes.*

Raptors entering USAF service have diminished to about 180, pushing the unit cost over $177 million. Export sales were permitted by Congress in 2006, but restrictions on transfer of technology seem likely to drive away even those few nations, such as Saudi Arabia and Japan, that might be able to afford them.

More affordable, and already sold to a number of nations, is Lockheed Martin's Joint Strike Fighter, the F-35 Lightning II. The F-35 is intended to replace F-16s and A-10s serving with the USAF, Harriers with the Marines and F/A-18 Hornets with the US Navy. Partners in a number of friendly nations will produce parts. This includes the United Kingdom, which proposes to replace Harriers and Sea Harriers with the F-35B short takeoff and vertical landing (STOVL) version. The F-35 resembles a mini-F-22, with twin vertical tails, a diamond-like wing planform and an internal weapons bay. The side-mounted intakes contrast with the unsuccessful JSF contender, the Boeing X-32, with its gaping mouth of an intake. Although it met all of the JSF competition's performance targets, it is possible that aesthetics had a role in the choice of the Lockheed Martin product by

*The Northrop YF-23 was one of two prototypes produced for the ATF contract.*

the Pentagon. With several NATO nations as well as Australia signed up to buy F-35s, even before a real example (as opposed to the X-35 prototypes) has flown, the Lightning II is destined for sales to rival that of the F-16 (more than 4000 to date) over the next few decades.

Nighthawk was first able to do using 1980s technology. The price of being theoretically unbeatable in air combat is that even the US defence budget is too tight for more than a relative handful of such 'silver bullets' to be purchased. Initial prospects of around 750

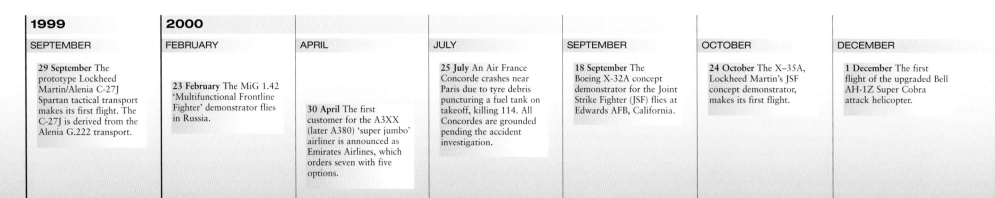

| 1999 | 2000 | | | | | |
|---|---|---|---|---|---|---|
| SEPTEMBER | FEBRUARY | APRIL | JULY | SEPTEMBER | OCTOBER | DECEMBER |
| **29 September** The prototype Lockheed Martin/Alenia C-27J Spartan tactical transport makes its first flight. The C-27J is derived from the Alenia G.222 transport. | **23 February** The MiG 1.42 'Multifunctional Frontline Fighter' demonstrator flies in Russia. | **30 April** The first customer for the A3XX (later A380) 'super jumbo' airliner is announced as Emirates Airlines, which orders seven with five options. | **25 July** An Air France Concorde crashes near Paris due to tyre debris puncturing a fuel tank on takeoff, killing 114. All Concordes are grounded pending the accident investigation. | **18 September** The Boeing X-32A concept demonstrator for the Joint Strike Fighter (JSF) flies at Edwards AFB, California. | **24 October** The X–35A, Lockheed Martin's JSF concept demonstrator, makes its first flight. | **1 December** The first flight of the upgraded Bell AH-1Z Super Cobra attack helicopter. |

One of the new technologies that promises to revolutionize air combat is thrust vectoring control, or TVC. Using the diversion of engine thrust to exert additional control is an idea that has been around for some time. Aircraft such as the Harrier used it as a means of vertical or short takeoff and landing before it was discovered to offer advantages in air combat. As legend has it, a US Marine Corps pilot, Captain Harry Blot, decided to see what would happen if he pivoted his Harrier's nozzles fully forward while travelling at high speed. The resulting extraordinary deceleration was something that no other combat aircraft could match. Further investigation showed that careful use of the nozzles could point the nose of the Harrier outside the normal plane of flight, allowing it to bring weapons to bear on a manoeuvring target that was otherwise out of its sights. This ability was dubbed 'vectoring in forward flight', or VIFFing, and was soon applied by Marine and RAF and Royal Navy pilots in mock dogfights.

VIFFing was a by-product of the Harrier's power system, and not immediately applicable to conventional jets. It was not until the late 1980s that practical tests began into a system

*The F-35A and F-35B have very similar airframes, including the aft cockpit bulge and associated doors for the lift-fan, which is fitted only to the F-35B.*

## 2001

| FEBRUARY | MARCH | JULY | SEPTEMBER | OCTOBER | DECEMBER |
|---|---|---|---|---|---|
| **21 February** An AGM114 Hellfire missile is fired from an RQ-1 Predator, the first time an armed UAV is tested. | **7 March** The EHI Merlin HC3 helicopter enters service with the RAF. | **20 July** The X-35B becomes the first aircraft to make a short takeoff, level supersonic dash and vertical landing in a single flight. | **8 September** The last VC-137, known as *Air Force One* when transporting the US president, makes its last flight. | **25 October** The Lockheed Martin X-35 is declared the winner of the JSF competition. It will be the F-35A, B and C, depending on service. | **4 December** It is announced that UAVs such as the Predator have been used to attack time-critical targets in Afghanistan – the first use of unmanned craft in an active combat role.<br><br>**December** The Dassault Rafale M enters service with the Aéronavale. |

*The Rockwell/MBB X-31 was developed specifically to investigate multi-axis thrust vectoring.*

that could be made to work with an afterburning jet. NASA tested an F-15 with single-axis (up and down) moving exhausts, mainly to improve take-off performance. The Multi-Axis Thrust-Vectoring (MATV) F-16 was tested in 1993-4 with a variable nozzle on its General Electric F110 engine. This could swivel by 17 degrees in any axis, allowing the aircraft to fly at an angle-of-attack of 86 degrees, meaning that it could fly with its nose pointed nearly at a right angle to the direction of travel. Further experiments followed with the Rockwell/MBB X-31, a purpose-built TVC testbed that used large paddles in the exhaust flow, permitting some previously impossible manoeuvres.

Meanwhile, Russian industry was working on the same problems. The Sukhoi Su-37 was a one-off derivative of the Su-27 'Flanker' with two-dimensional (2D) thrust-vectoring nozzles. It first flew in 1996 and astonished Western observers at that year's Farnborough Air Show with its manoeuvres at an angle-of-attack of up to 180 degrees, performing complete backflips and other startling gyrations for such a large fighter. A version of the two-seat Su-30 model

with 3D (yaw, pitch and roll) thrust-vectoring, designated the Su-30 MKI, was ordered by India in 1996, and the Indian Air Force (IAF) subsequently became the first air arm in the world to field an operational TVC fighter. Although the IAF has flown its standard Su-30s in exercises with Western types, it has kept its MKIs to themselves since they entered service.

The F-22 is the first US fighter with TVC and the first anywhere to be designed with it from the outset. Its exhausts are also designed for low heat signature, making them flat boxes rather than truncated cones as on the Sukhoi, MiG-29OVT and other TVC aircraft. Thrust vectoring presents a considerable technical challenge given the heat and vibration environment in which complex mechanical parts, such as actuators and afterburner petals, must operate.

### Russian Fighters

The fall of the Soviet Union caused turmoil among the makers of the former superpower's combat aircraft. No longer guaranteed orders from a seemingly unlimited defence budget and exports to supine client states, the great design

| 2002 | | | | | 2003 |
|---|---|---|---|---|---|
| FEBRUARY | APRIL | JUNE | JULY | AUGUST | JANUARY |
| **21 February** The first flight of the EMBRAER 170 regional airliner. | **24 April** Deliveries of the Eurocopter EC145 begin to France's Sécurité Civile agency. | **19 June-3 July** Steve Fossett makes the first solo balloon circumnavigation in the *Spirit of Freedom*, taking 14 days and 20 hours to fly to and from Australia, a journey of 33,195km (20,626 miles). | **18 July** The YAL-1 airborne laser aircraft, based on a 747-200, flies after modification. | **August** The Airbus A340-600 enters service with Virgin Atlantic Airways.<br><br>**29 August** The first flight of the Airbus A318, a 100-seat 'shrink' of the A319. | **14 January** The first F/A-22 Raptors are delivered to a USAF evaluation squadron at Nellis AFB, Nevada. |

bureaux MiG, Sukhoi, Yakovlev, Mil and others were forced to try to sell their products on the world market in direct competition with more canny Western manufacturers and their salesmen. In a few cases, the original designer's factory found itself competing with a plant continuing to build its product, but now based in a separate nation or state inside or outside of the new Commonwealth of Independent States (CIS). New developments had to be funded by foreign sales, which could be far and few between. The major fixed-wing types available for export were the Mikoyan-Gurevich MiG-29 'Fulcrum', the Sukhoi Su-27 'Flanker' and Sukhoi Su-25 'Frogfoot'.

The MiG-29 caused a sensation when it was first revealed to the Western public in the late 1980s. Although the aircraft had first flown in 1977, little was known or released about it by Western intelligence agencies for a decade. A visit by a squadron to a Finnish air base in 1986 gave the first clear glimpse of the MiG-29, which at once appeared to be more sophisticated than the familiar Soviet fighters. With twin tails, side intakes and a large bubble canopy, the 'Fulcrum' seemed optimized for

*Despite its size, the Su-27 is an extremely agile aircraft, and is capable of some astonishing combat manoeuvres. The Su-35 is a second-generation version with improved agility and enhanced operational capability.*

dog-fighting rather than operating under strict ground control. Multiple pylons for a range of infrared and radar-guided missiles and a powerful modern radar completed the package. Demonstration flights at Farnborough and Paris air shows from 1988 emphasized the MiG's

manoeuvrability and power. The MiG was a short-range fighter and interceptor, and it was soon stationed on the Warsaw Pact front line in East Germany and Poland.

Sukhoi's counterpart was the Su-27, a much larger aircraft in the class of the F-15, designed

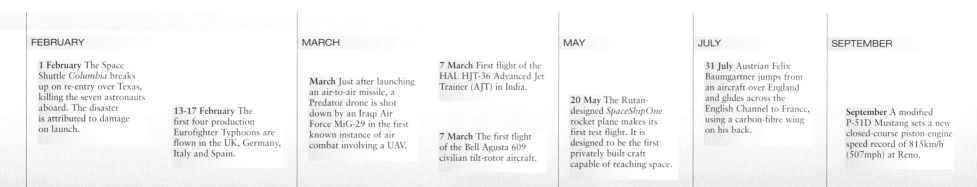

### FEBRUARY

**1 February** The Space Shuttle *Columbia* breaks up on re-entry over Texas, killing the seven astronauts aboard. The disaster is attributed to damage on launch.

**13-17 February** The first four production Eurofighter Typhoons are flown in the UK, Germany, Italy and Spain.

### MARCH

**March** Just after launching an air-to-air missile, a Predator drone is shot down by an Iraqi Air Force MiG-29 in the first known instance of air combat involving a UAV.

### MAY

**7 March** First flight of the HAL HJT-36 Advanced Jet Trainer (AJT) in India.

**7 March** The first flight of the Bell Agusta 609 civilian tilt-rotor aircraft.

**20 May** The Rutan-designed *SpaceShipOne* rocket plane makes its first test flight. It is designed to be the first privately built craft capable of reaching space.

### JULY

**31 July** Austrian Felix Baumgartner jumps from an aircraft over England and glides across the English Channel to France, using a carbon-fibre wing on his back.

### SEPTEMBER

**September** A modified P-51D Mustang sets a new closed-course piston-engine speed record of 815km/h (507mph) at Reno.

as a long-range fighter and first flown in 1981. It was first encountered during intercepts by NATO patrol planes over the Baltic Sea, but soon followed the MiG onto the international airshow circuit, where it proved even more impressive.

The MiG-29 was supplied to a number of Communist nations, usually with simplified avionics and downgraded radar, before the fall of the Soviet Union. In the new environment, MiG-MAPO – the commercial entity that followed the old design bureau – has worked hard to offer versions with ever more sophisticated radars and systems to any nation with the cash, whatever its current or former political alignment.

The latest versions on offer include the MiG-35, which is competing with the Gripen, F-16 and others for a large Indian contract, and the MiG-29OVT, with thrust-vectoring control.

Due to its greater cost and more specialized roles, the Su-27 and its offspring has not spread as widely as the MiG-29, but has been bought and licence-built by both India and China in significant numbers. Other customers include Vietnam and Eritrea. During fighting between Ethiopia and Eritrea in the 1990s, the Su-27 scored its only known kills to date when several Ethiopian fighters were destroyed – most of them MiG-29s.

*The German Luftwaffe acquired a number of MiG-29 interceptors, from the former East Germany.*

**2003**

OCTOBER

24 October Concorde is formally retired with the arrival of the last commercial services in quick succession into Heathrow Airport.

DECEMBER

17 December *SpaceShipOne* becomes the first privately built, manned aircraft to fly faster than sound.

**2004**

APRIL

26 April An order from Japan's All Nippon Airlines (ANA) launches the Boeing 7E7 programme, renamed the 787 in April 2005.

JUNE

21 June Flown by Mike Melville, *SpaceShipOne* makes a flight to 100.124km (62.2 miles) and is regarded as the first privately funded human space flight.

OCTOBER

4 October *SpaceShipOne* makes the second flight above 100km (62 miles) in two weeks and wins the $10,000,000 Ansari X-Prize for the first privately funded space flight.

27 October Steve Fossett sets a new absolute speed record for airships, flying a Zeppelin NT at an average of 115km/h (71.5mph).

**2005**

FEBRUARY

24 February The first Boeing KC-767 tanker is rolled out. It is delivered to the Italian Air Force.

MARCH

5 March The Virgin Atlantic *GlobalFlyer*, flown by adventurer Steve Fossett, lands at the completion of the first nonstop solo circumnavigation of the world.

APRIL

6 April The first Eurocopter Tiger is delivered to the Franco-German training unit in France.

27 April The first Airbus A380 flies at Toulouse. The A380 is the largest airliner ever flown.

The next and perhaps final step in the evolution of combat aircraft is the UCAV, or Unmanned Combat Air Vehicle. Conflicts in Afghanistan, Iraq and Palestine have already seen the use of armed UAVs (unmanned air vehicles) or drones firing missiles at ground targets, particularly those out of the range of a conventional aircraft or those which would be alerted by its presence. The long loiter time of an umanned aircraft allows a surveillance mission to turn into an attack at the flick of an operator's switch from a control cabin that may be thousands of miles away. Even air combat involving UAVs has taken place in a limited way. In the run-up to the 2003 Iraq war, an Iraqi MiG got off the first shot against a Predator drone that was moving to attack it with a missile, and in July 2006 an Israeli F-16 used a missile to bring down a Hizbollah UAV that had crossed the Lebanese border. Future UCAVs, which will be stealthy and designed from the start for weapons carriage, will have a greater degree of autonomy to seek and identify a target. Hopefully, though, a person will be kept in the loop to make the final critical decision whether or not to release weapons over a distant target.

*The RQ-1 Predator is a medium-altitude long-endurance UAV. It can carry and fire two AGM-114 Hellfire missiles, and when armed it is designated MQ-1. The aircraft has been in use since 1995.*

## 2006

| NOVEMBER | | DECEMBER | FEBRUARY | MARCH | JUNE | JULY | |
|---|---|---|---|---|---|---|---|
| **10 November** The record for the longest nonstop flight by a commercial jet is broken by a Boeing 777-200LR, which flies 23,309km (12,586 miles) from Hong Kong to London in 22 hours 42 minutes. | **14 November** Boeing announces that it will build the 747-8, a stretched, new technology development of the 747-400. | **December** The F-22 Raptor (the 'A' part of the designation having been dropped) enters frontline squadron service with the USAF at Langley Air Force Base, Virginia. | **11 February** Steve Fossett takes 76 hours 45 minutes to fly westbound from Cape Canaveral, Florida, to Bournemouth, England, a distance of 42,469km (26,389 miles). In doing so, he breaks three world records, including absolute distance. | **28 March** The Sea Harrier FA.2 is retired from Fleet Air Arm service. The Harrier GR.9 takes over as the strike component for Royal Navy carriers. | **27 June** The Rafale B enters squadron service with the French Air Force, the Armée de l'Air. | **7 July** The first prototype of the F-35 JSF is rolled out and given the official name 'Lightning II'. | **8 July** The first successful manned powered ornithopter is flown for 14 seconds in Toronto, Canada.<br><br>**10 July** An MV-22 Osprey is the first tilt-rotor aircraft to cross the Atlantic, landing at Farnborough. |

# Index